Women in Motion

Women in Motion
Alexa L. Foreman

Bowling Green University Popular Press
Bowling Green, Ohio 43403

Acknowledgements

Special thanks are due to Alice Gambrell and Luck Gambrell Davidson. Also thanks to the gang in Mexico, Frank Thompson, Jemi Nicoll, Lee Tsiantis, Christine Sigety for her patience, and Marie Christiansen and Laura McCrary for their humor.

Library of Congress Catalogue Card No.: 83-72435

ISBN: 0-87972-266-5
      0-87972-267-3

To
My Family

Who Has Always Kept
A Sense Of Humor Even
In The Worst Of Times

"Isn't it wonderful you've had such a great career when you had no right to have a career at all?"
> —Telegram from Katharine Hepburn to Dorothy Arzner, 1975

CONTENTS

INTRODUCTION

Women In Motion is concerned with the women who have
been active within the motion picture industry as well as
independent filmmakers. Since I could not include all of
the women who have made contributions to film, I have attempted to list the most representative women involved
with motion pictures from the birth of films to the present.
The manuscript is divided into four categories: Directors,
Independent and Avant-garde Filmmakers, Editors, and Screenwriters.

All films included are 16mm. Only the motion pictures
available for rental and/or sale are listed under the filmmakers' names within the chapters. (So, for example, a
filmmaker may have made a total of ten motion pictures, but
if only five are available for rental or sale, only five
will be listed.) Filmographies of some of the women are
included in the back of the book as are sources for Canadian filmmakers and video information.

EXPLANATION OF ENTRIES

Under each woman's name, films are listed as
follows: title, release date (when furnished), co-
worker (if the woman did not work alone), running
time, color or black and white or both, and company
where the film may be rented or bought. In Chapter I,
a summary of the film will follow this information.
In Chapter 2, 3, and 4, the cast, director, and
a summary will be listed. Cross-references will
be denoted by the direction "See" and the woman's
name will follow. Rental distributors may be denoted by a series of three initials and the initials
will be listed in the book's appendix with the
distributor's complete address.

CHAPTER ONE:

INDEPENDENT AND AVANT-GARDE FILMMAKERS

INDEPENDENT AND AVANT-GARDE
FILMMAKERS

This chapter does little justice to the courageous and frustrated filmmakers who work for years with no money or recognition purely for their love of film and in order to express their personal visions. These women cannot be classified in any one category as director, editor, or screenwriter, because out of necessity, an independent filmmaker is usually all three.

The films listed in this chapter are generally about women. Women's joys, sorrows, problems, and memories are effectively visualized in films which are for the most part positive, enlightening, and touched with a sense of humor. Other films included concern topics ranging from dance to the effects of radiation. Though each filmmaker may have a different way of expressing herself visually, whether by straight interview, stop action, story telling, animation, documentary, slow motion, or computer visuals, all have taken the time and effort to put their personal ideas and feelings on film to share with ohters.

Claudia Weill and Joan Micklin Silver are two examples of independent filmmakers who have become successful commercially, and , even though they now are known as industry directors, both are listed within this chapter because they have made more independent films than feature films.

NOTE: These films are not in chronological order because many films did not have release dates listed. Therefore, they are in alphabetical order. All films are available for rental and/or sale. Filmographies for some of the filmmakers are listed in the appendix of the book.

<u>WOMEN IN MOTION</u>

CHAPTER I

AARON, JANE
  <u>In Plain Sight</u> (1977)
  3 min, r, s: SBC.
  Animation and real world combined. <u>In Plain Sight</u> is a
  uniquely inventive film that is fun for children while
  adults can ponder its paradoxes of life vs. art, and real
  vs. synthetic time." -SBC

ACUNA, JUDY SHAW
  <u>For Better Or Worse</u> (1973)
  7 min, b/w, r, s: WMM.
  "Before and after the marriage, or how a woman pediatri-
  cian changes her marriage into a partnership." -WMM

ADAMS, NORMA
  <u>. . . And Everything Nice</u>
  20 min, c, r: UCE.
  "Follows a married woman in her mid 30's as she joins
  a women's consciousness-raising group. Scenes of the group
  are intercut with commentary by feminist Gloria Steinem."
  -UCE

ADATO, PERRY MILLER
  <u>Frankenthaler: Toward A New Climate</u> (1977)
  30 min, c, r, s: FNC.
  "At the age of 24, Helen Frankenthaler invented the
  stained canvas which influenced a whole generation of
  'color field' painters. Since that time, she has matured
  into one of the most durable and inventive of contemporary
  American artists. . . .the highlight of the film is a
  sequence in which the camera follows the actual creation
  of a Frankenthaler painting." -Program, 21st Annual American Film Festival.

  <u>Georgia O'Keeffe</u> (1977)
  60 min, c, r, s: FNC.
  "Georgia O'Keeffe appears on camera for the first time
  to talk candidly about her work and life. . . ." -FNC

  <u>Gertrude Stein: When This You See, Remember Me</u> (1970)
  90 min, c, r: COR, UCE.
  "The thoughts, words, and compelling presence of Gertrude Stein flows richly through this portrait of the
  author's Paris years from 1905 through the 1930's. The
  tremendous urge that swept through Paris during that era
  is reflected in mementoes and remembrances of Gertrude as
  author, hostess, art collector, and friend (including home
  movies of her and Alice B. Toklas, and a recording of
  the only radio interview she gave)." -C/McG-H

Mary Cassatt: Impressionist From Philadelphia (1977)
30 min, c, r, s: FNC.
Documentary portrait of Mary Cassatt. "Her personal
story - her years in Paris, her relationship with Degas,
the influence of her family - is told with on-location
footage and stills of the places she lived and painted."
-FNC

ADLER, JANET
Looking For Me (1970)
29 min, b/w, r, s: MUL, UCE.
"This moving documentary about dance therapy illustrates
a therapeutic approach using body and movements. The
most powerful sequence shows the therapist working individually with two autistic girls." -MUL

ALLEN, CATHERINE
Self-Health (1974)
See LIGHTHOUSE FILMS.

ANDERSEN, YVONNE
Fat Feet (1966). Co-makers: Dominic Falcone, Red Grooms
20 min, c & b/w, r: FMC. r, s: TBW.
Stars Dominic Falcone and Mimi Gross using animation on
pixillation. "A magical, exotic portrait of various people
in the city." Y.A.

Meow, Meow (1969). Co-makers: Dominic Falcone, Red Grooms
6 1/2 min, c, r: FMC. r, s: YBW.
"Animated cut-outs. A man finds a cat which turns into
a lion. The lion becomes a famous singer who is kidnapped by gangsters." -Y.A.

ANDERSON, AMELIA
Scott Joplin (1977)
15 min, c, r, s: PYR.
"This film biography of the originator of the ragtime
rhythm traces the sources of black music. . .and follows
Joplin's life from his discovery in a dance-hall by a
music publisher, his great initial success, his turning
to serious composition, the failure of the opera 'Tree-
monisha,' and his early death in poverty and obscurity."
-Pyramid.

Tender Images
6 min, c, silent, r: CAN.
"Fifteen imaginative stable images in black, sepia, and
white light. Serene and yet stimulating in spirit." -Canyon

What Is A Man? (1956)
10 min, c, r: CAN.
Inspired by the writings of James Joyce. "I consider
What Is A Man? a sophisticated humorous exploration of
the Experimental film medium." -Shirley Clarke

ASHTON, MARIE
Coming To Know (1976)
9 min, b/w, r, s: MUL, SBC
"Two young women discuss how they discovered their interest in women. In a straightforward, candid manner they
relate early experiences through which they became aware
of being gay." -SBC

The Yellow Wallpaper (1978)
14 min, c, r, s: WMM.
This film, set in the 1890's and based on the redis-
covered literary masterpiece by Charlotte Perkins Gil-
man, is the story of a woman's mental breakdown.

ANDERSON, MADELINE
Being Me (1975)
20 min, c, r, s: PNX.
"Being Me explores the many areas and origins of personal identity, and reveals how children perceive themselves in terms of their surroundings, family, and eth-
nicity." -Phoenix

I Am Somebody (1970)
28 min, c, r: UCE.
The struggle between black hospital workers and whites
in South Carolina.

A Tribute To Malcolm X (1969)
15 min, b/w, r: UCE.
Malcolm X is recalled by his widow.

The Walls Come Tumbling Down (1975)
29 min, c, r, s: FNC, PNX.
"Public-housing residents in St. Louis conducted a
nine month rent strike in 1969 to protest the latest in
a series of rent raises they considered intolerable. Since
then, residents have assumed the management of their develop-
ments to a degree unprecedented in the country." -Phoenix

ARLEDGE, SARA KATHRYN
Interior Garden
7 min, c, silent, r: CAN.
"Seventeen brilliantly colored stable images of an abstract and semi-abstract nature." -Canyon

Interior Garden II
6 min, c, silent, r: CAN.
"Nineteen imaginative stable images in black, sepia, and
white light." -Canyon

Introspection
7 min, c, r: CAN.
"This was the first filmic dance undertaken in 1941." -S.K.A.

ASHUR, GERI
   Janie's Janie (1971) Co-maker: Peter Barton
   25 min, b/w, r: ODE.
   Sudy of a woman's struggle for independence.

ASTON, JULIA
   The Bond Of Breastfeeding (1978)
   20 min, c, r, s: PRE.
   "A documentary film, based on the experiences of breastfeeding mothers, imparts the facts so that expectant
   mothers can readily decide whether or not to breast-
   feed." -Perennial

BACH, MARGARET
   Sam (1971)
   20 min, b/w, r, s: UCE.
   Film study of a Japanese-American who lived in an American
   detention camp during World War II.

BAER, NANCY
   Alice Neel: Collector of Souls (1977)
   30 min, c, r, s: CIN.
   Film documentary about artist Alice Neel "Neel is heard
   here speaking about the problems of being a woman artists,
   giving a glimpse of those resources of the soul that sus-
   stained her through the years of struggle before she
   achieved public recognition." -Maryse Holder, Art and Cinema

BAKER, DIANE
   One Of A Kind (1978)
   58 min, c, r, s: PNX.
   Diane Baker produced and starred in ". . .this drama
   about the love and conflicts between a mother and her
   daughter." -Program, 21st Annual American Film Festival.

BALFOUR-FRASER, ANNE
   Women Of The Toubou (1975)
   25 min, c, r, s: PNX.
   Film about the Sahara dwelling Toubou, a tribe in which
   the women are treated as equals by the men.

BANK, MIRRA
   Anonymous Was A Woman (1977)
   30 min, c, r, s: FNC.
   "An exploration of the origins of our current folk art
   traditions in the everyday creative spirit of the 18th
   and 19th centuries. Frequently when a piece of folk art
   has been given the attribution 'Anonymous,' it was the
   work of an unknown woman." -Program, 21st Annual American
   Film Festival

The Tap Dance Kid. Co-maker: Barra Grant.
33 min, c, r, s: LCA.
"Eight-year-old Willie wants to dance more than anything.
His father, a successful lawyer who 'shuffled' his way
through the Depression, disapproves." -Program, 21st
Annual American Film Festival.

Uncommon Images: The Harlem of James Van DerZee (1977)
22 min, c, r: FML.
Film portrait of the 90-year-old photographer.

BARTLETT, FREUDE
  See FREUDE

BAUMAN, SUZANNE
  The Cabinet (1972)
  14 min, c, s: CAR.
  Different objects in a woman's cabinet suggest various
  elements of her life.

  Manhattan Street Band
  24 min, c, s: CAR.
  A New York band "takes to the streets."

  Spirit Catcher: The Art of Betye Saar (1977)
  30 min, c, r, s: FNC.
  "Assemblage artist Betye Saar's fascination with the
  mystical merges with social concerns of significance to
  her as a black American. Probes the art, spirit, symbols
  and revelations of this complex personality." -Program,
  21st Annual American Film Festival

BEAMS, MARY
  Drowning Moon (1975)
  45 sec, b/w, r, s: SBC.
  "A short poem written by Beams' uncle during her childhood is illustrated in a vision of bright nocturnal
  memory: the rippling reflection of moon on water as it is
  crossed by the fluttering flight of a moth." -SBC

  Going Home Sketchbook (1975)
  3 min, c, r, s: SBC.
  " A cine-poem to the filmmaker's family, based on a reunion with them. The film begins with largely representational images and transforms into an abstract mood piece
  in which the mysterious quality of the familial relations
  is explored." -SBC

  Paul Revere Is Here (1976). Co-maker: Susan Rubin
  7 min, c, r, s: SBC.
  "A masterful rotoscope filmed focusing on the equestrian
  statue of Paul Revere in his hometown of Boston. En-
  couraged to comment upon the significance of Revere's ride,
  neighbors say some hilarious, irreverent things about
  silver polish and our relationship to American history."
  -SBC

Yudie (1974)
20 min, b/w, r, s: NDF.
"A film about the past and the present seen through the
eyes of a woman who grew up on New York's Lower East
Side. She is salty, irreverent, comic, and unsentimental."
-Program, Festival Of Women's Films, 1976.

BAREY, PATRICIA
Jane Kennedy - To Be Free (1972) Co-maker: Gloria Callaci
27 min, c, r: UCE.
"Though-provoking, humanistic portrait of a Chicago
nurse who has risked her personal freedom and been imprisoned for participating in civil rights demonstrations
and in protests against the Vietnam War." -UCE

BAROSS, JAN
The Computer Said
2 min, c, r: CAN.
"Comedy set to a much-edited version of a Bell Telephone
record. . .a computer learns to speak, to sing, and to
engage in the pursuit of happiness in this case wooing
a female computer who is musically inclined." -Canyon

The Scratch
3 min, c, r: CAN.
"In this film the scratch plays the antagonist and at
last has its due if not its revenge." -Canyon

BARRETT-PAGE, SALLY
Ain't Nobody's Business (1977)
54 min, c, r, s: TOM.
Documentary film on female prostitution featuring scenes
with six different prostitutes, a male member of the vice
squad, and Margo St. James. Made with an all-female crew.

Like a Rose (1975)
23 min, b/w, r, s: TOM.
Documentary about two women serving twenty-five year
sentences in a Missouri penitentiary. Made with an all-
female crew.

BARRON, EVELYN
Birth And Death (1968). Co-maker: Arthur Barron
119 min, b/w, r: UCE.
Film study of birth and death.

Factory (1972) Co-maker: Arthur Barron
56 min, b/w, r: UCE.
"Cinema verite study of the world of the blue-collar
worker and the economic and psychological bind in which
he is caught. Stark and powerful." -UCE

Piano Rub (1975)
3 min, c, r, s: SBC.
"The keyboard and strings of a piano are transformed
into graphic linear patterns of visual music, as the
sounds of 'piano rubbing' rise and fall." -SBC

Seed Reel (1975)
4 min, b/w, r, s: SBC.
"A three-part animated fantasy of sensuality in which
female and male genitalia have a life of their own and
like nothing better than dancing to the tune of 'Turkey
in the Straw' or engaging in a friendly, graceful minuet."
-SBC

Solo (1975)
2 min, b/w, r, s: SBC.
"An abstract film that is also warm, friendly and gentle. . ."
-SBC

Tub Film (1971)
2 min, b/w, r: BUD. s: SBC.
"A charming little tale of a woman and her sweet-voiced
kitten. Both are playful and carefree, but one is in for
a surprise." -BFA Educational Media

BEESON, CONI
Ann, A Portrait (1971)
19 min, c, r: CAN.
Documentary of Anna Halprin, the founder of the S.F. Dancer's
Workshop.

Daria And Dennis (1972)
10 min, c, s: apply to filmmaker.
The wedding of Daria Halprin and Dennis Hopper.

Dione (1968-73)
6 min, c, s: apply to filmmaker.
A pregnant woman's fantasies intercut with the delivery
of her baby.

The Doll (1974)
7 min, c & b/w, s: apply to filmmaker.
"Young woman fantasizes that she is nothing in this
psychic struggle for identity." -C.B.

Firefly
4 min, b/w, r: CAN.
"Abstract variations of a dancer." -C.B.

Five (1967). Co-maker: Ronald Chase
5 min, b/w, s: apply to filmmaker.
Film study of a young man in different costumes.

Fourteen (1974)
7 min, c, s: apply to filmmaker.
"Quick images of an ingenue, the filmmaker's daughter,
Kim Beeson." -C.B.

Grow Old Along With Me
12 min, c, r, s: apply to filmmaker.
"A positive, poetic statement to reaffirm that love and
sex know no age." -FOC

High On Drag (1974)
6 min, b/w, s: apply to filmmaker.
Two men, dressed in drag, act out their fantasies.

Health On Wheels (1967)
15 min, c, r: CAN.
Study of health care for cannery workers in California.

Holding (1974)
16 min, c, r, s: GRO, SBC.
"A lyrical and explicit documentary about lesbian love."
-Program Notes, Pacific Film Archive

The Moon Is My Balloon (1967-73)
10 min, c, s: apply to filmmaker.
Beeson's daughter and her balloon.

Prelude to Medical Care (1968). Co-maker: Ray Andersen.
13 min, c, s: apply to filmmaker.
Study of health care for cannery workers in California.

Sir (1973)
7 min, c, s: apply to filmmaker.
"Psychic struggle, ghetto escape featuring a black
dancer, Sir Lawrence Washington." -C.B.

Stamen (1972)
6 min, c, r, s: MUL, SBC.
"Erotic film of males in love." -C.B.

Taos (1973)
6 min, c, r: CAN.
"Dance fantasy in nature with Daria Halprin." -C.B.

Thenow (1970)
16 min, c & b/w, r: CAN. r, s: MUL
"A flight of fancy, autobiographical, dedicated to eros,
of my image of myself and my lovers, as black and as white
and as male and as female. As in a dream, all of the
characters are myself." -C.B.

Unfolding (1969)
16 min, b/w, r, s: FOC, MUL.
"Education film as art." -C.B.

Watercress (1972)
9 min, c, r, s: MUL.
"Filmed in the country on communes. . . communal together-
ness inlcudes sauna, music, mud bath and a love-in, the
touching and being touched collage of a woman and 3 men."
-C.B.

Women (1974)
12 1/2 min, c, r: CAN. r, s: FOC, MUL.
"Images of women, in the grass, shopping, belly dancing,
bumping and grinding, and more, are interspersed with
some of the thousands of names used through time to praise
or degrade 'the fair sex.'" -MUL

BENN, JANET
Pictures (1978)
3 min, c, r, s: WMM.
"Pictures is a short animated film made to commemorate
International Women's Year." -WMM

BEROES, STEPHANIE
Light Sleeping (1975)
4 min, c, r: CAN.
"Light Sleeping is an erotic fantasy of sensual love between a human and an animal. . .a woman and a cat." -SBC

BEST OF THE NEW YORK WOMEN'S FILM FESTIVAL, THE (1974)
103 min, r: NLC.
This package includes Crocus, Opening/Closing, Dirty
Books, Commuters, Cover Girl: New Face in Focus, Cycles,
Gibbous Moon, and Holding.

BILLIAN, CATHEY
Wash (1976)
3 min, c, r: apply to filmmaker.
"Abstract patterns of water and color gradually transform
themselves into a representational image." -Independent
Film/Video Guide

BINGHAM, ELEANOR
The New Klan (1978)
58 min, c, r: COR.
"A startling portrait of a movement within the Ku Klux
Klan which is bent on bringing the Klan into the mainstream
of American politics." -Program, 21st Annual American Film
Festival

BLAUSTEIN, SUSANA
Susana (1980)
25 min, b/w, r: WMM
"Susana is an autobiographical portrait of a young
Argentine lesbian growing up in a homophobic environment. . ."
-WMM

BOHLEN, ANNE
With Babies And Banners: The Story Of The Women's Emergency Brigade (1978). Co-makers: Lyn Goldfarb, Lorraine
Gray
46 min, c, r, s: NDF.
"The dramatic story of the women's role in the General
Motors sit-down strike of 1937 in Flint, MI. Rare historical footage reconstructs the event, including the life and
labor of the times as seen through the eyes of Flint's
wives and working women. In a surprise action, the women
show how their experience is relevant to today's working
woman." -Program, 21st Annual American Film Festival

BOOTH, MARLENE
By Themselves (1977)
34 min, b/w, r, s: UCE.
"Portrait of three single women, one divorced, one widowed,
and one unmarried." -UCE

BOSTROM, DENISE
Healthcaring From Our End Of The Speculum (1976).Co-
maker: Jane Warrenbrand
32 min, c, r, s: SBC, WMM.
"Healthcaring is a bold and sensitive documentary in
which women of different ages and backgrounds speak in
candid and often alarming terms of their experiences
with the present health care system. Their stories reveal the abuse and exploitation of women by doctors and
drug companies. . .Healthcaring helps the viewer
examine feelings about her body and her medical treatment without shame, fear, or despair. The positive, warm
style of the film encourages women to share their own
experiences and gain a better sense of their rights to
better medical attentions." -SBC

Musereel #1. Co-makers: Carol Clement, Ariel Dougherty,
Nancy Peck, Marilyn Ries
17 min, c, r, s: WMM.
"Musereel #1 is a documentation of the first women's
spirituality conference, Through the Looking Glass: A
Gynergenetic Experience, a gathering of over 2000 women
in Boston, 1976." -WMM

BOTTNER, BARBARA
*Note: Animated Women package, 15 min, c, includes Bottner's
Later That Night, Made For Each Other, Deborah Healey's
Brews and Potions, Monique Renault's A La Votre!, and Ian
Moo Young's The Ballad of Lucy Jordon. Except for Later That
Night, all are available separately. r,s: TEX.

Later That Night (1978)
3 min, c, s: TEX.
"In a hilarious nighttime fantasy, a woman finds that
she can transform her sexuality into real muscle power."
-TEX

Made For Each Other (1978)
3 min, c, s: TEX.
"A witty look at the impossibility of woman being everything, but everything, to her man." -TEX

BOURKE-WHITE, MARGARET
Eyes On Russia, From the Caucasus to Moscow (1934)
10 min, b/w, r: KPF.
"An extremely rare subject by the famed still photographer." -KPF

BRANDON, LIANE
Anything You Want To Be
8 min, b/w, r, s: NDF.
Film about pursuing the goal of being what you want to
be - whether you are a woman or a man.

Betty Tells Her Story
20 min, b/w, r, s: NDF
". . .When Betty tells her story the first time, she is
amusing, witty, comfortable. . .Later in the day Betty
tells her story again: the facts, the circumstances are
all the same, but Betty has subtly changed and the pain
of the memory emerges, with an aura of reflective self-
realization. Seldom in a film does the warmth and the
human spirit of an individual come across as it happens
here; seldom does a person reveal herself so honestly
and openly."-Patricia H. Black, Film Library Quarterly

Not So Young Now As Then (1974)
18 min, c, r, s: NDF.
"Changing moods captured at the filmmaker's 15th high
school reunion, ranging from excitement, humor, and
anxiety to nostalgia and a hint of sadness." -L.B.

Sometimes I Wonder Who I Am
5 min, b/w, r, s: NDF.
Film about facing one's identity.

BURST-TERRANELLA, FRAN
Another Chance (1983). Co-maker: Cheryl Gosa
24 min, c, r: IAI.
"Another Chance is a documentary film about an alternative
to prison." -F.B-T. and C.G.

<u>Cathy</u> (1982). Co-maker: Cheryl Gosa
14 min, c, r: IAI.
<u>Cathy</u> is a thought-provoking look at stereotypes about phy-
sical handicaps as seen in the story of a teenager with
cerebral palsy who decides to try out for cheerleader.
Cathy's courage and humor as she pursues her goal in-
spire discussion and lively dialogue among viewers of
all ages. In this short fiction film, Cathy is played
by Geri Jewell, a young actress and comedienne who has
cerebral palsy." F. B-T. and C.G.

<u>Lila</u> (1980). Co-maker: Cheryl Gosa
28 1/2 min, c, r,: IAI.
"<u>Lila</u> is an inspiring look at the life and work of 80-
year-old practicing psychiatrist Lila Bonner-Miller, who
is at once a doctor, a church leader, an artist, a great-
grandmother and a remarkable example to all who know her."
-F. B-T. and C.G.

<u>Meli</u> (1980). Co-maker: Cheryl Gosa
21 min, c, r: IAI.
"<u>Meli</u> is a film about juggling and struggling with a career
and a family and the realities and joys of having both."
- F. B-T. and C.G.

BUTE, MARY ELLEN
<u>Color Rhapsodie</u> (1951)
7 min, c, r: CFS.
"Beautiful abstract film visually interpreting Liszt's
'Hungarian Rhapsody #2'." -CFS

<u>Mood Contrasts</u>
7 min, c, r: CFS.
"Pioneer computer abstract film by a pioneer filmar-
tist, in which Rimsky-Korsakov's 'Hymn to the Sun' and
'Dance of the Tumblers' are visually interpreted by a
multitude of abstract and surreal visual images." -CFS

<u>Passages From Finnegan's Wake</u> (1965)
97 min, b/w, r: UCE. r,s: GRO.
"To Edmund Wilson ('The Dream Of H.C. Earwicker'),
<u>Finnegan's Wake</u> is an attempt to render the dream fan-
tasies and the half-conscious sensations experienced
by a single person in the course of a night's sleep. . ."
-GRO
See SCHOONMAKER, THELMA (Editors).

<u>Polka Graph</u>
6 min, c, r: CFS.
"Spritely abstract film visually interpreting Shosta-
kovich's polka from the 'Age of Gold' ballet suite."
-CFS

Spook Sport (1956). Co-maker: Norman McLaren
9 min, c, r: CFS.
"Semi-abstract stylized cartoon interpretation of Saint-
Saëns' 'Danse Macabre.'" -CFS

CALLACI, GLORIA
Jane Kennedy - To Be Free
See BAREY, PATRICIA.

CAMP, LIZABETH
Dream Your Own Dreams (1978)
21 min, c, r, s: FFC.
"In this informal look at Gwen Frostic's accomplishments
as poet, artist, businesswoman, philosopher, and lecturer,
the basic themes of each person's uniqueness. . .are shown
in both her own life and in her writings. . ." -FFC

CANNON, DYAN
Number One (1976)
42 min, b/w, available from Vince Cannon.
"An everyday story of everyday children - big ones and
little ones." -Program, 2nd International Festival of
Women's Films, New York

CARSON, JO
Himalayan Pilgrimage(1974)
16 min, c, r, s: SBC.
"Shot with a totally subjective eye, Himalayan Pilgrimage
conveys the mythic life sense and social elements of a
people who live in the world's highest mountains." -SBC

CARSON, KIT
Due to Ya Ya (1971)
10 min, c, r: CAN.
Study of the grandmother of the filmmaker. "A look
into the private world and special memories of an
86-year-old Greek immigrant. Set in a tiny New England
mill town near the seacoast." -CAN

The Long Distance Soft Shoe
3 1/2 min, b/w, r: CAN.
"Super light lyrical entertaining quickie film (no sex)
of a Golden Gate soft shoe crossing." -CAN

CHANGAR, MYRNA
The Neighborhood (1969)
18 min, b/w, r: FMC.
"Captures the spirit of the classic comedies in a contemporary setting. . .cops, sex, religion, film stereotypes." -FMC

Sempre Libra
15 1/2 min, c, r: FMC
"Misadventures of an astrological Everyman." -FMC

CHANGAS, ESTELLE
  Farenthold: A Texas Chronicle (1977)
  35 min, c, r, s: available from Farenthold.
  Documentary on the political career of Frances "Sissy"
  Farenthold of Texas.

CHAPELLE, POLA
  Fishes In Screaming Water (1979)
  5 1/2 min, c, r: FMC.
  "Stars Georgecat, with music composed and performed by
  his brother, Mamacat." -P.C.

  Going Home (1972)
  60 min, c, r: NYF
  Adolfas Makas goes home to Lithuania.

  How To Draw A Cat (1973)
  2 1/2 min, c, r: FMC.
  Film showing how to draw a cat.

  A Matter Of Baobab - With One Growth (1966-70)
  2 1/2 min, c, r: FMC.
  "Experiment in compression on film." -P.C.

  Those Memory Years (1972)
  8 1/2 min, c, r: FMC.
  "Autobiographical trivia. A short musical film which re-
  creates in full color, the longings and dreams of a woman
  of the past, replete with trembling blue mornings and
  the anxieties of a woman in search of Ful-film-ment."
  -P.C.

CHASE, DORIS
  Circles I (1971)
  7 min, c, r: FMC, W/A/F.
  The first film in the circle series.

  Circles I Variation II
  7 min, c, r: CFS.
  "The central theme of spiraling, revolving circles is rem-
  iniscent of Duchamp's 'anemic cinema' and enlists the viewer
  in a very pleasurable game of distinguishing color and shape."
  -Joan Braderman, Art Forum

  Circles II (1972)
  14 min, c, r: W/A/F.
  "Dance/sculpture film that explores new dimensions in
  color and space. . .develops like a fugue with dancers
  moving through themes that are repeated with variation
  ard multiplication." -D.C.

  Circles II Variation II (1973)
  8 min, c, r, s: PER.
  "Uses dancers, the Mary Staton Dance Ensemble of Seattle
  . . .primarily as elements in a rich semi-abstract movie in

which post-production work is almost as important as the
lovely rolling and dancing with circles (sculptures by
Doris Chase) that takes place in front of the camera. . ."
Roger Greenspun, <u>NYT</u>

<u>Conversation</u> (1981)
5 1/2 min,b/w, r: apply to filmmaker.
"Multiple overlapping images combine with still-frames
in a filmmaker's conversation with the repairman." -D.C.

<u>Dance Frame</u> (1978)
7 min, c, r: apply to filmmaker.
"The human form is used in composition with geometric
form in an exploration toward a third dimension through
juxtaposition of color and line." - D.C.

<u>Dance Out Line</u> (1978)
4 min, c, r: apply to filmmaker.
"An outline drawing animation on a black background of a
dancer's multiple image." -D.C.

<u>Jazz Dance</u> (1980)
4 min, c, r: apply to filmmaker.
Technology and art move to a jazz rhythm.

<u>Moon Gates</u> (1973)
5 1/2 min, c, r: W/A/F. r, s: PIC.
Sculpture combined with dance.

<u>Moon Gates Three Versions</u> (1974)
15 1/2 min, c, r: W/A/F
"Three 5-minute versions of a handsome dance piece. The
first version is original footage, the second, the same
footage optically printed, the third version, the film
video-synthesized. . .for dance and film study." -Freude
Bartlett

<u>Moon Redefined</u> (1980)
5 1/2 min, b/w, r: apply to filmmaker.
"Chase uses the architectural forms of her sculpture as an
integral element in this film. The image is video
synthesized and sequenced at variable speeds to create a
sensual rhythmic pattern. <u>Moon Redefined</u> was produced
at the Experiemental Television Center in Binghampton,
N.Y. with Peer Bode; music is by Bruce Ditmas." -D.C.

<u>Plexi Radar</u> (1981)
7 1/2 min, b/w, r: apply to filmmaker.
"<u>Plexi Radar</u> involves the filming of a revolving, cir-
cular plexi-glass sculpture which is then computer-sequenced.
The image of the sculpture is alternating and dividing
into numerous horizontal planes -- hypnotic in that the
subconscious imposes the illusion of an ever-changing
screen." -D.C.

<u>Rocking Orange I</u> (1974)
4 1/2 min, c, r: W/A/F
Dance and sculpture.

Rocking Orange III (1974)
4 1/2 min, c, r: W/A/F
Dance with sculpture.

Rocking Orange Three Versions (1975)
12 min, c, r, s: PIC.
"Based on the kinetic sculpture designed by Doris Chase
for the Seattle Opera Company Ballet. . .The first version
is a straight-forward presentation of dancers and sculpture in motion. . .The second part is the identical film
put through a video synthesizer and transferred back
to film. The third variation is achieved with the creative use of optical processing." -Pictura

Sculpture for Children (1974). Co-makers: Laurie Steig,
Elizabeth Wood
5 1/2 min, c, r: W/A/F. r, s: PIC.
"A NYC classroom of children ages 6-9 playing and learning
with Chase-designed set of 'Sculpture For Children'." -D.C.

Squares (1973)
6 min, c, r: W/A/F. r, s: PIC.
"Computer-generated abstract film in which multi-images
of squares in both positive and negative colors float
gracefully in space." -CFS

Tall Arches III (1974)
6 min, c, r, FNC
"Simple motions are multiplied in visual echoes of the
primary colors as the dancers reach, glide, and gesture,
their images finally resolved into one."-Mac

Variation Two (1978)
11 min, c, r: apply to filmmaker.
"A choreographic statement designed for film in which
numerous effects serve to enlarge the aesthetic concept."
-D.C.

CHEN, BETTY
  Marguerite
  4 min, r, s: SBC.
  "Poetic, animated film about a woman breaking up with
  her husband." -Freude Bartlett

CHILD, ABIGAIL
  Daylight Test Section (1975-78)
  4 min, c, silent, r: CAN.
  "Recurring emergence of narrative despite attempts at
  their destruction. The 'loaded' image becomes the deter-
  minant feature for reading otherwise unemotional footage;
  a first experiment in what is an ongoing investigation."
  -CAN

Game (1972). Co-maker: Jonathan Child
38 min, b/w, r: UCE.
The game between a pimp and prostitute.

Pacific Far East Line (1978-79)
15 min, c, silent, r: CAN.
"A year's view of the changing skyline of Downtown San
Francisco. My windows become a sun dial; the footage re-
ordering time and memory." -A.C.

Peripeteia I And II (1977-78)
12 min, c, silent, r: CAN.
"Navigation spiralling sunward; exploring the movement
of forest and body. . .Peripeteia II continues this exploration of space, contrasting more severely the fixed
camera (frames' sight) with the moving body (in site)." -A.C.

Some Exterior Presence (1977)
8 min, c, silent, r: CAN.
". . .the film is largely red, black, and white. The effect is one of starkness, yet tempered by the richness
of the red and its alternating suggestions of violence,
church, and ritual." -L. Dackman, Cinemanews.

CHOPRA, JOYCE
Clorae And Albie (1975)
36 min, c, r: EDC.
Two women discuss their careers.

Girls At 12 (1974)
30 min, c, r: UCE. r,s: EDC.
"A look at 2 girls, just on the edge of childhood, and
the many ways in which the rituals of being feminine are
passed along to them." -J.C.

Happy Mother's Day (1964). Co-maker: Richard Leacock
26 min, b/w, r: UCE.
"Documentary on Mary Ann Fischer of Aberdeen, South
Dakota who became the mother of quintuplets (on top
of five other children)." -Women's Film Co-op.

Joyce At 34. Co-maker: Claudia Weill
28 min, c, r: NDF.
The birth of her daughter causes Chopra to examine her
life and career at age 34.
See WEILL, CLAUDIA (Directors, Chapter I).

Matina Horner: Portrait Of A Person (1973). Co-maker: Claudia
Weill
16 min, c, r: UCE. r, s: PNX.
"Excellent portrait of the noted educator and president
of Radcliffe College. Employs still photographs, old home
movies, and an animated sequence to convey warmth, and
innovative ideas." -UCE

Sally Garcia and Family (1978)
35 min, c, r, s: EDC.
"Sally Garcia and Family is an unscripted documentary
about a growing phenomenon of our time - the woman returning to work as she enters middle age, despite her
satisfaction with home and family." -EDC

That Our Children Will Not Die (1978)
60 min, c, r, s: FOR.
"A look at community-based primary health care services
in five locations in Nigeria." -Program, 21st Annual
American Film Festival

CHOY, CHRISTINE
From Spikes To Spindles (1976)
50 min, c, r, s: TWN.
"Formerly depicted by Western filmmakers as exotic and
mysterious. . .the Chinese Americans, known as the 'silent
minority', are emerging from a period of isolation. . .
director Chris Choy has broken through that barrier of
stereotypes, bringing to the screen a genuine portrait
of the Chinese community. . ." -TWN

Inside Women Inside (1978). Co-maker: Cynthia Maurizio
28 min, c, r, s: TWN.
"How does a woman cope with such common occurrences as
illness, pregnancy and family conflicts when she is sent
away to prison? At the North Carolina Correctional
Center for Women and the Correctional Institute for
Women at Riker's Island, New York, a number of women
answer these questions quite candidly." -TWN

CHURCHILL, JOAN
Sylvia, Fran And Joy (1973)
25 min, b/w, r: UCE. r,s: CHU.
Study of three women.

Tattooed Tears (1978). Co-maker: Nick Broomfield
88 min, c, r, s: CHU.
"Shows life in a California prison for youthful offend-
ers, recording the pressure and intensity of an enclosed
space, a life totally without privacy. Shown are the se-
curity measures, the meaningless rows, the rituals and
retreats into private realities, indoctrination, training
and education. The film concentrates on five prisoners
as they do their time." -Program, 21st Annual American
Film Festival

CHYTILOVA, VERA (Czechoslovakian)
The Ceiling
40 min, b/w, r, s: ICA.
"The Ceiling is a drama of a young woman who discovers
she has set for herself a low 'ceiling' of attainment
by dropping out of school to become a fashion model."
-Icarus

Daisies (1966)
74 min, c, Czech with English subtitles, r: FNC.
"Daisies attempts the construction of an artificial
reality in the story of two young, reckless anti-heroines. . .
Daisies utilizes sophisticated editing of motion filmed
at an unreal speed, of superimposition, optical printing,
frame tinting and combining black and white and color."
-Milos Stehlik

Something Different (1963)
80 min, b/w, r, s: ICA.
"Something Different compares the quest for meaning in
life as it evolves in the life of two very different
women. . .a harried middle-aged housewife, and. . .a
champion gymnast." -Icarus.

CITRON, MICHELLE
Daughter Rite (1978)
48 min, c, r, s: NWU.
"Explores the mother/daughter and sibling sister relationships as seen from ther perspective of the daughters
of two different families, dealing with the themes of
anger, love, grief, betrayal, manipulation, and pat-
terning." -Program, 21st Annual American Film Festival

CLARKE, SHIRLEY
Bridges-Go-Round (1958)
3 1/2 min, c, r: CAN. r, s: SBC.
8 min, c, r: MMA. (8 minute includes two versions:
electronic sound, as well as jazz soundtrack).
Clarke animates the bridges around New York City.

Bullfight (1955)
9 min, c, r: MMA.
A bullfight combined with dance.

The Connection (1960)
103 min, b/w, r: NYF.
"Classic of improvisational cinema - eight junkies
waiting for a fix in a Greenwich Village loft." -NYF

Cool World (1963
100 min, b/w, r: ZPH.
Film study of Harlem street gangs from Warren Miller's novel.

Dance In The Sun (1953)
6 min, b/w, r: MMA.
"Two renditions--one in the rehearsal hall, the other on
a beach--of the same dance (edited together)." -MMA

In Paris Parks (1955)
15 min, c, r: MMA.
"A dance film of children playing in Paris parks." -S.C.

A Lover's Quarrel With The World (1964)
52 min, b/w, r: KPF, UCE
Film study of the poet Robert Frost.

A Moment In Love (1958)
8 min, c, r: MMA.
"A boy and a girl meet in a romantic wooded glen and with
a leap into space take off into a dance. Multiple images
and controlled color turn the lovers into blossoming
flowers." -MMA

Mysterium (1978)
11 min, c, r, s: SPI.
"The enigma of the masculine-feminine is explored from
its primordial beginnings. The filmmaker takes the
choreography and gives it a new existence as a dance film."
-Program, 21st Annual American Film Festival

Portrait of Jason (1967)
105 min, b/w, r: NYF.
Jason Holliday,a black homosexual prostitute, opens his
life to Shirley Clarke's camera. "The most extraordinary
film I've seen in my life is certainly Portrait of Jason."
-Ingmar Bergman

A Scary Time (1960)
20 min, b/w, r: MMA.
This touching plea for the United Nations Children's Fund
"begins as a Halloween celebration and continues to show
these nightmares come true in the intercut scenes of
children starving. . ." -MMA

Skyscraper (1959)
20 min, c & b/w, r: MMA, UCE.
Clarke "goes to work" on a skyscraper with her camera.

CLEMENT, CAROL
Luna Tune (1979)
2 1/2 min, c, r: WMM.
"Luna Tune, a sand animation, celebrates women's spiritua-
ality with 80-year-old lesbian poet Elsa Gidlow reading her
work, 'What If. . .the Million and First Meditation. . .'"
-WMM

Musereel #1
See BOSTROM, DENISE. (Directors, Chapter I).

Surviva (1980). Co-maker: Ariel Dougherty
35 min, c, r: WMM.
"Centering on one woman artist, Surviva combines animation and nature montage with documentary and narrative
sequences. . ." -WMM

COLLACHIA, JEANNE
Robert Frost's The Death Of The Hired Man (1979)
21 min, c, r, s: EBE.
"A dramatization of a poem by Robert Frost. The story
has been adapted for film using Frost's dialogue word for
word, and visually translating the spirit and texture
of Frost's poetry." -Program, 21st Annual American Film
Festival

COLLINS, JUDY
Antonia: A Portrait Of The Woman (1974). Co-maker: Jill
Godmilow
58 min, c, r: BUD, UCE. r,s: PNX.
Moving documentary concerning Antonia Brico, who dis-
cusses her debut in the 1930's and her life as a woman
conductor.
See GODMILOW, JILL (Directors, Chapter I).

CONRAD, BEVERLY
Coming Attractions (1970). Co-maker: Tony Conrad
77 min, c, r: FMC.
". . .looks backward into the memories and forward into
the future of Francis Francine, an elegantly dowdy trans-
vestitite of, and indeed beyond, a certain age." -Roger
Greenspun, NYT

Four Square (1971). Co-maker: Tony Conrad
18 min, c, silent, r: FMC.
"Designed for simultaneous projection by 4 projectors on
4 screens arranged in a square, enclosing the audience. . .
basically a film about red, the space and time. . ." -T. & B.
Conrad

Straight And Narrow (1970). Co-maker: Tony Conrad
10 min, b/w, r: FMC.
". . .A study in subjective color and visual rhythm, the hypnotic poetry of the images will cause viewers to experience
a programmed gamut of hallucinatory color effects. " -T. & B.
Conrad

COOLIDGE, MARTHA
  Bimbo (1978)
  17 min, c, r, s: FNC.
  "Kenny is 30 when he meets his two best friends from
  high school for a private reunion. They have changed.
  Seeing them forces Kenny to reevaluate his career choice
  . . ." -Program, 21st Annual American Film Festival

  David: Off And On (1972)
  42 min, c, r: VIE. r, s: FNC.
  "Martha Coolidge's remarkable documentary about her drug-
  addicted brother, David. David is gentle, good-humored,
  handsome, obviously intelligent. In his twenty-one years,
  he has been a schoolboy, an alcoholic, a heroin addict,
  a convict, a mental patient, a resident of purgatory and
  hell." -VIE

  More Than A School (1973)
  55 min, c, r, s: FNC.
  Film study of the Community School in Long Island, New
  York.

  Not A Pretty Picture (1973)
  81 min, c, r: FNC.
  "A woman's perspective on rape based on the filmmaker's
  own experience in boarding school. . .The young actors
  alternate between acting their roles and discussing with
  the director the disturbing personal connections they
  feel with the characters they play. The film is a
  devastating portrait of how people are trapped into sex
  roles that shape their lives." -Program, 2nd International
  Festival Of Women's Films, New York. Beautifully edited by
  Suzanne Pettit.

  An Old Fashioned Woman (1974)
  49 min, c, r, s: FNC.
  Coolidge's study of her grandmother.

  Passing Quietly Through (1971). Co-maker: Dinitia
  McCarthy
  26 min, b/w, r, s: GRO.
  "Blunt and human encounter between a nurse and an aging
  man." -Films on Death and Dying, EFLA

COUZIN, SHARON
  Roseblood
  7 1/2 min, c, r: CAN.
  "Images of a woman in dance, in flora, in picture, in
  eyes, in architecture, in sunshine, in color, in crystal,
  in space, in confusion, in danger, in disintegration, in
  her hand, in birth, in the valley of Sorrow, in the sea,
  in repetition, in sculpture and in herself." -CAN

COX, NELL
  A To B (1970)
  36 min, c, r: UCE.
  Film view of a Southern girl's adolescence.

CRAFTS, LISA
  Desire Pie (1977.)
  4 1/2 min, c, r, s: MUL, SBC.
  "Suggesting the possibility of a 'cosmic rhythm,' Desire
  Pie is explicit in its sexuality; a sensual rendering
  of a woman's imagination. Excellent as an erotic short,
  this film would also be a lighthearted addition to classes
  in human sexuality and awareness." -SBC

CROMMIE, KAREN
  The Life And Death Of Frida Kahlo (1975).Co-maker: David
  Crommie
  40 min, c, r, s: SBC.
  "The film focuses on the events that molded Kahlo's life:
  the childhood spinal injury which resulted in her being
  childless and eventually crippled; her marriage to (Diego)
  Rivera; and endurance of constant physical and emotional
  turmoil, which became the focal point of her art." -Linda
  Gross, L.A. Times

  V.D. And Women (1978). Co-maker: David Crommie
  17 min, c, r, s: PRE.
  "Produced by a woman, for women, and with an all-women
  cast, the film has a woman-to-woman intimacy that makes
  it successful where other films on the same subject may
  fail." -PRE

CRUIKSHANK, SALLY
  Chow Fun
  4 1/2 min, c, r, s: SBC.
  "Influenced by the fluid, oozing motion of 30's cartoons
  and the bright colors and designs of Chinese food pack-
  aging." -S.C.

  Fun On Mars
  4 min, c, r, s: SBC.
  Two people travel to Mars for a visit.

  Make Me Psychic (1979)
  8 min, c, available from filmmaker.
  "Make Me Psychic. . .features a . . .heroine, who somehow
  acquires psychokinetic powers, with the result that she can
  eat cookies, drink, and extract money from men's pockets
  by magnetic attraction. There is a prime little sequence
  in which she passes a powder puff over her face and magically
  assumes the features of a vamp, and buffs her nails into
  flaming blowtorches." -Edgar Daniels, American Film

Quasi At The Quackadero (1975)
10 min, c, r, s: SBC.
"The wacky adventures of a couple of science fiction
ducks who visit an amusement park in the future, where
concessions exploit time travel and psychic discoveries."
-S.C.

CURRY, TARA ALEXANDER
The Imaginarium (1978)
15 min, c, r, s: MMA.
"Presents the Imaginarium, a team of artists, arts spe-
cialists and museum educators who design unique partici-
patory experiences for children, integrating movement,
music and visual arts. . ." -Program, 21st Annual American
Film Festival

DANCOFF, JUDITH
Judy Chicago And The California Girls
27 min, c, r: CFS.
Film concerning artist Judy Chicago.

DAVENPORT, REBECCA
The Upperville Show. Co-maker: Tom Davenport
10 min, b/w, available from filmmaker.
"Smooth and creamy finesse of the skilled, very rich at
leisure." -NLC. Filmed at a horse show in Upperville,
Virginia.

DAVEY, FLORENCE
Indian Holy Men (Darshan). Co-maker: Satyam Shivan
Sandaram
28 min, c, r: NLC.
Four Indian Holy Men and their beliefs are examined.

DECOLA, SHEILA
Mrs. Cop (1973). Co-maker: Joe DeCola
16 min, c, r: UCE.
"Mary Ellen Albrecht is a regular police sergeant in the
Washington, D.C. force. The film shows her working in
various areas, in the cells of the prison, in court. . .
Interviews with Mary Ellen, her husband, and fellow police
officers, who discuss their feelings about working with
a woman." -Alternatives, EFLA

DEEN, NEDRA
7 1/2 Minute Film (1974)
7 1/2 min, c, r, s: SBC.
"A story of paralysis and waste set in Colfax, Louisiana. It is a beautifully shot film of a contemporary
Southern belle packing and leaving home to wait for a man
at a bus stop - the man who never comes." -Siew Hwa
Beh, Women And Film

DE HIRSCH, STORM

Cayuga Run (1967). Hudson River Diary: Book I
18 min, c, r: CAN, FMC.
The Cayuga train makes its run along the riverbank of the
Hudson from NYC to Poughkeepsie, "celebrating the seasons
and the river Hudson." -S.D.H.

The Color Of Ritual, The Color Of Thought
26 min, c, r: FMC.
Trilogy consisting of Divinations, Shaman, and Peyote
Queen. "Multiple voyages into varied continents of the
self, exploring. . .areas of no-time, new space. All three
are inter-related and best experienced together. " -S.D.H.
(Each film is a unit in itself and may be rented separately.)

Divinations (1964)
6 min, c, r: FMC.
"Delicately wrought fantasies combining photographed and
brilliantly hand-painted objects and abstractions." -Ken
Kelman, The Nation

Experiment in Meditation (1971)
18 min, c, silent, r: FMC.
"Zooming in on the rose becomes a figure of vision for
the act of meditation; in and out, and back again for a
closer, more inspective, introspective look." -Casey
Charness

Goodbye In The Mirror (1964)
80 min, b/w, r: FMC.
Thoughts and actions of three women living in Rome, Italy.

Journey Around A Zero (1963)
3 min, b/w, r: FMC.
"A phallic invocation. An abstract occasion of image
and sound." -S.D.H.

Lace of Summer (1973)
4 min, c, silent, r: FMC.
"Cine-sonnet #1" -Bonnie Dawson, Women's Films In Print

Newsreel: Jonas In The Brig
5 min, b/w, silent, r: FMC.
"A newsreel of Jonas Mekas shooting his filmed version
of 'The Brig' on the set of the Living Theatre's production."
-S.D.H.

Peyote Queen (1965)
8 min, c, r: CAN, FMC.
"A journey through the underworld of sensory derangement
. . .where the Mysteries are enacted in the Theatre of the
Soul." -S.D.H.

River-Ghost (1973) Hudson River Diary: Book IV
9 min, c, r: FMC.
"Reflections on a haunted cove along the banks of the
Hudson River." -S.D.H.

September Express (1973)
6 min, c, silent, r: FMC.
"Layers of visual movement and stationary objects en-
twine with memory-traces to structure the shape of
motion in time." -S.D.H.

Shaman, A Tapestry For Sorcerers (1967)
12 min, c, r: FMC.
"Dedicated to all the magic makers of the world who
weave a talisman for man's rebirth in his house of breath."
-S.D.H.

Sing Lotus (1966)
14 min, c, r: FMC.
"18th century Indian miniatures enact a traditional wedding ceremony of a Hindu Prince and Princess. An exotic
landscape of the mind; fable-fantasy of childhood-man-
hood." -S.D.H.

Tattooed Man (1969)
35 min, c, r: CAN, FMC.
"Children of the Water World drift the ocean in an empty
crystal ball. . .then come to watch the Tattooed Man,
marked for life, tattooed by tears running down the womb..."
-S.D.H.

Third Eve Butterfly (1968)
10 min, c, dual screen projection, r: FMC.
"A kind of atonal visual rhythm...Butterflies are image
motifs in a series of semi-abstract color pattern that
vibrate, jump and change frequently..." -Parker Tyler,
Understanding Films

Trap Dance
1 1/2 min, b/w, r: FMC.
"An Angry Arts 'protest film' with Black and White visuals."
-S.D.H.

Wintergarden (1973). Hudson River Diary: Book III
5 min, c, r: FMC.
"Tonight is a snowbird with heart hung hostage in a water
drop, its iceflaked starfeet remembering the gargoyle's
empty threat to drown in rivulets of melting feather
frost." -S.D.H.

DEITCH, DONNA
Berkeley 12-1
5 min, b/w, r: CAN.
Police versus protestors in Berkeley.

Memorabilia
4 min, c, r: CAN, FMC.
"A toy robot shoots the world but finds that it can no
longer function at the feet of Richard Nixon, who is
stuck to the fence around a cemetery." -FMC

P.P.1
7 min, c, r: CAN.
"Once upon a Mayjune (1969) many of the people of Berkeley planted a part of a vacant land with trees and flowers
and other living things for children and other living people."
-D.D.

Portrait
14 min, c, r: CAN.
"An awe-inspiring surreal allegory of man's destruction
of himself and his environment, expressed through haunting,
superimposed images of overwhelming power and authority."
-Kevin Thomas, L.A. Times

She Was A Visitor
2 min, c, r: CAN, FMC.
"An autobiographical space trip across the bridge of the
midnight color." -D.D.

Woman To Woman (1975)
55 min, c, r, s: SBC.
"A documentary film about hookers, housewives and other
mothers." -D.D. "Woman To Woman could become the
Potemkin of the women's movement." -David Rosenbaum,
Boston Phoenix

DEMETRAKAS, JOHANNA
Celebration At Big Sur (1971). Co-maker: Baird Bryant
85 min, c, r: FNC.
Benefit concert with Joni Mitchell, Joan Baez, John
Sebastian, and Crosby, Stills, Nash and Young.

Right Out Of History - The Making Of Judy Chicago's
Dinner Party (1980)
75 min, c, r: KPF.
"This document of feminist/artist Judy Chicago's labor of
love is an artistic tribute to important and often for-
gotten creative women of history. As an activist, Chicago
has her moments of shrillness...but the final result of her
perseverance is exalting and Demetrakas' monumental task
of filming and editing four years of excitement is as
striking as the event itself." -KPF

See DEMETRAKAS, JOHANNA (Editors).

DEREN, MAYA
At Land (1944)
15 min, b/w, silent, r, s: GRO.
"A searching out, at any cost, for control over one's
destiny." -Jeanne Betancourt, Women In Focus

Meditation On Violence (1948)
12 min, b/w, silent, r, s: GRO.
Film showing examples of Chinese boxing.

Meshes Of The Afternoon (1943). Co-maker: Alexander
Hammid
14 min, b/w, r: FNC, r, s: KPF. 20 min, s: REE.
"Deren's first work which sparked the post-war experimental film revival in U.S. Noted for its imagery and
symbolism, preoccupation with the unconscious, and
shifting transitions between dream, nightmare, and reality."
-Bonnie Dawson, Women's Films In Print

The Private Life Of A Cat
30 min, b/w, r: GRO.
How to take care of kittens.

Ritual In Transfigured Time (1946)
15 min, b/w, silent, r, s: GRO.
"Ritual is about the nature and process of change."
-M.D.

A Study In Choreography For Camera (1945)
4 min, b/w, silent, r, s: GRO.
"Classic experiment in film-dance. Through an exploitation of cinematic techniques, camera creates its own
space and time." -GRO

The Very Eye Of Night (1959)
18 min, b/w, r, s: GRO.
"A celestial cine-ballet of night, filmed in the negative. The dancers become cosmic and four-dimensional,
advancing, as if planets in the night sky, by the blind
incalculable accuracies of sleepwalkers." -GRO

DOLAN, MARIANNE
  Damages. Co-maker: Maurice Levy
  9 min, c, r: CAN.
  "Director Robert Altman exchanges roles with his star
  Susannah York in a re-enactment of Altman's film Images."
  -CAN

  Zinc Ointment. Co-maker: Maurice Levy
  9 1/2 min, c, r: CAN.
  "Warren Beatty and Julie Christie have last laugh on
  director Robert Altman on set of McCabe And Mrs. Miller."
  -CAN

DOOGAN, MARGARET BAILEY
  Screw (1977)
  3 min, c, r, s: SBC.
  "Set to the words of a 'technical love poem' ("Screw" by
  Diane Wakowski), this film is one woman's visual interpretation of the word 'screw.' Graphically elegant and imaginative, Screw is a witty bedroom fantasy - a personal
  questioning of male/female relationships that strikes a
  a chord at the very heart of our being." -SBC

DORE, O.
  Alaska (1968)
  18 min, c, silent, r: CAN.
  "An emigration film. A dream of myself, the consequence
  of the act with society." -D.O.

  Blonde Barbarei (1972)
  25 min, c & b/w, r: CAN.
  "A film for the liberation of sensuality - a film against
  the hospitalisme of society." -Andreas Weiland

  Jum-Jum. Co-maker: Werner Nekes
  10 min, c, r: CAN.
  "Dimensions of movement:
  1. Swinging movement
  2. Changes of light
  3. Constellations of persons and objects." -CAN

  Kaldalon (1970-71)
  45 min, c, r: CAN.
  ". . .one of the most beautiful pieces of 'personal' filmmaking. . .attempt to recreate the light of that place on
  film. . ." -Tony Reif, Vancouver Cinematheque.

  Kaskara (1974)
  21 min, c, r: CAN.
  "A balance of enclosed beings in divided space. Winglike
  displacements through different kinds of settings in
  distinct planes of multiple exposures, of facades and of
  spaces in which a person enters and exits. . ." -D.O.

Lawale (1969)
30 min, c, r: CAN.
"Dore O.'s Lawale is a strange succession of tableaux of
four women and a man which gives the sense of a sort of
dream family locked in an antiseptic world of endless
afternoon teas, dinners and waiting. Often her images
seem to be stills either before or after something has
been said." -Michael Reynolds, Berkeley Barb

DOUGERTY, ARIEL
Musereel #1
See BOSTROM, DENISE (Directors, Chapter I).

Surviva (1980)
See CLEMENT, CAROL (Directors, Chapter I).

Sweet Bananas (1972)
30 min, c, r, s: WMM.
"An unsettling documentary portraying the love/hate
ambivalence of contemporary women." -WMM

DOURMASHKIN, BARBARA
Help, I'm Shrinking (1975)
12 min, c, r, s: FNC.
"A defeatist child and an advice-giving butterfly are
the stars of this animated fable." -FNC

Isabella And The Magic Brush (1976)
14 min, c, r, s: FFC.
"This animated fantasy, adapted from a Chinese tale,
tells of little Isabella whose desire to be an artist
is thwarted by poverty, a tyrant king, her own parents,
who think she should be a cook, and by the court painter
who fears competition." -FFC

Petronella (1978)
14 min, c, animated, r, s: FFC.
"In this humorous twist of the timeless fairytale plot
of prince rescues princess, Princess Petronella feels
that she deserves equal opportunity, to go forth and
rescue a prince. . ." -FFC

DRUKS, RENATA
A Painter's Journal
10 min, c, r: CFS.
"A subjective documentary in semi-surrealistic style of
a painter's approach to her art." -CFS

DUGA, IRENE
Pesca Picsa (1968)
3 1/2 min, c, r: FMC.
"Animated and live. A sensual film of continuous orgasm
of pulsating color and image." -I.D.

Turtle Soup (1967)
5 1/2 min, c, r: FMC.
"Animated and live...dream experience of childhood, youth,
old age; past, present, future; child, parent, grand-
parent; beauty, vanity, despair; dream, reality, illusion." -I.D.

DUIGNAN, PATRICIA ROSE
  Women On Orgasm (1974)
  15 min, c, r, s: MUL.
  Women discuss orgasm.

DU LUART, YOLANDE
  Angela Davis: Portrait Of A Revolutionary (1971)
  60 min, b/w, r: NYF.
  Film study of Angela Davis.

DUNLAP, MONICA
  Katy (1974)
  16 min, c, r: UCE.
  "Dramatic portrayal of a preteen girl's fight to be permitted to deliver newspapers along with the boys. Made
  for CBS." -UCE

DUPREE, NANACY
  Afghan Women (1975). Co-makers: Herbert DiGioia, Louis
  Dupree, David Hancock, Josephine Powell, Toryali Shafak,
  Judith von Daler
  17 min, c, r: UCE.
  "Secluded as they are, these women have strong personal-
  ities and play a dominant role in certain aspects of do-
  mestic affairs. They discuss marriage, dowries, polygamy,
  birth control, education of boys and girls." -American
  Universities Field Staff

  Women In A Changing World (1975). Co-makers: George
  Chang, Richard Chen, Herbert Digioia, Louis Dupree,
  Loren Fessler, David Hancock, Norman Miller, Patrick
  Mok, Josephine Powell, Toryali Shafak, Judith von Daler
  48 min, c, r: UCE.
  Women from different cultures and their equal rights
  are examined.

DURAS, MARGUERITE (French)
  Destroy, She Said (1969)
  100 min, b/w, French with English subtitles, r, s: GRO.
  "Marguerite Duras has created a hypnotic, and haunting
  film about five alienated people, isolated in an unworld-
  ly hotel. Enmeshed in a ritualistic power game, they
  inexorably assume interchangeable personalities as each
  acts out his own ambiguous charade..." -GRO

Nathalie Granger (1972)
83 min, b/w, r: BAU.
Nathalie Granger is about an afternoon in the lives of
two women, two children and a salesman. It is also about
the relationships between parents and children, between
women and between society and the individual." -BAU.
With Jeanne Moreau and Lucia Bose.

The Truck (Le Camion) (1978)
80 min, c, r: BAU.
"Le Camion is about a filmmaker going over the script of
a movie she wants to make with the other leading player.
They are the only two people we see: the other footage is
on the 5-axle truck itself rolling through the desolately
beautiful countryside outside Paris." -BAU

DURRIN, GINNY
Hard Work (1978)
29 min, c, r, s: MTI.
"Film about...Margo St. James and her fight to have prostitution decriminalized. Hard Work revolves around the
Hooker's Convention in Washington, D.C. ...The action
takes place over a five-day period and includes a visit to
the Women's Detention Center, TV and press interviews,
a congressional cocktail party...and a sunrise walk
around the White House." -MTI

EDELHEIT, MARTHA
Camino Real (1972)
3 min, c, silent, available from the filmmaker.
"Dreams: to have the courage to make something useless
(to sleep fiercely) endlessly." -M.E.

Hats,Bottles, and Bones, A Portrait Of Sari Dienes (1977)
22 min, c, r, s: W/A/F.
"A poetic interpretation of the life and work of the 79
year old artist." -W/A/F

Sno-White (Crimson) (1975)
7 min, c, r, s: W/A/F.
"A mini introduction to part of The Albino Queen And
Sno-White In Triplicate also made by Edelheit. Split-
screened." -W/A/F

ERLICH, GRETEL
Jockey (1973)
25 min, c, r: UCE.
Film concerning the first female jockey, Penny Ann
Early.

ELAM, JOANN
Rape
35 min, b/w, r: CAN.
"In Rape, three rape victims speak to the filmmaker and
to each other about their experiences." -CAN. "Rape is
a rare film for its refusal to co-opt a feminist subject
with a reactionary patriarchal form." -Ruby Rich

EMSWILER, SHARON
Included Out (1973)
2 min, c, r: UCE.
"Humorously animated comment on the sexist bias of the
English language and its effect on social values. A
woman is told that 'man' includes 'woman' as well - until she tries to enter a men's room." -UCE

FADIMAN, DOROTHY
Radiance: The Experience Of Light (1978)
22 min, c, r, s: PYR.
"Radiance is a journey from the light in nature to the
radiant spirit in all life. Using a stunning array of
religious art, video images, nature photography and kinetic mandalas, the filmmaker communicates her own encounter
with the phenomena of inner light." -PYR

FANSHEL, SUSAN
Nevelson In Process (1977). Co-maker: Jill Godmilow
30 min, c, r, s: FNC.
"Louise Nevelson is know for her innovative environmental
art. Her 'process' is dramatically demonstrated on camera
as she creates two sculptures, one of wood and one of
metal." -FNC
See GODMILOW, JILL (Directors, Chapter I).

Voulkos And Company (1975)
42 min, c, r: ODE.
Film study of the sculptor Peter Voulkos.

FAYMAN, LYNN
Greensleeves
4 min, c, r: CFS.
"Pure color forms float lyrically across the screen in
this abstract film exercise to the music of 'Greensleeves.'"
-CFS

Sophisticated Vamp
4 min, c, r: CFS.
"Pure color forms glide across the screen to the music
of a vamp in this abstract exercise." -CFS

FEFERMAN, LINDA
  Dirty Books (1971)
  14 min, c, r: NLC.
  "Spoof on a young woman making a living from writing
  pornography when her serious work won't sell." -Bonnie
  Dawson, Women's Films In Print

  Elizabeth Swados: The Girl With The Incredible Feeling
  39 min, c, r: VIE.
  "Possibly the best film for introducing modern classical
  music to a rock-oriented group, this is a witty portrait
  of the increasingly famous young composer Elizabeth
  Swados." -VIE

  Linda's Film - Menstruation (1974)
  18 min, c, r, s: FOC, PNX.
  An examination of menstruation - fact and fiction.

FEINER, LISA
  On A Question Of Justice
  29 min, c, r, s: GRO.
  "A number of recent court cases and studies have drama-
  tized numerous cases of rape and brutalization of women
  that have gone unpunished. This remarkable film deals
  with the physical oppression of women and the unjust
  penalties sometimes faced by women who have been convicted of crimes." -GRO

  Three
  18 min, c, r, s: GRO.
  "This film examines the subject of bisexuality in women.
  Through a series of illuminating interviews, a number of
  women offer candid views of what they expect from their
  own sexual and emotional relationships as well as how
  they define their own femininity and their assessments
  of the woman's role in contemporary society." -GRO

FELTER, SUSAN
  Pescados Vivos
  20 min, c & b/w, r: CAN.
  "A warm and comic vision of life with the aid of the magical optical printer." -CAN

FIRESTONE, CINDA
  Attica (1973)
  80 min, c & b/w, r: UCE.
  Film study of the prison.

Mountain People (1978)
52 min, c, r, 1: CIV.
"...John and Nora Sturgill, in their eighties, Myrtle
Thomas and Lula McCloud, in their seventies, know no way
of life other than self-sufficiency...Mountain People
examines this disappearing way of life and breed of elderly people in rural America." -CIV

Retirement (1978)
50 min, c, r, 1: CIV.
"Retirement examines the growing controversy concerning
the ultimate damage that restricted adult retirement
communities may have on our society..." -CIV

South Beach (1978)
30 min, c, r, 1: CIV.
"South Beach focuses on the everyday life of retirees
living in South Miami Beach, Florida who are forced to
stretch their $140 Social Security checks to cover their
rent, food and doctor bills and who must deal with isolation as their friends die and their families ignore them."
-CIV

FISHER, HOLLY
Psssht
6 min, c, r: CFS.
"Delightful topical spoof on the use of aerosol cans in
the average American household." -CFS

FLEMING, LOUISE
Just Briefly (1976)
15 min, b/w, r, s: PNX.
"Just Briefly is a glimpse of a young black woman's
search for emotional fulfillment." -PNX

FRANCO, DEBRA
A Wedding In The Family (1978)
22 min, c, r, s: NDF.
Film about the filmmaker's sister and her wedding.

FREDRICKSON, LINDA
New Man
5 min, b/w, r: CAN.
"Based on a true story of a child who shoots and kills
his younger brother. Film is a montage of T.V. violence
intercut with children playing at killing each other and
scenes in toy stores." -CAN

FREEMAN, JOAN
Toilette (1977)
7 min, c, r: FNC.
"A dilemma of identity, Toilette is a funny account in
clay animation of a woman uncertain of who she is." -FNC

FREEMAN, MONICA J.
A Sense Of Pride - Hamilton Heights (1978)
15 min, c, r, s: available from filmmaker.
"The Hamilton Heights neighborhood in Harlem is explored
through interviews and visuals which show how the residents' sense of pride, struggle and pulling together make
it the landmark area that it is today." -Program, 21st
Annual America Film Festival

Valerie: A Woman! An Artist! A Philosophy Of Life! (1975)
15 min, c, r, s: PNX.
Film portrait of sculptor Valerie Maynard.

FREUDE
Folly (1972)
3 min, c, r: CAN. r, s: SBC.
"Woman endlessly sweeping the sand back into the sea!"
-F.B.

One And The Same (1972-73). Co-maker: Gunvor Nelson
4 min, c, r: CAN. r, s: SBC.
"Two friends, both filmmakers, had a terrific time making
and playing in this movie." -Programme, "Women and Film
Festival," Toronto

My Life In Art (1968-74)
40 min, c, r: CAN, SBC.
Includes Sacred Heart Of Jesus, Promise Her Anything But
Give Her The Kitchen Sink, Shooting Star, Standup And Be
Counted, Adam's Birth, Sweet Dreams, Folly, Women And Chil-
ren At Large, and One And The Same. Some of these
films are available for rental individually - Sacred Heart
Of Jesus and Adam's Birth can only be rented on this reel.

The Party (1969). Co-maker: Scott Bartlett
3 min, b/w, r: CAN.
"Going down on American television." -CAN

Promise Her Anything But Give Her The Kitchen Sink (1969)
3 min, c, r: CAN. r, s: SBC.
"An inter-balancing of opposing emotions, a beautiful
love-poem to her husband, a journey of mind-expansion and
woman's statement of rebellion." -Kirk Tougas, Georgia
Straight

Shooting Star (1970)
5 min, c, and b/w, r: CAN. r, s: SBC.
"Humour as an agent of de-mystification...the multi-layers
of video within film and film within film comment, with
great jest, upon the nature of these pre-occupations."
-Kirk Tougas, Georgia Straight

Standup And Be Counted (1969). Co-maker: Scott Bartlett
3 min, c, r: CAN. r, s: SBC.
No summary available.

Sweet Dreams (1971)
3 min, c, r: CAN. r, s: SBC.
"Structures child/mother and child/dolphin relationships
and links the balletic movement of dolphins within a water
womb to the movement of the child...the soundtrack (hump-
back whales) emphasizes a primeval language of communi-
cation, finding union with the natural languages of the
child." -Kirk Tougas, Georgia Straight

A Trip To The Moon. Co-maker: Scott Bartlett
30 min, b/w, r: CAN.
No summary available.

Women And Children At Large (1973)
7 min, c, r: CAN. r, s: SBC.
No summary available.

FRIEDMAN, BONNIE
Chris And Bernie (1974). Co-maker: Deborah Shaffer
25 min, c, r, s: NDF.
"Focusing on the special needs and problems of single
parents, Chris and Bernie is a moving documentary about
two 25-year-old women, both working and divorced with
young children. The problems they face, the solutions
they've found, and their hopes for the future are clear
and powerful in this warm, lively, and well-made film."
-Media And Methods

The Flashettes (1977). Co-maker: Emily Parker Leon
20 min, c, r, s: NDF.
"A documentary about the members of a black girls' track
club from Brooklyn. It captures the shared sorrows and
joys of competitions and the friendships of the girls."
-NDF

How About You? (1973). Co-makers: Marilyn Mulford, Deborah
Shaffer
25 min, b/w, r, s: TEX.
"Birth control and sexuality...young adults in a world of
changing roles and responsibilities." -TEX

The Last To Know (1981)
45 min, c, r: NDF.
Documentary concerning women alcoholics.

FRIEDMAN, ROBERTA
<u>Amusement Park: Composition And Decay</u>
12 min, b/w, r: CAN.
"...The film is made up of three parts: the first tries
to show the essence of amusement parks by visual simile;
the second alternates the human and mechanical elements;
and in the third, the park is empty, decaying, and finally demolished." -CAN

<u>Bertha's Children</u> (1976)
8 min, sepia, r: CAN.
"...The film is constructed out of a set of contrasts and
similarities: between the five siblings, between each one
and the environment in which he is photographed, between
'real' and 'filmic' motion, and between the visual and
verbal presentation of information." -CAN

<u>The Making Of Americans</u>
15 min, b/w, r: CAN.
"<u>The Making Of Americans</u> is based on the idea that the
essential nature of a thing can be revealed in an appropriate presentation of surface features..." -CAN

FROEMKE, SUSAN
<u>Grey Gardens</u> (1976). Co-makers: David and Albert Maysles,
Ellen Hovde, Muffie Meyer
94 min, c, r: MAY.
"Edith Bouvier Beale, 79 (Jackie Onassis' aunt) and her
daughter, Little Edie, 56 (Jackie's cousin): an aristo-
cratic mother and daughter lock out the world and spend
two and a half decades in a dilapidated seaside mansion
stoking lost fantasies, momentary glories, and mutual
antagonism. . ." -<u>Ms. Magazine</u>
See MEYER, MUFFIE (Editors).

FRYER, ELLEN
<u>Girls' Sports: On The Right Track</u> (1976)
17 min, c, r: BUD. r, s: PNX.
"The first film to summarize the recent changes in girls'
sports, featuring archive footage of past women athletes.
The experiences of three high-school girls...demonstrate
the opportunities for girls in sports today." -BUD

GALLANT, DENISE
<u>Koan</u>
2 min, c, r: CAN.
"Prayer made into animated art. The unfolding hand gives
birth to a butterfly which bursts into a prism of wing.
They dance, are reabsorbed into the one and reenter the
hand." -CAN

GERSTEIN, CASSANDRA M.
Kali
4 min, c, r: MC.
"Four-image media, using flowing bodies and female forms
with a sensual Indian sountrack by Calo Scott..." -C.G.

Mai East (1968)
5 min, c & b/w, r: FMC.
Male sexuality versus female sexuality.

Strange Lands
6 1/2 min, b/w, r: FMC.
"An erotic audio homage to Ingmar Bergman." -C.G.

Tales (1970)
70 min, c, r: NLC.
Several people reveal their sexual experiences.

Undine
4 1/2 min, c & b/w, r: FMC.
"Mythical image film portrait of Calo Scott, following
the myth of the Undine who will teach the violin each
midsummer's night at the water's edge." -C.G.

GIFFARD, ELLEN
Christo's Valley Curtain (1972). Co-makers: Maysles
Brothers
28 min, c, r, s: MAY.
Film study of Christo's curtain which hangs in a Colorado
valley and is 18 feet high and 24 miles long.

GIRITLIAN, VIRGINIA
Barbara
6 min, b/w, r: CAN.
"In this film I wished to film my friend using the events
of my own life to create, with poetry and film, a sexy
three-part story of growing up." -V.G.

Cumulus Nimbus (1973)
6 min, b/w, r: CAN. r, s: SBC.
"Soft, lyrical look at a young woman making up her mind
about a woman lover." -Freude Bartlett

Eggs And Elevators (1974)
3 1/2 min, b/w, r: CAN.
"Comedy of a woman cracking up, flipping out." -Freude
Bartlett

Footlights (1974)
11 min, c, r: CAN.
A ghost comforts a nervous performer.

81 Bacon
6 min, b/w, r: CAN.
"Young man tries to talk to passengers on a San Francisco bus." -Bonnie Dawson, Women's Films in Print

New York - Miami Beach
6 min, b/w, r: CAN.
". . .It is a document of a trip to New York and to Miami
Beach, my home town, showing its beauty and vulgarity."
-V.G.

Undertow
12 min, c, r: CAN.
"Undertow explores a middle-aged man's emotional chaos
and descent into self-destruction. Based on a real incident, the subject was an acquaintance of the filmmaker."
-CAN

GODMILOW, JILL
Antonia: A Portrait Of The Woman (1974)
See COLLINS, JUDY (Directors, Chapter I).

Nevelson In Process (1977)
See FANSHEL, SUSAN (Directors, Chapter I).

The Popovich Brothers Of South Chicago (1978)
60 min, c, r, s: BAC.
"A musical portrait of the small, blue-collar Serbian-
American community of South Chicago as seen through the
lives of The Popovich Brothers - one of the best of the
old-time "tamburitza" orchestras." -Program, 21st Annual
American Film Festival

GOLDFARB, LYN
With Babies And Banners: Story Of The Women's Emergency
Brigade (1978)
See BOHLEN, ANNE (Directors, Chapter I).

GOLDSMITH, SILVIANNA
Destructive Relationships: Homage To Tye Eulenspiegel
10 - 20 min, c, r: W/A/F.
"An addition film, a film to be added to continually."
-S.G.

Lil Picard: Art Is A Party
10 min, c, r: W/A/F.
Film portrait of the 78-year-old artist.

Nightclub, Memories Of Havana In Queens
6 min, c, r: W/A/F.
Three dancers in a nightclub in Queens, N.Y.

Orpheus Underground II
30 min, c, r: W/A/F.
An edited version of Orpheus, "Legend of the poet and musician who had to go to the underground to bring his wife back." -S.G.

The Transformation Of Persephone
10 min, c, r: FMC.
The story of Persephone.

GOMEZ, ANDREA
  Nigun (1977)
  9 min, c, r, s: SBC.
  "Nigun by Andrea Gomez uses the story of a primordial couple and the birth of their child as the vehicle for the retelling of a myth..." -Ron Epple

GOSA, CHERYL
  Another Chance (1983)

  Cathy (1982)

  Lila (1980)

  Meli (1980)
  See BURST-TERRANELLA, FRAN (Directors, Chapter 1).

GOTTLIEB, LINDA
  The Case Of The Elevator Duck (1974). Co-maker: Joan Micklin Silver
  17 min, c, r, s: LCA.
  Film taken from Polly Berrien Berrends' story.

  The Fur Coat Club (1973). Co-maker: Joan Micklin Silver
  18 min, c, r, s: LCA.
  Two 9-year-old girls get more than they bargain for when they are locked in a mink coat vault while playing a game.

  The Immigrant Experience: The Long Long Journey (1973). Co-maker: Joan Micklin Silver
  31 min, c, r, s: LCA.
  Polish family comes to the United States.

GRANT, BARRA
  The Tap Dance Kid
  See BARRON, EVELYN (Directors, Chapter I).

GRANT, LEE
  Tell Me A Riddle
  90 min, c, r: SWA.
  Melvyn Douglas, Lila Kedrova. The love-hate relationship between an aging husband and wife is examined as the wife questions her dependence on her husband. Edited by Suzanne Pettit.

GRAVES, NANCY
   *Note: Package including Isy Boukir, Goulimine and 200
   Stills At 60 Frames. 31 1/2 min, c, r: FMC. Goulimine
   (1970), 8 min. of camels in the Sahara was extended into
   Isy Boukir. 200 Stills At 60 Frames is 8 min, silent.

   Aves: Magnificent Frigate Bird, Great Flamingo (1973)
   23 min, c, r, s: SBC.
   Study of birds.

   Isy Boukir (1971)
   16 min, c, r, s: SBC
   A study of camels.

GRAY, LORRAINE
   With Babies And Banners: Story Of The Women's Emergency
   Brigade (1978)
   See BOHLEN, ANNE (Directors, Chapter I).

GREENFIELD, AMY
   Dirt (1970-71)
   4 min, c, r: FMC.
   "A woman is dragged, struggling, with increasing violence, across dirt. The motion, energy and way of
   filming came largely from my need to personally deal
   with the actions on news of the violence in the riots of
   the 1960's. The sound, rasping and loud, was made optically by the film actually passing over photocells." -A.G.

   Element (1970-73)
   12 1/2 min, b/w, silent, r: FMC.
   "The female person in motion, nude and covered with wet,
   black, claylike mud. This one exploration of the single
   human being falling into, sliding along and rising out of
   this glistening substance over and over, summons up spec-
   ific sensations from a very primitive and visceral part
   of the human being." -A.G.

   Encounter (1968-69)
   8 1/2 min, c, silent, r: available from filmmaker.
   "A conflict, a struggle for possession, within one woman
   or between two women...this psychic 'story' is told in
   terms of a dance." -A.G.

Tides (1982)
12 min, c, r: FMC.
A slow-motion vision of woman and ocean.

Transport (1970-71)
6 min, c, available from filmmaker.
"An exploration of one movement cycle: a man then a
woman are lifted from the ground and carried through
space. The man and woman never meet. Their relationship
is made entirely through the way the film is edited. The
man and woman move (are moved) between ground and sky
with an increasing violence which is an attempt to be
transported, lifted out of oneself." -A.G.

GREGORY, MOLLIE
ERA And The American Way (1974)
26 min, r, s: SBC.
Film about the Equal Rights Amendment.

GROSSMAN, ANN-CAROL
Speaking Of Men (1977). Co-maker: Christine M. Herbes
20 min, c, r, s: POY.
"Three women talk about men: their attitudes toward
men, their relationships with men, how men are important
to them. Seen in individual portraits, the women, who
are similar (young, single professionals) express very
different, very personal points of view on how men have
affected their lives and on what they are looking for in
their relationships with men." -POY

HALEFF, MAXINE
The Forbidden Playground
10 1/2 min, b/w, r: FMC.
"Dance film photographed in a modern playground, with
documentary sequences of NASA astronauts." -M.H.

The Magic Lantern Movie (1976)
9 min, c, r, s: SBC.
"This informative film traces the roots of the film
medium in magic and vaudeville using a crowd of lovely
images from the turn of the century...The film includes
a humorous turn-of-the-century trick film entitled The
Magic Lantern made by the French movie pioneer George
Melies." -SBC

HALLECK, DEE DEE
Mr. Story(1973). Co-maker: Anita Thacher
28 min, c, r, s: PNX.
Film concerning Albert Story, a chair repairman.

HAMILTON, NANCY
  Helen Keller In Her Story (1973)
  45 min, r: BUD. s: PNX.
  Film portrait of Helen Keller.

HAMMER, BARBARA
  Arequipa (1981)
  12 min, c, r: available from filmmaker.
  Fantasy about 16th-century nuns in Peru.

  Audience (1983)
  30 min, b/w, r: available from filmmaker.
  "...A series of international interviews with my
  audiences as I tour." -B.H.

  Dyketactics (1974)
  4 min, c, r: CAN. r, s: MUL, SBC.
  "Lesbian commercial. Highly edited according to texture."
  -B.H.

  A Gay Day (1973)
  3 min, c, r: CAN.
  "A satire on lesbian monogamy." -B.H.

  Jane Brakhage (1974)
  10 min, b/w, r: CAN.
  "An expressionistic documentary of the influential and
  vividly self-reliant woman who combines creation, pioneer
  spirit, and motherhood in a totally unique individual
  manner as well as being a nurturing and innovative force
  in the works of filmmaker Stan Brakhage." -B.H.

  Machu Piccu (1981)
  15 min, c, r: available from filmmaker.
  Film study of the Peruvian temple.

  Menses (1974)
  3 min, c, r, s: IFC.
  "A comedy of ritualistic women's activity, play and
  satire, around and about the monthly flow. A really fun
  movie with feelings of bonding and trust evident among
  participants." -B.H.

  Our Trip (1980)
  4 min, c, r: available from filmmaker.
  "...an animated film based on a hiking trip in the Andes..."
  Martha Gever, New Women's Times.

Pond and Waterfall (1982)
30 min, c, r: available from filmmaker.
"Experimental cinema exploring the verdant pond under-
water growth and in the waterfall leaping from pool to
pool..." -B.H.

Psychosynthesis (1975)
9 min, c, r: CAN.
"Personal artistic attempt to delve into the psyche of
women. Hammer delves into her own psyche as mother, witch,
sexual being, and child." -INS

Sisters! (1973)
12 min, c & b/w, r: CAN.
"A celebration of lesbian women including footage of the
Women's International Day march in S.F. and joyous
dancing from the last night of the Lesbian Conference
at UCLA when 'Family of Women' played." -B.H.

Synch Touch (1981)
10 min, c, r: available from filmmaker.
"A series of film experiments proposing the aesthetic
connection between touch and sight to be the basis of
feminist filmmaking." -B.H.

Women's Rites (1974)
15 min, c, r: CAN.
"Impressionistic, langorous study of rituals of regener-
ation and renewal among women set in autumnal foliage
of a country weekend." -B.H.

HANNEMAN, YVONNE
Getting Tough
22 min, c, r: RFL.
"Variety is the spice of a fitness program. New ideas
such as bounding and mountain running, and new competitions
like Ride and Tie. Plus a ski camp for runners. U.S.
Ski Team members introduce cross-country skiing to top
runners." -Y.H.

I Am A Runner
22 min, c, r: RFL.
"Boston Marathon winners Bill Rodgers and Jacqueline
Hansen, together with coach John Babington, give inspiration and advice about training and racing; with slow
motion analysis of running styles and form." -Y.H.

Looking Good
22 min, c, r: RFL.
"Designed to motivate those people who should run, but
don't. We discuss the importance of fitness, and show
how to start a running program. Advice on what to wear,
how to train, and running the first race." -Y.H.

Mini-Marathon
24 min, c, r: RFL.
"The story of 2500 women running a 10 kilometer (6.3
mile) race in New York's Central Park." -Y.H.

Muruga (1973)
23 min, c, r: SBC.
A study of the Muruga Festival in Sri Lanka.

Scraps (1973)
6 min, c, r: SBC.
An Indian woman makes something from nothing.

Vesak (1973)
17 min, c, r: SBC.
Buddha's birthday.

The Work of Gomis (1973)
50 min, c, r: SBC.
Film portrait of Dr. M.H. Gomis in Ceylon.

HASLANGER, MARTHA
Focus (1973)
3 min, c & b/w, silent, available from filmmaker.
"Black and white movement, disorienting up and down,
quiets to a stable viewpoint of slow jerking movement
in a playground. The movement becomes less mutidirectional
until finally a face on the merry-go-round suddenly
changes to real-life color and real-life speed, grounded
by the staring of a child." -M.H.

Frames And Cages And Speeches
13 min, c, r: CAN.
"About frames and framing, about cages and caging, about
speeches and speaking...an experimental film (a seven-act
'play') dealing with a medium's narration of us and our
narration of it." -CAN

June (1972-74)
8 min, b/w, available from filmmaker.
"Slow-paced preparation for an evening out by a 50-year-
old woman. Clothes, make-up, hair, all a somber ritual.
As June saw the film one year after it was made, her com-
ments were recorded and inserted into the film at the
points they refer to." -M.H.

Syntax
13 min, c, r: CAN.
"This apparently simple film is in reality an elaborate
exercise in movement, lighting and editing, which eventually creates the visual climaxes of the film - trying
to approach our subconscious." -Mira Liehm

Your Home Is You (1973)
15 min, c, available from filmmaker.
"Farcical depiction of interior decoration dicta and
wifely life styles. How we should live (according to
mass advertising myths)." -M.H.

HEALEY, DEBORAH
Brews And Potions (1978)
1 min, c, r: available in Animated Women package from
Texture, s: TEX.
"Tongue-in-cheek suggestions for love potions, and
soothing remedies for the pains of love." -TEX
See also BOTTNER, BARBARA

HELLER, LINDA
Album (1976)
5 min, c, r, s: SBC.
"Growing up female in the nuclear family and surviving
with a sense of humor intact is the story of this
charming, brightly-colored family album of pop-deco
drawings." -SBC

HENNESSEY, SHARON
What I Want (1971)
10 min, c, r: CAN. r, s: SBC.
"All the things ever wanted and a few dozen probably never
thought of before...the list is both personal and universal, incorporating all those silent wishes and hopes
we rarely consider worthy of verbalizing." -"Women
Filmmakers Program," -Whitney Museum

HERBES, CHRISTINE M.
Speaking of Men (1977)
See GROSSMAN, ANN-CAROL (Directors, Chapter I).

HERSHEY, ANN
Never Give Up: Imogen Cunningham (1971-74)
30 min, c, r: BUD, UCE. r, s: PNX.
"The 92-year-old photographer, her wit, work and history." -A.H.

We Are Ourselves
15 min, c, r, s: MUL.
"A joyful, entertaining and explicitly sexual film about
two thoughtful and independent women who have followed
their individual desires to seek a fulfilling and creative lifestyle together." -MUL

HILL, MARY
Barrier Beach (1971)
20 min, c, r: UCE.
"Unique photographic study of the changes in a barrier
beach over a period of a year." -ACI

HITCHCOCK, VICTRESS
What Can I Tell You (1978)
55 min, c, r, s: CEN.
"A portrait of three generations of women in an Italian-
American family, which explores both the changes in the
roles of the three women, as well as the essentially
timeless quality of family life." -Program, 21st Annual
American Film Festival

HOCHBERG, VICTORIA
Boz Scaggs (1977-79)
20 min, c, r: FRO.
A New Year's Eve concert by Boz Scaggs.

The Eagles (1978)
15 min, c, r: FRO.
Concert performances from the Eagles' 1978 tour.

The Eagles (1980)
30 min, c, r: FRO.
The Eagles recorded on film while working in the studio.

Metroliner (1975)
35 min, c, available from filmmaker.
Metroliner is the visual story of a train's high-speed
run from New York to Washington." -V.H.

The Right To Die (1974). Co-maker: Marlene Sanders
56 min, c, r: UCE. r, FNC.
"No subject is more intensely personal yet more universal
in concern than Death...The Right To Die uses interviews
with dying patients to open up this subject for serious
consideration by all of us." -MAC

A Simple Matter Of Justice (1978)
26 min, c, r: FNC.
"Fast-paced, visually exciting, emotionally honest, A
Simple Matter Of Justice is an examination of the most
hotly debated issue facing women today, the Equal Rights
Amendment. It highlights the history of the ERA and
covers the oppositions, both historical and current." -FNC

El Teatro Campesino(1971). Co-maker: Janet Sternburg
61 min, b/w, r: UCE.
"The theatre of the farmworkers which supported the 1965
United Farmworkers strike in California. . ." -Bonnie
Dawson, Women's Films In Print.

A Woman's Place (1973). Co-maker: Marlene Sanders
52 min, c, r: UCE. s: XEX.
"Traces the influences that create and perpetuate the
'traditional' role of women, including children's books
and toys, film clips and advertising." -UCE

HOCHMAN, SANDRA
The Year Of The Woman (1973)
80 min, c, r: NLC.
"The acclaimed poet Sandra Hochman has created in this
remarkable film an unforgettable fusion of politics, the
woman's movement, and fantasy. It is a documentary of
the 1972 Democratic National Convention, made by an all
woman crew and featuring many of the outstanding figures
in the women's movement." -NLC
With Bella Abzug, Shirley Chisholm, Gloria Steinem,
Shirley MacLaine, Flo Kennedy, Norman Mailer, John
Lindsey, Art Buchwald, and Warren Beatty.

HOLMES, KAREN
You, Mother
9 1/2 min, b/w, r: CAN.
"An examination, both visual and in word, of some of the
reasons women give for having children. Uppermost is the
question of women's obligation to bear children. The
film takes no point of view but that of asking, 'Do you
think about the why of your child?' The film presents
motherhood not as a sacrosanct state above question but
rather as the serious reality that it is." -CAN

HOLT, NANCY
Pine Barrens (1975)
32 min, c, r: CST.
A look at the Pine Barrens area in New Jersey.

Sun Tunnels (1978)
26 min, c, r: CST.
Holt's recording of her sculpture and its changing
relationship to the sun.

Swamp (1971). Co-maker: Robert Smithson
6 min, c, r: CST.
Study of a swamp.

HOVDE, ELLEN
Grey Gardens (1976)
See FROEMKE, SUSAN (Directors, Chapter I).

See KLINGMAN, LYNZEE (Editors).

HUBLEY, FAITH
   Adventures Of An * (1957). Co-maker: John Hubley.
   10 min, c, animated, r: FNC, KPF, UCE, VIE.
   "Man, represented by the asterisk symbol *, is introduced
   as a baby enjoying the visual excitement of the world
   about him. As he grows, his ability to see and enjoy
   life becomes lessened. He emerges as an adult who is un-
   able to see and feel freely. Through the eyes of his
   own child, however, he is able to rediscover the world
   of life and beauty." -Hubley Filmography

   Children Of The Sun (1960). Co-maker: John Hubley
   10 min, c, animated, r: KPF, UCE.
   "Story of a happy child - his fun, pleasures, his growing
   up; in contrast to a hungry unhappy child." -Association-
   Sterling.

   Cockaboody (1973). Co-maker: John Hubley
   8 1/2 min, c, animated, r: VIE. r, s: PYR.
   "The role of imaginative play of children in their
   growing adjustment to reality."   -FNC

   The Doonesbury Special (1977). Co-maker: John Hubley
   26 min, c, animated, r: VIE. r, s: PYR.
   "In a few short years, Garry Trudeau's comic strip
   'Doonesbury' has become a part of the American culture...
   In this ironic look at contemporary society, Zonker
   Harris and his friends come face to face with shifting
   values and the conclusion of an era - the age of the
   activist sixties..." -PYR

   Eggs (1970). Co-maker: John Hubley
   10 min, c, animated, r: VIE.
   "Death and Fertility are visualized as giant ethereal
   figures arguing over what they can do with our world.
   Death is a kind of hip Grim Reaper. Fertility is a sexy
   cartoon woman. One, of course, wants to propagate, the
   other reduce the population...Perched on the Brooklyn
   Bridge like a giant hammock, they are pleased to discover
   how much of their work is being done for them by man."
   -VIE

   Everybody Rides The Carousel (1976). Co-maker: John Hubley
   72 min, c, animated, r, s: PYR.
   Animated study of psychologist Erik Erikson's 8 stages of
   life theory. Part I covers three periods of life: the
   newborn, the toddler and childhood. Part II covers the
   emergence of a sense of competence, feelings of inferiority,
   adolescence, the search for identity, and young adulthood: intimacy versus isolation. In Part III, the last two
   stages of development are discussed: adulthood and old age.

Harlem Wednesday (1957). Co-maker: John Hubley
10 min, c, r: FNC.
Harlem viewed on a Wednesday.

The Hat (1964). Co-maker: John Hubley
18 min, c, animated, r: UCE.
A soldier becomes involved in a political discussion
with his enemy when he drops his helmet in enemy ter-
ritory.

The Hole (1962). Co-maker: John Hubley
14 min, c, animated, r: KPF, UCE. r, s: FNC.
The hole is in New York City where two men are at work.

Moonbird (1959). Co-maker: John Hubley
10 min, c, animated, r: FNC.
"In 1959, John and Faith Hubley won an Academy Award for
this cartoon, in which they invented the technique of
making a sound track from the spontaneous humor of
small children talking to each other. Using their own children, they made pictures of what must be going on in the
minds of two small boys who dig a hole to capture the
moonbird. The result is significant and very funny - so
funny in fact that this film played as a theatrical short
film for many years." -VIE

People, People, People (1976). Co-maker: John Hubley
5 min, c, animated, r: BUD. r, s: PYR.
"Within its five minutes running time, this film takes a
look at the millions of people who have inhabited our
country starting from 17,760 B.C. and moving on (at
whirlwind speed) to the present." -BUD

Second Chance: Sea
11 min, c, animated, r, s: PYR.
"This timely animated film, produced and directed by
Faith Hubley, is a refreshing serenade to the sea, celebrating its glories while moving us to care about the
ocean crisis." -PYR

Step By Step (1978)
11 min, c, animated, r, s: PYR
"In Step By Step, Faith Hubley uses the animated film as
a means of personal, artistic expression as she inter-
prets the world of childhood - as its was, as it exists
and as it might be." -PYR

54

Tender Game (1958). Co-maker: John Hubley
6 min, c, animated, r: FNC, UCE.
"Free association of popular music and popular images to
the tune of 'Tenderly' sung by Ella Fitzgerald." -Hubley
Filmography. "Semi-abstract graphics perform the ballet
of young adults falling in love. An entertaining short,
utilizing the special techniques that elevate Hubley
films from animated production to a separate level of
art." -FNC

Urbanissimo (1966). Co-maker: John Hubley
6 min, c, animated, r: FNC, KPF.
"Comic allegory of a runaway 'city' devouring its
environs." -FNC

Voyage To Next (1973). Co-maker: John Hubley
9 1/2 min, c, animated, r: FNC.
A discussion between Father Time and Mother Earth.

W.O.W. (Women Of The World) (1975). Co-maker: John Hubley
11 min, c, animated, r, s: PYR.
"Produced in honor of International Women's Year, W.O.W.
uses an animated collage of world art to present a creative history of the earth from the feminist point of
view. From opening to closing, with a richness of symbolism and relationships between females and males in
ancient matriarchal times." -PYR

A Windy Day (1967). Co-maker: John Hubley
9 1/2 min, c. animated, r: FNC.
"This is, in a way, a sequel to John and Faith Hubley's
Moonbird. The same children grown older, live an older
child's fantasy...The fantasy is of what it must be like
to be adults." -VIE

Zuckerkandl (1968). Co-maker: John Hubley
14 min, c, animated, r: FNC.
"Alexander Zuckerkandl...mythical philosopher, created
by Robert Hutchins to satirize the middle class view that
the anaesthetized life is the best life." -GRO

IRIS FEMINIST COLLECTIVE
  In The Best Interests Of the Children(1977)
  55 min, c, r, s: IFC.
  "Documentary portrait of eight lesbian mothers, their
  children, attorneys and social workers; also deals with
  the issue of child custody problems for lesbians." -IFC

IROLA, JUDY
  Self-Health (1974)
  See LIGHTHOUSE FILMS.

IRVINE, LOUVA
Blue Moment (1976)
10 min, c, available from filmmaker.
"Soft focus, multiple-exposed, edited-in-the camera film
portraying the natural choreography of Guggenheim Museum
director, Thomas Messer, on the ramp at the Bolotozsky
opening." -Program, 2nd International Festival Of Women's
films, New York

Dig We Must
10 min, b/w, available from filmmaker.
"Improvisational dramatic satire. A surreal artist's
attempts to overcome Con Edison and find his inner light."
-L.I.

Elegy For My Sister (1972)
10 min, c, available from filmmaker.
"Slowed-motion suspension tone poem filmed at Jones Beach
upon the passing of my sister, Jane. Edited in the camera."
-L.I.

Murray Hill Morning
10 min, c, available from filmmaker.
"Film about New York neighborhood." -L.I.

Three Lives (1971). Co-makers: Susan Kleckner, Robin
Mide, Kate Millet.
70 min, c & b/w, r, s: ICA.
As the title suggests, Three Lives concerns the lives of
three people: Mallory Millet-Jones, Kate Millet's sister,
Robin Mide, one of the directors of the film, and Lillian
Shreve, the mother of one of the crew members. The "three
lives" are varied. Millet-Jones has just gone through a
divorce and is now experiencing a new independent lifestyle. Shreve, on the other hand, appears happy with her
long marriage and her role as a mother. Mide is a lesbian
who conveys to the viewer her restlessness and energy
technically, through jump cuts, and physically, in the way
she chooses to be filmed.

Waterdance (1972)
10 min, c, available from filmmaker.
"Slowed-motion suspension of the play of light on the
ocean's waves, filmed while crossing the Aegean." -L.I.

JAFFE, PATRICIA
Who Does She Think She Is? (1974). Co-maker: Gaby Rodgers
60 min, c, r: NYF.
"About, starring and improvised from the unusual world of
Rosalyn Drexler - novelist, playwright, painter, ex-
wrestler, night-club singer, wife and mother." -NYF

JASPER, SUZANNE
Being A Prisoner (1975)
28 min, c, r, s: WMM.
"The film focuses on a 'model prison': the prison keepers
comparatively humane; the women can wear their own clothes
and decorate their own rooms. Yet the superficiality of
this humane treatment is all too apparent...Being A Prisoner
is a moving glimpse into black, white and Puerto Rican women's
lives and their response to incarceration." -WMM

JASSIM, LINDA
Cycles (1971)
11 min, c, r: CFS, NLC. (available in package from NLC).
"Mysterious and dynamic visualization of a woman's rape and
her subsequent return to the womb." -NLC

JOEL, SHIRLEY
Woman: Who Is Me? (1977)
See TRICEPTS PRODUCTIONS.

JOHNSON, KAREN
Hands
2 min, b/w, r, s: SBC.
"A thumb, a finger, two fingers, a hand all move in a
fascinating way impelling the audience to take part."
-Programme, "Women And Film Festival," Toronto

Orange (1969)
3 min, c, r: CAN. r, s: MUL.
"Using nothing more than soft music and the close-up,
this film classic shows nothing more than the eating
of a navel orange. The excellent film editing and sensual
macrophotography of the inner orange can produce erotic
excitement." -SBC

JOHNSON, PHYLLIS
Two Worlds To Remember
40 min, c, r, s: FOC.
"The central theme of this documentary: the worlds we remember are the past that shaped us, and the present that
holds us...The two elderly women consented to participate
because 'there's nothing more important that we who are old
can do than share our experiences to help others.'" -FOC

JOINT PRODUCTIONS
We're Alive (1975)
50 min, c, b/w, r, s: IFC.
"Women incarcerated at the California Institution for Women
relate their experiences as inmates and discuss conditions in
the prison in moving and political statements." -IFC

JOKEL, LANA
  Andy Warhol (1973). Producer: Michael Blackwood
  53 min, c, r, s: BKW.
  Interview with Warhol which includes film sequences from
  some of his motion pictures: Trash, Chelsea Girls, Heat,
  and Women In Revolt.

KAPLAN, NELLY (French)
  Abel Gance: Yesterday And Tomorrow (1963)
  28 min, e, r: IMA.
  Documentary on one of the pioneers of filmmaking.

  Beloved Woman (A La Source La Femme Aimee) (1965)
  12 min, c, and b/w, r: FMC.
  A study of the erotic drawings of Andre Masson.

  Nea (1977)
  101 min, c, subtitles, r: CIV.
  Sami Frey, Ann Zacharias
  Based on the novel by Emmanuelle Arsan, this satirical
  film concerns a young woman who decides to live her desires and fantasies.

  A Very Curious Girl (La Fiancée Du Pirate) (1969)
  105 min, c, subtitles, r: FNC.
  Bernadette Lafont, Georges Geret
  "Bernadette Lafont gives a rousing performance as a
  peasant girl who, following the death of her mother,
  decides to charge for the sexual favors that were pre-
  viously extorted." -Janus Films

KARTEMQUIN FILMS
  All Of Us Stronger (1976)
  9 min, c, r, s: SBC.
  "All Of Us Stronger is a film about women and young girls
  learning to defend themselves. Participants in a woman's
  class talk about self-defense and their own experiences
  as we watch them learn to punch, kick and block, break
  out of grabs and free spar." -SBC

  The Chicago Maternity Center Story (1977)
  60 min, b/w, r, s: WMM.
  Part I - 30 min, concerns the history of the 75-year-old
  Chicago Maternity Center and the possibility of its closing
  because of plans for a new hospital. Part II - 30 min, "A
  concrete historical analysis shos why modern medicine re-
  jects the Center's approach in favor of high-cost, hospital-
  based care...Though supported by the community and the staff,
  the women fail in their effort to keep the Center open." -WMM

KAY, ELIZABETH
Dream Your Own Dreams (1978)
21 min, c, r, s: FFC.
"Gwen Frostic has created her own business built around
her writing and art work. We see her at work and hear her
ideas on the beauty of nature, the need to preserve natural
resources, and the importance of personal growth." -Program,
21st Annual American Film Festival

KELLER, JUDITH
Woman: Who Is Me? (1977)
See TRICEPTS PRODUCTIONS.

KENDALL, NANCY
Almira 38
20 min, b/w, r: FMC.
"A dance poem, a tribute to a woman who sought a freedom,
an abstract film..." -FMC

Coming Attraction
4 min, c, r: W/A/F.
"A segment of a saga of a woman's love for her sportscar."
-Art and Cinema

Crewel Stitches
30 min, c, r: W/A/F.
"Scraps, textures, and colors from an industrious camera
worked into a folk design; an autobiographical frame."
-W/A/F

Painting
6 min, c, r: W/A/F.
"Things are reversed in this plain event." -W/A/F

Radio
4 min, c, r: W/A/F.
"A simple melody first heard in filmmaker's childhood
evokes images of city blossoms: a nostalgic revery."
-W/A/F

Womben
5 min, c, r: W/A/F.
"A juxtaposition of two dissonant views of femininity
evoking a third sense." -W/A/F

KENNEDY, SHELBY
The Bruce Nauman Story. Co-maker: Don Whitaker
10 min, b/w, r, s: CAN.
"...The true artist helps the world by remaining anonymous. The true artist helps the world by remaining..."

I Change, I Am The Same (1969). Co-maker: Anne Severson
1 min, b/w, r: CAN. r, s: MUL, SBC.
"Whimsical commentary on changing roles between the sexes."
-Freude Bartlett. Camera work by Severson's daughter, April.

Lightning Waterfall Fern Soup
10 min, c, r: CAN.
"The flashing of light produced by a discharge of atmos-
pheric electricity from a cloud to earth/a perpendicular or
very steep descent of the water of a stream/a potent magic
that satisfies not only the hunger of the body but the
yearnings of the soul/mysterious gnawings restorative soup
fulfillment." -CAN

Riverbody (1970). Co-maker: Anne Severson
7 min, b/w, r: CAN. r, s: MUL, SBC.
"A continuous dissolve of 87 male and female nudes." -CAN

KISH, ANNE
Can Anybody Hear The Birds
10 min, b/w, sound on tape, r: CAN.
"Made in three seasons adjacent to each other, in wonder
at the extraordinary quality of sculpture in proximity to
human beings and the rest of nature." -CAN

Duos - Combinations For A Portrait
11 min, b/w, sound of tape, r: CAN.
"Portrait of two college roommates, filmed spontaneously,
with a sound collage organized as an aural mirror of the
interplay which is seen on the screen." -CAN

Umatilla '68
37 min, b/w, r: CAN.
"An anthropological film of the life and work of the Umatilla Indians, whose reservation is adjacent to the town
of Pendleton, Oregon." -CAN. Narration and music by the
tribes.

KLECKNER, SUSAN
The Birth Film (1974)
35 min, c, r: NYF.
Birth of a couple's child that takes place at their home.
"Spontaneous film celebrating childbirth and woman." -NYF

Three Lives (1971)
See IRVINE, LOUVA (Directors, Chapter I).

KONNER, JOAN
  Danger! Radioactive Waste (1977)
  50 min, c, r: FNC.
  "The horrors of radioactive overexposure - possible gen-
  etic damage, increased incidences of cancer and leukemia,
  and others - are further heightened by an apparent inability of both government and industry to solve the nuclear waste disposal problem." -FNC

  Mary Jane Grows Up (1976)
  52 min, c, r: FNC.
  "No longer the symbol flaunted by young counter-culture
  rebels, marijuana smoking, if not completely respectable,
  has become part of the social scheme of millions, including
  parents, teachers and professionals, as well as young
  people...Whether we like it or not, marijuana is here to
  stay and somewhere, somehow the 'pros' have got to meet
  the 'cons' on common ground." -FNC

  What Man Shall Live And Not See Death? (1971)
  57 min, c, r, s: FNC.
  The politics of dying are discussed in interviews.

KOPPLE, BARBARA
  Harlan County, U.S.A. (1976). Co-maker: Anne Lewis
  103 min, c, r, l: CIV.
  "Portraying a classic twentieth-century conflict between
  labor and management, Harlan County, U.S.A. chronicles
  the efforts of 180 coal mining families to win a United
  Mine Workers contract at the Brookside Mine in Harlan
  County, Kentucky. The real beauty of Harlan County, U.S.A.
  is the intimacy with which we come to know those 180 families..." -CIV

KRASILOVSKY, ALEXIS RAFAEL
  La Belle Dame Sans Merci (1973)
  4 min, c, r: CAN.
  A woman looks back at her life.

  Blood (1975)
  21 min, c, r: CAN.
  "In its stream-of-consciousness way Blood evokes Manhattan
  street life even more powerfully than Martin Scorcese's
  Taxi Driver. Ms. Krasilovsky brings into camera an array
  of furtive, frustrated people...and allows them to talk
  about themselves as we watch them in action. As a depiction
  of contemporary urban despair Blood...is an angry, outraged
  protest of the exploitation of women and men." -Kevin
  Thomas, L.A. Times

  Charlie Dozes Off And The Dog Bothers Him (1973)
  3 min, c & b/w, silent, r: CAN.
  "A visual poem about sleep and wakefulness." -Bonnie Dawson,
  Women's Films In Print

Commiseration Moon (1976)
6 min, c, r: CAN.
"Shot in part with holographic lenses by Alexis Krasilovsky,
Commiseration Moon is a filmed poem for women driven to the
ground by love." -CAN

Cows (1972)
3 min, c, r: CAN.
"Handpainted film about women's relation to the media and
cows at the McNulty Dairy Farm." -Bonnie Dawson, Women's
Films In Print

End Of The Art World (1971-72)
40 min, c & b/w, r: CAN.
Interviews with several artists.

The Guerrilla Commercial (1973)
1 min, c, r: CAN.
"A studio production employing an all-woman crew. About
discrimination faced by women filmmakers." -A.R.K.

KREPS, BONNIE
  After The Vote (1972)
  22 min, b/w, r: UCE.
  "Serious and comic picture of the effects of sex role stereo-
  types. Professor Ron Lamert, a Canadian psychologist, and
  Ti-Grace Atkinson provide the perspective." -ODE

  Portrait Of My Mother (1974)
  30 min, c, r: UCE.
  "The gentleness and strength of an older woman leading a
  group of younger women through the mountains and rivers of
  Wyoming. A daughter's appreciation of her mother's life."
  -ODE

KRESS, JUDITH
  If Trees Can Fly (1976)
  12 min, c, r, s: PNX.
  "If Trees Can Fly is a visual essay on the random thoughts
  of two 10-year-old children as they witness nature unfolding -
  bird eggs hatching, swans preening themselves and birds in
  flight." -PNX

KRUMINS, DAINA
  The Divine Miracle
  5 1/2 min, c, r: CAN.
  "An intriguing composite of what looks like animation and
  pageant-like action is The Divine Miracle, which treads a
  delicate line between reverence and spoof as it briefly
  portrays the agony, death, and ascension of Christ in the
  vividly colored and heavily outlined style of Catholic de-
  votional postcards..." Edgar Daniels, Filmmakers' Newsletter

LAMOUR, CATHERINE
  The New Opium Route. Co-maker: Marianne Lamour
  54 min, r, s: ICA.
  "...study of the fierce proud Pashtus, who have lived for
  centuries unmolested in the wild region of the Khyber Pass
  on the border of Afghanistan and Pakistan. This unique
  film, the first document from this isolated region, available in this country, does not only show us the source of
  most of the 'hard drugs' in the U.S., but it is a fascinating
  document on the gap between the two cultures, their values
  and their social systems." -ICA

LANGELD, GRETCHEN
  The Cloister
  19 min, b/w, silent, r: FMC.
  "A woman's experience at the NYC House of Detention for
  Women." -G.L.

LASKOWICH, GLORIA
  Killing Time
  11 1/2 min, c & b/w, r: FMC.
  "...in reality and fantasy a female relates ambivalently
  to the males around her." -G.L.

LASSNIG, MARIA
  Art Education
  9 min, c, r: W/A/F
  Hand-drawn animation.

  Baroque Statues
  16 min, c, r: W/A/F.
  Live dance film.

  Chairs (1971)
  "Chairs behave like people." -Cinema Femina. Hand drawn
  animation.

  Couples
  9 min, c, r: W/A/F.
  "A woman's tragic love affair." -Cinema Femina. Hand drawn
  animation.

  Iris
  10 min, c, r: W/A/F.
  A film about the filmmaker's friend, Iris. Cinema Femina.
  Hand drawn animation.

  Palmistry
  10 min, c, r: W/A/F.
  "A fat girl is singing about her refusal to get thin.
  Juxtaposing superstition and science." -W/A/F. Cinema
  Femina Hand drawn animation.

Self Portrait
4 1/2 min, c, r: FMC.
"Filmmaker's psyche and its relationship with men."   -Film
Forum

Shapes
10 min, c, r: W/A/F.
"Male and female silhouettes are moving with Bach music."
-W/A/F

LAUGHLIN, KATHLEEN
Disappearance of Sue (1972)
2 1/2 min, c, r, s: SBC.
"A whimsical pixillated story of a lady in a black coat
disappearing, via a soda-cracker ritual in the park and a
floral experience in the famous Como Park Conservatory."
-K.L.

Interview (1974)
7 min, c, r: CAN.
"An impression of a friend who lives the dichotomy of discipline and freedom through his violin experience." -K.L.

Madsong(1976)
5 min, c, r, s: SBC
"Madsong combines natural photography, animation, optical
printing, and multiple voices to convey the introspection
of a girl between childhood and womanhood..." -Edgar Daniels,
Filmmakers Newsletter

Opening/Closing (1972)
4 1/2 min, b/w, r: CAN, NLC, r, s: SBC.
The doors of washers at a laundromat are used as metaphors.

A Round Feeling (1974)
5 1/2 min, r, s: SBC.
The rides at a fair are used to convey "a round feeling".

Some Will Be Apples (1974). Co-producer: Phyllis Poullette-
MacDougal
15 min, c, r, s: SBC.
"Based on the writings of Zona Gale, a Wisconsin-born
writer, very popular in the early 1900's. She wrote novels
based on the ideas and problems of the midwestern women
of the time and this film brings to life (through old
photos, animation, and live-action) some of those characterizations and situations." -K.L.

Susan Through Corn
2 min, c, r, s: SBC.
"Simple film giving an exhilarating sense of a young woman
entering a large corn field, being followed with a single-
framed camera, and emerging on the other side, then disappearing...triple flute soundtrack." -K.L.

LAZARUS, MARGARET
Taking Our Bodies Back: The Women's Health Movement
(1974)
35 min, c, r, s: CAM.
"Demonstrates the inadequate and discriminatory health care
that women are receiving and the movement to improve health
care: including self-help, home birth and the role of women
in the breast cancer controversy." -M.L.

LEDERER, SUE
Charles Darden: Conductor (1972)
13 1/2 min, c, r: UCE.
"Charles Darden, young black music teacher, founder and con-
ductor of the Berkeley Free Orchestra, apprentice to Seiji
Ozawa, talks about being black, about his career, the role
of music in today's society, about working with children..."
-BFA Education Media

LEON, EMILY PARKER
The Flashettes (1977)
See FRIEDMAN, BONNIE (Directors, Chapter I).

LEVERINGTON, SHELBY
The Detour (1977)
13 min, c, r: BUD. r, s: PNX.
"A film shown entirely from the viewpoint of one person,
Catherine Hamilton, age 83, a dying patient in a large hospital. Modern medicine struggles to keep her alive as she
struggles to die in peace..." -BUD

LEVINE, NAOMI
At My Mother's House
6 min, c, silent, r: FMC.
"A still life dedicated to Vermeer and to my mother."
-N.L.

From Zero To 16
7 min, c, r: FMC.
"An autobiographical attempt, both visually and audioly...
including shots of the 6th Rite of Opposite Forces and family
album snap shots." -N.L.

Jeremulu
2 min, b/w, r: FMC.
"Visual word poem in white images..." -Bonnie Dawson,
Women's Films In Print

l.A.l. a London Bridges Falling Down
4 1/2 min, c, r: FMC.
"What it is visually like to be the Waterloo Bridge or
the Battersea." -N.L.

Optured Fraiken Chaitre Joe
3 min, b/w, silent, r: FMC.
Joe Chaikin's Open Theatre is examined.

Premoonptss
15 min, c, silent, r: FMC.
"The name Premoonptss: to put a footmark on the events
up to the time of the first moon landing, on July 14, 1969,
...photographic images change, grow and dramatize the
overall feeling of Man in the 1960's.

Prismatic
19 1/2 min, c, silent (16 fps), r: FMC.
"A rainbow film...a visual geometric film study using the
prism...What is not permitted in or by life is permitted
here...to have our moments all over again...even coated
with a rainbow." -N.L.

The Story Of A Dot
2 min, c, silent, r: FMC.
"This is a very colorful, directly, short account of a
pin-scratched scribble of a Dot that turns into a square,
and then into a rectangle, and then into a triangle, and
finally becoming a scribbly mess." -N.L.

Zen, And The Art Of Baseball
5 1/2 min, c, r: FMC.
"A Homage To The Hudson River School Of Painting. This
little gem is an attempt to cinematize the style of the
Hudson Rivers painters of the late 1800's and early
1900's." -N.L.

LEVITT, HELEN
In The Street (1952). Co-makers: James Agee, Janet Loeb
16 min, b/w, silent, r: MMA.
Film which documents the lifestyle of Harlem in the 1940's.

The Quiet One (1948). Co-makers: James Agee, Janet Loeb,
Sidney Meyers
67 min, b/w, r: BUD, FNC. r, s: REE, TEX.
Film study of a black youth who grows up in New York's
Harlem and becomes a juvenile delinquent. In a reformatory,
he becomes the 'quiet one' until a psychiatrist helps him.
With Donald Thompson, Sadie Stockton, Clarence Cooper,
Estelle Evans.

LEWIS, ANNE
  Harlan County, U.S.A. (1976)
  See KOPPLE, BARBARA (Directors, Chapter I).

LIGHT, ALLIE
  Self-Health (1974)
  See LIGHTHOUSE FILMS.

LIGHTHOUSE FILMS
  Self-Health (1974). Co-makers: Catherine Allen, Judy
  Irola, Allie Light, Joan Musante
  23 min, c, r, s: MUL, SBC.
  "No meaningful understanding of sexuality is possible for
  women without an understanding and acceptance of their
  bodies. Made with the S.F. Women's Health Center, this
  film provides clear and enlightened instruction on methods
  of self-examination and imparts a sense of discovery and
  celebration in the process of self-health." -Program Notes,
  Pacific Film Archive

LIIKALA, ISABELLE
  Feels Of Blue (1969)
  6 min, c, r: FMC.
  "Fragmented lake landscape; willows, rain, sun, and snow...
  with multiple electronic-concrete sound overlays light love
  and humor." -Bob Liikala

LINKEVITCH, BARBARA
  Chinamoon (1975)
  15 min, c, r, s: SBC.
  "Chinamoon conveys the sequinned nightmare world inhabited
  by four prostitutes. The film focuses on the bed, men and
  experiences that the women share and the room they never
  leave..." -Linda Gross, L.A. Times

  Goodman
  12 min, b/w, r: CAN.
  "Film about 2 women with separate capacities for laughter;
  utilizing mime to the slight extent that we all do." -CAN

  Silverpoint (1974)
  25 min, c, r, s: SBC.
  "An intense psychological portrait of a young woman dancer
  experiencing conflict about her dance mixed with jealousy in
  her relationships with other women." -SBC

Thought Dreams
3 min, b/w, r: CAN. r, s: SBC.
"Game of hide and seek." -CAN

Traces (1973)
12 min, c, r: SBC.
"A dramatic reverie conveys the experience of growing up."
-Bonnie Dawson, Women's Films In Print

The Facts In The Case Of M. Valdemar (1976)
12 min, c, r: CAN.
"Two trains dominate the film...one celebrates a delight
in the mesmeric state induced by the random repetitive
movements of a mechanical toy car with its flickering
colored light and the second traces recollections of the
humorous process of shooting the film." -CAN

Flapping Things (1974)
10 min, c, silent, r: CAN.
"A metaphor of a yoga experience which speaks delicately
to the human." -CAN

L.A. Carwash (1975)
8 1/2 min, c, r: CAN.
"A film evolving out of my experiments with dual screen
projection and concerned with transformations suggested
by the sensual qualities of light and sound at the Village
Carwash in Los Angeles. The sound and picture exist as
complete and separate entities coinciding only for four
seconds." -J.C.L.

Other Reckless Things (1983)
25 min, c, r: CAN.
Reaction to the news media's tendency to dwell on violent
and bizarre events. "The film intends to lay bare the
rhythmic invasion of these media-distorted events into
our lives." -J.C.L.

Periodic Vibrations In An Elastic Medium (1973-76)
16 min, c, silent, r: CAN.
"Discrete images are modelled into a filmic form which
grows out of visual kinetic linkages rather than linguistic
modes, musical notations, or anecdotal concerns...A con-
tinuing work composed from several thousand feet of film
collected since 1973 in a variety of geographical sites."
-J.C.L.

Visible Inventory Nine: Pattern Of Events (1981)
12 min, b/w, r: CAN.
"A non-fiction narrative which touches on a basic tenet
of evolutionary theory..." -J.C.L.

Visible Inventory Six: Motel Dissolve (1978)
15 min, c, r: CAN.
"A space of time filled with moving...the camera coolly
surveys the interiors of motel rooms in which I stayed..."
-J.C.L.

LITTLEFIELD, NANCY
And Baby Makes Two (1978)
27 min, c, r, s: FNC.
"By turning the stage over to pregnant teenagers and teenage mothers, (the film) effectively conveys their innocence,
sadness and resignation at what they've done with their
lives." -L.A. Times

LOEB, JANET
In The Street (1953)

The Quiet One (1948)
See LEVITT, HELEN (Directors, Chapter I).

LONGINOTTO, KIM
Theatre Girls (1978). Co-maker: Claire Pollak
80 min, b/w, r: WMM.
"Theatre Girls Club is a hostel in Soho, London for destitute
women. Once a theatrical club, it is now the only shelter
in London that will take in any woman at any time..." -WMM

LYNCH, PATRICIA
High School High (1977)
23 min, c, r, s: FNC.
"This film study of cocaine and its use covers the historical
background and the cultivation of the coca plant from which
it is derived." -FNC

MACCALLUM, ELIZABETH
Portrait Of Christine (1978)
"28-year-old orthopaedically handicapped Christine shares
the philosophy and values which have contributed to her becoming a successful and appreciated member of her society."
-Program, 21st Annual American Film Festival

MACLAINE, SHIRLEY
The Other Half Of The Sky: A China Memoir (1974). Co-
maker: Claudia Weill
74 min, c, r, s: NDF.
"In 1973 Shirley MacLaine visited China with a delegation
of seven disparate American women - a rock-ribbed Republican,
a Navajo Indian, a Puerto Rican sociologist, a 12-year-old
minister's daughter, a California sexologist, a black Mississippi civil-rights worker and a Texas clerical worker...
The film, a collaborative effort by MacLaine and award-
winning filmmaker Claudia Weill, resembles the usual
travelog about as much as Peking duck resembles hamburger."
-Maureen Orth, Newsweek. Edited by Suzanne Pettit.

MALANAPHY, KATHLEEN
Livia Makes Some Changes (1974). Co-makers: Anne Sandys,
Sheelah Weaver
7 min, b/w, r, s: WMM.
"Livia, the mother, has the courage to move outside the
routines which have come to stifle her and, in doing so,
sets off a marvelous chain reaction to her son and husband
who then are induced to participate in the life of the
household. This is a really upbeat movie." -Emma Cohen,
Film Library Quarterly

MALDOROR, SARAH (Portuguese)
Sambizanga (1972) (Portuguese)
102 min, c, Portuguese with English subtitles, r: NYF.
"Filmed in 1961 (at the time of the first anti-Portuguese
uprising) by a woman, Sarah Maldoror, making her first
feature...Sambizanga has lost none of its power and rele-
vance today. The story focuses on a happy young black
couple; one day the husband is arrested for political
reasons...the central movement of the film is the search
of the young wife from village to village for her lost
husband." -NYF

MANDLIN, DOTTY
60 Second Spot (1974). Co-maker: Harvey Mandlin
25 min, c, r, s: PYR.
"This gallant, funny, and extremely well-made account of
the unknown epic struggles that lie behind the major television commercials delights everyone who sees it, from the
Bogart fan to the aspiring film student. In the high-
pressure world of major ad agencies, cinematic art comes
to grips with success or disaster." -PYR

MANGOLTE, BABETTE
The Camera: Je-Or(Ou) - La Camera: I (1977)
88 min, c & b/w, available from filmmaker.
"Using a subjective camera, the film describes the act of
making photographs." -Independent Film/Video Guide

MARNER, CAROLE
Phyllis And Terry (1964-65). Co-maker: Eugene Marner
36 min, b/w, r: FMC, UCE.
"Phyllis And Terry is a cinema verite portrait of two teenage Negro girls who live in the slums of New York's Lower
East Side...Their great dignity, their charm, their hope,
their despair are the poignant and compelling lines in
the portrait." -C. and E. Marner

MARX, PATRICIA
Obmaru
4 min, c, r: CFS.
"Study of West Coast experimental film movement."
-Films By/Or About Women

Things To Come
4 min, c, r: CFS.
"Spritely abstract animation film in which the basic
visual images were created by painter Marx and then
animated by Jonathon Belson. Music by Dizzy Gillespie."
-CFS

MARX, SUE
John Glick: An Artist And His Work (1978)
9 min, c, r, s: available from filmmaker.
"John Glick, a potter, speaks of himself, his feelings,
his work, as we watch him enter his studio and complete
the making of a large bowl." -Program, 21st Annual American Film Festival

MAURIZIO, CYNTHIA
Inside Women Inside (1978)
See CHOY, CHRISTINE (Directors, Chapter I).

McCARTHY, DINITIA
The New Sexuality (1975)
26 min, c, r, s: FNC.
"Nude encounter groups, bisexuality, homosexuality,
non-monogamous marriages - unmentionable, even un-
thinkable, a generation ago - are now discussed,
openly participated in. This sensitive exploration of
the changing attitudes of Americans, particularly in
urban areas, deals not only with the possible causes -
the pervasiveness of sex in the media, the women's
liberation movement, and the alienation of youth."
-FNC

Passing Quietly Through (1971)
See COOLIDGE, MARTHA (Directors, Chapter I).

McKAY, ELIZABETH
The Man And The Snake (1975). Co-maker: Sture Rydman
26 min, c, r, s: PYR.
"Loosely based on one of Ambrose Bierce's famous short
stories of ironic horror, 'The Man And The Snake,' this
is a tale of the unsettling struggle between the common
sense of the day and the subtle abduction of the mind
by the eerie effects of nightfall." -PYR

The Return (1976). Co-maker: Sture Rydman
30 min, c, r, s: PYR.
"This compelling film, adapted from stories by Ambrose
Bierce and A.M. Burrage, has been lavishly produced...
Rumors of the appearance, in a brooding country mansion,
of a murdered woman's ghost provide the basis for this
suspenseful tale." -PYR

McLAUGHLIN-GILL, FRANCES
Cover Girl: New Face In Focus (1968)
29 min, c, r: available in package, NLC.
Just what title says.

MEDINA, ANN
Inflation (1975). Co-producer: Stan Opotowsky
54 min, c, r, s: PNX.
"By familiarizing us with the history and concepts behind the current Inflation, the report provides us with
the basic knowledge necessary to make any attempt to
control the inflationary spiral and revitalize the
economy. Interviews with economist Paul Samuelson,
corporate business, politicians, workers and consumers."
-PNX

MENDELSOHN, JANET
Common Ground: Changing Values And The National Forests
(1978)
29 min, c, r, s: COF.
"Examines complex forest policy issues - harvesting of
old growth timber, wilderness designation, recreation
development, and protection of local lifestyles and
values - through the eyes of backpackers, loggers,
foresters, and residents of forest communities." -Program,
21st Annual American Film Festival

MENKEN, MARIE
*Note: Package including Arabesque For Kenneth Anger,
Bagatelle For Willard Maas, and Moonplay. 15 min, c &
b/w, r: FNC.
Package including Visual Variations On Noguchi, Hurry!
Hurry!, Glimpse Of The Garden, and Dwightiana. 16 min,
c & b/w, r: FNC.

Andy Warhol (1965)
20 min, c, silent at 24 fps, r: FMC, GRO.
"A long day in the life of Pop artist Andy Warhol." -M.M.

Arabesque For Kenneth Anger (1961)
4 min, c, r: FMC.
Film study of the Alhambra.

Bagatelle For Willard Maas (1961)
5 min, c, r: FMC.
"New version of the now famous film made for her hus-
band, the poet and filmmaker. Returning from the Brussels
Fair, she shot this at Versailles and the Louvre."
-Charles Boultenhouse, FMC

Drips In Strips (1961)
2 1/2 min, c, silent at 24 fps, r: FMC.
"Spattered paint responding to gravity, forming its
own patterns and combinations of color." -M.M.

Dwightiana (1959)
3 min, c, r: FMC.
"Charming, frivolous animation made to entertain a
sick friend." -Cinema 16

Excursion
5 min, c, silent at 24 fps, r: FMC.
No summary available.

Eye Music In Red Major
4 min, c, silent at 24 fps, r: FMC.
"Study in light based on persistence of vision and
enhancement from eye fatigue." -M.M.

Glimpse Of The Garden (1957)
5 min, c, r: FMC.
"Lyric, tender, intensely subjective exploration of
a flower garden, with extreme magnification, flashing
color harmonies." -Cinema 16

Go, Go, Go (1962-64)
12 min, c, silent at 24 fps, r: FMC
No summary available.

Hurry! Hurry!
3 min, c, r: FMC.
"Daring film ballet danced by human spermatozoa under
powerful magnification...dance of death made from scientific footage, printed over murky fire." -Cinema 16

Lights (1964-66)
6 1/2 min, c, silent at 24 fps, r: FMC.
"Made during the brief Christmas-lit season, usually
between midnight and 1:00 A.M....based on store decora-
tions, window displays, fountains, public promenades,
Park Avenue lights, buildings and church facades."
-M.M.

Mood Mondrian
7 min, c, silent at 24 fps, r: FMC.
"Film of a painting of a sound. Piet Mondrian's Broadway
'Boogie-Woogie' is translated into visual boogie rhythm."
-M.M.

Moonplay (1962)
5 min, b/w, r: FMC.
"Lunar fantasy in animated stop-motion." -M.M.

Notebook (1962-63)
10 min, c, silent at 24 fps, r: FMC.
"A very personal film which she keeps adding to...a
masterpiece of filmic fragments..." -P. Adams Sitney

Sidewalks (1966)
6 1/2 min, b/w, silent at 24 fps, r: FMC.
"Looking down instead of around while walking, finding
the magic patterns in the pavements of a city." -John
Hawkins

Visual Variation On Noguchi (1945)
4 min, b/w, r: FMC.
"Sculptures of the famous Japanese-American artist,
Isamu Noguchi are given audacious movement in a controversial art film experiment." -Cinema 16

Watts With Eggs
2 min, c, silent at 24 fps, r: FMC.
No summary available.

Wrestling
8 min, b/w, r: FMC.
"Crowd-sounds montage soundtrack, A T.V. 'concrete.'"
-M.M.

MEYER, MUFFIE
  Grey Gardens (1976)
  See FROEMKE, SUSAN (Directors, Chapter I).

  See MEYER, MUFFIE (Editors).

MIDE, ROBIN
  Three Lives (1971)
  See IRVINE, LOUVA (Directors, Chapter I).

MILLET, KATE
  Three Lives (1971)
  See IRVINE, LOUVA (Directors, Chapter I).

MOCK, FLORA
  Tom Tit Tot
  13 min, c, r: CFS.
  "Beautifully costumed actors performing in silhouette
  and pantomine against colorful stylized backgrounds
  dramatize this English version of 'Rumplestiltskin.'"
  -CFS

Waiting
12 min, c, r: CFS.
"Illustrates the frustration of women who wait from
birth to death for a state of happiness and fulfillment
that always seems to be waiting just around the next
corner..." -CFS

MOCK, FRIEDA LEE
Jung Sai: Chinese American. Co-maker: Terry Sanders
29 min, c, r, s: FNC.
"A young Chinese-American journalist seeks out her
ethnic origins, traveling through the West interview-
ing Chinese of all ages, on the early coolie labor
immigrations, the work on the transcontinental railway
and in the mines, and the formation of the great
Chinatowns." -Macmillan Catalog

MORRIS, GEORGIA
Careers And Babies (1976)
20 min, c, r, s: POY.
"Careers And Babies shows four women, two of whom have
children and two of whom do not, who have reacted to
this common question...(of choosing between a career
and children or both)." -POY

MORRISON, JANE
Children Of The North Lights (1976)
20 min, c, r: WES.
"A portrait of Ingri and Edgar D'Aulair, the noted
children's authors and artists..." -J.M.

Henry Strater, American Arist (1975)
28 min, c, r: WES.
"A documentary profile of this Maine painter, a contemporary of F. Scott Fitzgerald and noted portrait
painter of Ernest Hemingway." -J.M.

In The Spirit Of Haystack (1979)
10 min, c, r: available from filmmaker.
"...Impressionistic view of this noted crafts school
in Deer Isle, Maine." -J.M.

The Two Worlds Of Angelita (Los Dos Mundos De Angelita)
(1982)
73 min, c, r: available from filmmaker.
"A parable of Puerto Rican reality and the migration
experience told through the story of a young Puerto
Rican family." -J.M.

The White Heron (1978)
26 min, c, r, s: LCA.
Based on Sarah Orne Jewett's short story, the film concerns "...Sylvy, a solitary girl caught between the ad-
miration she feels for a young hunter and her overriding
love for nature..."   -LCA

MOURIS, CAROLINE
Coney (1975). Co-maker: Frank Mouris
5 min, c, r: BUD, VIE.   r, s: PNX.
"It is a view, using stop motion, fast cutting, fast
motion and cut-out animation of Coney Island, the decaying amusement park island in New York City." -View-
finder. "The harsh reality of Coney Island today is
seen through the unusual emotional/visual filter of
pink cotton candy." -BUD

Frank Film (1973). Co-maker: Frank Mouris
9 min, c, r: UCE. r, s: PYR.
"Entirely collage animation, thousands of color cutouts
fill the screen in an endless cornucopia of the objects
that have filled Frank's life." -PYR

Impasse (1978). Co-maker: Frank Mouris
10 min, c, r, s: PNX.
"An aggressive red arrow tries to get rid of a little
white dot from a totally black field...The artwork for
this film is made entirely with self-adhesive Avery
labels attached to the standard acetate cels of traditional animation." -Program, 21st Annual American Film
Festival

Screentest (1975). Co-maker: Frank Mouris
20 min, c, r: BUD. r, s: PNX.
"A candid look at an unusually gifted group of avante-
garde artists coming together to experience and share
each other's art." -PNX.

MUDGE, JEAN
Emily Dickinson: A Certain Slant Of Light (1977)
29 min, c, r, s: PYR.
"...Julie Harris takes the viewer on a tour of Dickinson's environment (Amherst, Mass.) - a place of natural
grandeur, devotion to religion and education, and a
toleration of individuality which inevitably shaped the
poet's thoughts and feelings..." -PYR

MULFORD, MARILYN
  How About You? (1973)
  See FRIEDMAN, BONNIE (Directors, Chapter I).

MURPHY, MARGARET
  They Are Their Own Gifts (1978). Co-maker: Lucille
  Rhodes
  52 min, c, r: NDF.
  "A biographical trilogy which documents the lives and
  works of three American artists - poet Muriel Rukeyser,
  painter Alice Neel and choreographer Anna Sokolow."
  -Independent Film/Video Guide

MUSANTE, JOAN
  Self-Health (1974)
  See LIGHTHOUSE FILMS.

NELSON, BARBARA
  Reentry
  9 min, b/w, r: CAN.
  "Ours is such a couple-oriented society that the prospect
  of divorce fills us with panic...Reentry's subject is a
  woman dealing with depression caused by such fears. Her
  alternatives seem limited as she focuses on suicide but
  out of crisis emerges growth and her 'reentry.'" -CAN

NELSON, GUNVOR
  Five Artists: Billbobbillbillbob (1970-71). Co-maker:
  Dorothy Wiley
  70 min, c, r: CAN.
  Just that.

  Fog Pumas (1967). Co-maker: Dorothy Wiley
  25 min, c, r: CAN, FMC. r, s: SBC.
  "Strange places in the filmmakers' minds mixed with
  strange places in reality make a third place on film.
  The subject of the film is that third place..." -G.N.

  Kirsa Nicolina (1970)
  16 min, c, r: CAN, FMC. r, s: SBC.
  "Deceptively simple film of a child being born to a
  Woodstock couple in their home is an almost classic
  manifesto of the new sensibility, a proud affirmation
  of a man amidst technology, genocide, and ecological
  destruction...birth is presented as a living through of
  primitive mystery, a spiritual celebration, a rite of
  passage..." -Amos Vogel, Village Voice

Moon's Pool (1973)
15 min, c, r: CAN, FMC, r, s: SBC.
"The search for identity and resolution of self. Photographed under water, live bodies are intercut with natural landscapes creating powerful mood changes...images
surface from the unconscious." -Freude Bartlett

My Name Is Oona (1969-70)
10 min, b/w, r: CAN, FMC, MMA. r, s: SBC.
"Captures in haunting, intensely lyrical images, fragments of the coming to consciousness of the child girl,
(the filmmaker's daughter)." -Freude Bartlett

One & The Same (1972-73)
See FREUDE (Directors, Chapter I).

Schmeerguntz (1966). Co-maker: Dorothy Wiley
15 min, b/w, r: CAN, FMC, FNC, UCE. r, s: SBC.
"Contrasts the 'glamour girl' ideal...with the discom-
fort of pregnancy, the tedium of child care, housecleaning and other unpleasant routines." -UCE

Take Off (1972)
10 min, b/w, r: CAN. r, s: SBC.
"A strip tease dancer makes a sardonic comment on attitudes toward the female body in a male-dominated culture." -Program, 2nd International Festival of Women's
Films, New York

Trollstenen (1976)
120 min, c, r: CAN. r, s: SBC.
"Trollstenen, laced with memories and dreams from the
past, is a multi-layered personal documentary of the life
of my parents and family in Sweden." -G.N.

NEWSREEL WOMEN
Makeout (1970)
12 min, b/w, r, s: SFN.
"The oppressive experience of making-out in a car..
from the woman's point of view." -Newsreel

She's Beautiful When She's Angry
17 min, b/w, r, s: SFN.
"A guerilla theatre piece on the role of women, performed at an anti-abortion rally in New York City in
1969. A beauty contestant is pressured into the roles
necessary to be the 'ideal woman,' 'a winner.'" -Newsreel

The Woman's Film (1971)
40 min, b/w, r, s: SFN.
"The Woman's Film was made entirely by women in San
Francisco Newsreel...It is a film which immediately
evokes the sights and sounds and smells of working
class kitchens, neighborhood streets, local super-
markets, factories, cramped living rooms, dinners
cooking, diaper-washing, housecleaning, and all the
other 'points of production' and battle-fronts where
working class women in America daily confront the
realities of their oppression. It is...a supremely
optimistic statement..." -Irwin Sibler

NOBLE, BARBARA
The River (1977)
29 min, c, r, s: PNX.
"Based on a short story by Flannery O'Connor, about a
neglected little boy who is befriended by the poor
woman who takes care of him. Zealously religious, she
introduces him to religion, and this experience of
baptism and religion has dramatic effects on him."
-Program, 21st Annual American Film Festival

NORRIS, MARIANNA
Women, Amen! (1973)
15 min, c, r: UCE.
"Examines the impact of the women's movement on churches
in the U.S. Shows a young woman activist who organizes
a consciousness-raising group, reforms worship services
and finally enters a seminary, while older women lobby
for bringing women into decision-making procedures."
-UCE

O, DORE
See DORE O (Directors, Chapter I).

OBERHAUS, PATRICIA
A-Day-In-The-Woods
3 min, b/w, silent, r: CAN.
"This is my first movie. It is I guess, a 'Victorian
Weed Commercial,' a picnic in the Berkeley Hills with
a magician, a milkmaid, a 'fashionable professionable
lady,' a wood pest,...and a 'Telegraph pirate lady'..."
-P.O.

Garhard Nicholsen
3 min, c, silent, r: CAN.
"...a personal portrait of sculptor Garhard Nicholsen.
Garhard is a metal sculptor; he casts bronze, takes
prints, makes stained glass walls..." -P.O.

Ham Hox
3 min, c, silent at 24 fps, r: CAN.
"This is a manipulative collage movie. Myself on camera, borrowed, and a Berkeley High School student, on
the movement of pieces at my command..." -P.O.

The Store On Telegraph
18 min, c, r: CAN.
"We opened the store...as a joke...a put-on, to ire
the money grabbers...on Telegraph. Sound track is
taken from our ol' juke box." -CAN

OMORI, EMIKO
Sculpture. Co-maker: Joshua Smith
3 min, c, r: CAN.
"A glint of light and off it soars; freed from its
pedestal, the aluminum sculpture moves and dances in
the nights." -CAN

The Space Between
7 min, b/w, r: CAN.
"...Impressions of the Marin County Civic Center designed
by Frank Lloyd Wright." -CAN

O'NEILL, BEVERLY
Skye Boat For Biscuit (1974)
3 min, c, r, s: SBC.
"Prompted by the death of the filmmaker's dog, Biscuit,
this film is a short and unsentimental addition to the
ranks of experimental film." -SBC

ORE, DIANE
The History Of Miss Annie Anderson (1976)
28 min, c, r, s: FNC.
Portrait of a 94-year-old pioneer.

OSTERTAG, SANDY
Woman Is (1975)
12 min, c, r, s: PNX.
"Woman Is uses a series of photographic stills in order
to explore the history and character of roles that women
occupy in society. Stressed is the contrast and individuality of the people within each role." -PNX

OXENBERG, JAN
A Comedy In Six Unnatural Acts (1975)
25 min, b/w, r, s: IFC.
"A loving satire of some of the stereotyped images of
lesbians, filmed in various styles which are spoofs
on different genres of Hollywood films." -IFC

Home Movie
10 min, c & b/w, r, s: IFC, MUL.
"An autogiographical film about lesbianism, combining
documentary footage of the lesbian community with actual old home movies of the filmmaker. Personal narration
about growing up as a lesbian and coming out." -IFC

I'm Not One Of 'Em
3 min, c, r, s: IFC.
"A woman spectator at the roller derby talks about her
unique experiences with lesbianism. Hilarious and also
painful." -IFC

PEARLMAN, JOAN
Back To School, Back To Work   (1973)
20 min, c, r: UCE.
"Examines the common forms of opposition faced by
wives and mothers who wish to return to school or
work." -UCE

PECK, NANCY
Musereel #1
See BOSTROM, DENISE (Directors, Chapter I).

Womancentering
8 min, b/w, r, s: WMM.
"Womancentering is a film that portrays with a sense of
humor, a young mother's first interest in feminism."
-WMM

PETTY, SARA
Furies (1977)
3 min, c, r, s: SBC.
"Furies is a sprightly feline romp set to Ned Rorem's
'Trio for Flute, Cello, and Piano.' Sara Petty employs
charcoal and pastels to create Cubist and Art Deco-in-
spired designs which evoke the joyous curiosity, grace
and beauty of two cats in constant motion." -Karen
Cooper, Film Forum

PIGORSCH, PHYLLIS
Mrs. Slattery's Stew
9 min, c, r: CAN.
Allegory on women.

PITT, SUZAN
Asparagus (1978)
19 min, c, r: CAN
"A sensual, beautifully animated interpretation of an
artist's inspiration and the artistic product." -Chris
Spilsbury.

Bowl, Theatre, Garden, Marble Game (1975)
7 min, c, r: CAN.
"Four Animated Anecdotes and a squeaky violin; a
selection of visual surprises." -CAN

Cels (1972)
6 min, c, r: CAN.
"Drawings of roomlike spaces with heavy doors that trun-
dle up and down to the sound of a typewriter. As each
door opens, it reveals a partial thought in a series of
film experiences: a spool unwinding, a guitar playing
itself, a chase into infinity..." -Minneapolis Tribune

A City Trip (1972)
3 min, c, r: CAN. r, s: SBC.
"Children interpret their impressions of city life with
cutouts and improvised sound effects." -Bonnie Dawson,
Women's Films In Print

Crocus (1971)
7 min, c, r: CAN, FMC. r, s: NLC, SBC.
"A funny poetic, animated act of married love includes
moths, birds, flowers, cabbages, cucumbers and crying
baby." -Program Notes, Pacific Film Archive

Jefferson Circus Songs (1973)
19 min, c, r: CAN. r, s: SBC.
"Love action pixillation and flat animation combine in
a magical train ride to another world - a musical fantasy
of absurd creatures and ceremonies of the imagination."
-CAN

Whitney Commercial
2 1/2 min, c, r: CAN.
"Commissioned by the Whitney Museum of American Art, to
gain support for their film program, the 'New American
Filmmakers Series'". -CAN

POLLAK, CLAIRE
Theatre Girls (1978)
See LONGINOTTO, KIM (Directors, Chapter I).

POPE, AMANDA
Cities For People (1975)
49 min, c, r, s: UCE.
This documentary "...explores the space left in a city -
for people - after the buildings are up." -UCE. Narrated
by Cloris Leachman.

PORTER, NANCY
Mr. Speaker: A Portrait Of Tip O'Neill (1978)
58 min, c, r, s: FNC.
"This cinema verite documentary offers an unprecedented
'inside look' at the nature of the Speaker's power and
his effect on national policy." -FNC

A Woman's Place Is In The House (1977). Co-maker: Mickey
Lemle
30 min, c, r, s: TEX.
Portrait of Elaine Noble, a member of the Massachusetts
House of Representatives who also happens to be a lesbian.

POULLETTE-MACDOUGAL, PHYLLIS
Some Will Be Apples (1974)
See LAUGHLIN, KATHLEEN (Directors, Chapter I).

POWELL, JOSEPHINE
Afghan Women (1975)

Women In A Changing World (1975)
See DUPREE, NANCY (Directors, Chapter I).

PRISADSKY, MARJORIE
Last Week
5 min, b/w, r: CAN.
"Apollo II - down 5 3/4 - 2 shares traded." -M.P.

White Susan
6 min, b/w, r: CAN.
"on being alone and aroused..." -CAN

PUGH, SALLY
You Don't Have To Buy This War, Mrs. Smith (1971)
28 min, b/w, r: KPF.
"The no-holds-barred speech by Bess Myerson Grant, then
Commissioner of Consumers' Affairs for New York City,
delivered before the 1970 World Mother's Day Assembly
in San Francisco, in which - for the first time - the
names and the profits of the leading war profiteering
companies in the United States were forever put upon the
public record...important addendum to the record of
those who did the most to bring the war to a close..."
-KPF

RAMSTAD, JOSIE
Bird Lady Vs. The Galloping Gonads (1976)
1 min, b/w, r, s: SBC.
"...Human forms irresistibly fly, change and mix with
plants, animals, birds, arrows, hands, phalluses, and
hungry suns as everything comes joyfully together in
mirthful mythic warmth." -SBC

Labor (1976)
2 1/2 min, c, silent, r, s: SBC.
"The birth experience is told from the mother's point of view
in this animated film drawn from the filmmaker's real life
experience." -SBC

RASMUSSEN, LORNA
Great Grand Mother (1978). Co-maker: Anne Wheeler
29 min, c, r, s: NDF.
"...a fascinating film about the lost history of the women who
pioneered the western frontier." Pater Briskin, Seven Days Magazine.

REICHERT, JULIA
Growing Up Female: As Six Become One (1971). Co-maker: James
Klein
60 min, b/w, r, s: NDF.
"Seeing Growing Up Female is one of those painful experiences
tha's good for you. With a minimum of comment, the film
shows how female human beings are brainwashed into passivity,
mental sluggishness and self-contempt." -Susan Sontag

Union Maids Co-makers: James Klein, Miles Mogulescu
48 min, b/w, r, s: NDF.
"Three women in their 60's - Sylvia, Kate and Stella - tell the
way they risked their jobs and lives to organize trade unions.
They are the 'stars' of Union Maids, a vivid slice of almost for-
gotten American history. By featuring the stories of these still-
vigorous and appealing women, intercut with newsreels of stormy
labor struggles, the film has recreated and humanized the spirit
of one of the most vital aspects of our times. What is expecially
moving is the way the film provides a quietly hopeful sense of
our continuity with the past and future." -San Francisco Chronicle

REINIGER, LOOTE (German)
The Adventures Of Prince Achmed (1923-26)
61 min, c, silent, r: EMG.
"The earliest feature-length animated film know to exist, The
Adventures Of Prince Achmed is a tour de force of charm, talent,
and originality. Adapting and interweaving several tales from
'The Arabian Nights,' Reiniger uses cut-out silhouettes against
hand-tinted backgrounds to tell the story of Achmed's long and
dangerous search for the bird princess...whom he loves but has
lost through the wiles of an evil sorcerer." -Macmillan catalog

Puss In Boots (1950)
10 min, b/w, r: KPF.
"...this award-winning 'cut-out' and silhouette film was done
with scissors, paste-brush, and black paper. The incredible
intricacy and detail of her cut-outs and the life-like movements have never been approached..." -KPF

RENAULT, MONIQUE
A La Votre! (1978)
2 min, c, r, available in Animated Women package, s: TEX.
"In elegant line drawing, woman is seen as gigantic and all-
powerful, in contrast to tiny, puny, ineffectual man." -TEX
See BOTTNER, BARBARA (Directors, Chapter I).

RESNICK, SUSAN
  Arcadia (1974)
  10 min, c, r: BAU.
  "In her first film, Resnick defines three worlds: the
  animal world, the city, and the realm of primitive
  music." -BAU

  Departure (1978)
  26 min, c, r: BAU.
  "The physical and psychic transformation of a woman who
  departs for a shopping day in New York City." -S.R.

  Island Between Three Silences (1977)
  12 min, c, r: BAU.
  "The unspoken emotions of three women in a cafe are the
  basis of this visually exciting film." -BAU

RHODES, LUCILLE
  They Are Their Own Gifts (1978)
  See MURPHY, MARGARET (Directors, Chapter I).

RIES, MARILYN
  Musereel #1
  See BOSTROM, DENISE (Directors, Chapter I).

ROCHLIN, DIANE
  Diane, The Zebra Woman (1962). Co-maker: Sheldon Rochlin
  24 min, b/w, r: FMC.
  "Grade Z home movie." -S.R.

  Vali. Co-maker: Sheldon Rochlin
  65 min, c, r: NLC.
  "A record of the experiences of an amazing, true-life
  witch..." -NLC

RODGERS, GABY
  Who Does She Think She Is? (1974)
  See JAFFE, PATRICIA (Directors, Chapter I).

ROSE, BARBARA
  Lee Krasner: The Long View (1978)
  30 min, c, r, s: AFA.
  "Critic Barbara Rose's film portrait of the seminal Abstract Expressionistic artist, focusing on Krasner's life,
  including her studies with Hans Hoffman and her marriage
  to Jackson Pollock. Krasner is also seen completing
  work for and hanging a show at New York's Pace Gallery."
  -Program, 21st Annual American Film Festival

Works In Series: Johns, Stella, Warhol   (1973)
30 min, c, r: BKW.
Study of the artists.

ROSE, KATHY
The Doodlers (1976)
5 min, c, r, s: SBC.
"...This is a whacky film whose creator envisions her
drawings coming to life: rebelling, socializing, and
engaging in the art of animation themselves." -Karen
Cooper, Film Forum

The Mirror People (1974)
4 min, c, r, s: SBC.
"The mirror people are gaunt, crayon-colored figures who
stretch themselves into the most impossible contortions.
Diving in and out of their mirrors, shaping themselves
into boxes and blocks, they are a race gone mad with
narcissisms, a chattering, whining pack of nabobs..."
-Rob Epple, Media and Methods

The Mysterians (1973)
6 min, c, r, s: SBC.
"Strange people-creatures soar and spin, shrink and
swell, as they miss and merge with clouds, trees, and
each other. Incredulous and zany, the mysterians are
our fantasies incarnate, off on a mad spree." -SBC

Pencil Booklings (1978)
14 min, c, r, s: SBC.
"Kathy Rose animates herself and her assortment of characters (Miss Nose, Miss Grundy, Noodle-Arm, Lionel, Oona,
Curly, Vicki, Hattie, Spiky, Pluto, Cat, Bird, Star, Moon,
Sun, Brush, Pencil) in a charming fantasy about the
art of animation. Each of her characters has a unique
personality as they take turns doing solo performances.
They even invite Kathy to join them in their cartoon
world, thus adding another playful dimension to the
theme of the relationship of an artist to her material."
-SBC

ROSE, LISA
The Hat Show
7 min, c, r: CAN.
"An exploration of identity through fantasy." -CAN

Headcheese
3 1/2 min, b/w, r: CAN
"Headcheese is a cinematic diary of one year of a life...
It was an attempt at capturing the spontaneous unfolding
of the unconscious..." -L.R.

ROSENBERG, ROYANNE
Autopsy (1972)
4 1/2 min, c, r, s: SBC.
"Shots in slow motion of an actual autopsy of a grey-
haired man, and a static outdoor show using a deep-
focus composition of a grey-haired man standing in the
distance down the pier...may have been about love or
separation." -Julia LeSage, Women And Film magazine

Roseland (1973)
12 1/2 min, c, r, s: SBC.
"Rose Oliver, an overweight, white welfare mother of
four talks about being a mother and her life in the
projects of Chicago." -Bonnie Dawson, Women's Films In
Print

ROSENFELT, JOAN
Blackout On Honeysuckle Lane (1983)
9 min, c, r, s: available from filmmaker.
"Dramatic fiction/narrative" -J.R.

The Nap (1979)
13 min, c, r, s: available from filmmaker.
"A well-earned afternoon nap turns into a nightmare."
-Program, 21st Annual American Film Festival

Plant A Seed (1976)
3 min, c, r, s: PNX.
"A film designed to encourage city people to improve
their environment by planting window boxes." -J.R.

ROTHSCHILD, AMALIE
It Happens To Us (1971)
30 min, c, r: UCE. r, s: NDF.
"It Happens To Us is a 30-minute documentary in which
women of different ages, marital status, and race
speak candidly about their abortion experiences. Their
stories reveal the problems of illegal versus legal
medically-safe abortions." -NDF

Nana, Mom And Me (1974)
47 min, c, r, s: NDF.
"Documentary look by the filmmaker, who is considering
having a child, into the interrelationships between herself, her mother and grandmother." -A.R.

Woo Who? May Wilson (1969)
33 min, c, r: UCE. r, s: NDF.
"When her husband informs her that his future plans no
longer include her, May Wilson, age 60, former 'wife-
mother-housekeeper-cook' and a grandmother, moves to
New York City and begins the painful process of working
out a new life in which the art that had once been a
hobby becomes central. With humor and insight the film
shows her acquiring new friends and a new self-image
in which she can accept herself as an artist, as we
watch her gain success as 'Grandma Moses of the Underground'". -NDF

RUBIN, SUSAN
Paul Revere Is Here (1976)
See BEAMS, MARY (Directors, Chapter I).

SAGAN, FRANCOISE
One More Winter
15 min, c, r, s: FNC.
"Francoise Sagan's One More Winter is a poignant
vignette of an old couple's romance which generates
envy in a blase young man, as yet untouched by love."
-FNC

ST. PIERRE, SUZANNE
A Dose Of Reality (1978)
16 min, c, r, s: CAR.
"A study of death and dying with emphasis on giving the
terminally ill patient a choice in making decisions
until the end." -Program, 21st Annual American Film
Festival

SAMUELSON, KRISTINE
Time Has No Sympathy (1975)
28 min, c, r, s: SBC.
"A humanistic portrait of women in prison made by a
woman. Without special emphasis on political or expo-
sitory material, Time Has No Sympathy conveys strong
emotion through detailed coverage of daily prison life
and the unfolding character of LaRue, a committed
spokeswoman for social change." -SBC

SANDERS, MARLENE
The Right To Die (1974)
See HOCHBERG, VICTORIA (Directors, Chapter I).

What's Happened Since Fire! (1976)
13 min, c, r, s: PNX.
What's Happened Since Fire! is an update of ABC-TV's
special, 'Close-up On Fire!,' and includes the controversial test burning of a baby's crib made from polysty-
rene." -PNX

A Woman's Place (1973)
See HOCHBERG, VICTORIA (Directors, Chapter I).

Women's Liberation (1970)
23 min, c, s: XEX.
Study of women's liberation.

SANDYS, ANNE
Livia Makes Some Changes (1974)
See MALANAPHY, KATHLEEN (Directors, Chapter I).

SAVAGE-LEE, CAROLINE
California Street Steps
3 1/2 min, silent, r: CAN.
"This is a lyrical exploration of a space filled with
physical opposition." -CAN

Channels
5 min, b/w, silent, r: CAN.
"An explanation of channel-changing on a radio with signals interfering with other signals, creating a system
of interference patterns that reassemble the inner
impulses of vision."   -CAN

Voyeur (1977)
7 1/2 min, c, r, s: CAN.
"A film that toys with illusionistic space and time from
a window perspective, allowing events to occur naturally
in combination with events juxtaposed for contrast and
comparison." -CAN

SCHILLER, GRETA
Greta's Girls. Co-maker: Thomas Seid
18 min, b/w, r, s: WMM.
"This film presents a day in the life of two women who
are just beginning their relationship together. The
paradox of the human experience is conveyed without
cliches." -WMM

SCHNEEMAN, CAROLEE
Body Collage (1964)
6 min, b/w, silent, r: W/A/F.
One of the films in the Kinetic Theatre series.

Falling Bodies (1967)
6 min, b/w, silent r: W/A/F.
Performance - Schneeman and James Tenney. Kinetic Theatre film.

Carl Ruggles Christmas Breakfast (1963)
7 min, b/w, r: W/A/F.
The distinguished, irascible New England composer at 86
years; his frank and considered opinions on Ives' sex
life, Schoenberg's temperament, the essence of rubato
..." -W/A/F

Fuses (1964-67)
22 min, c, silent, r: CAN, W/A/F. r, s: SBC.
"Presents the life of a man and woman together, their
bed as the life source of the house they inhabit."
-C.S.

Illinois Central (1968)
10 min, c, silent, r: W/A/F.
Performance by the Kinetic Theatre Troupe.

Meat Joy (1964)
12 min, c, r: W/A/F.
Performance - Schneeman. Kinetic Theatre film.

Plumb Line (1968-72)
18 min, c, r: CAN, W/A/F.
"Sounds: my cat, Kitch, singing: cries of 'no,' sirens,
song fragment, my voice describing a meal from maze of
breakdown: his voice 'tell me a story.'" -C.S.

Viet Flakes (1965)
7 min, b/w, r: CAN, W/A/F.
"Filmed from still atrocity images through various
lenses. Discrepancies between aesthetic perception
and literal information, emotion and detachment, dis-
location of time and space." -W/A/F

Waterlight/ Water Needle(1966)
12 min, c, r: W/A/F.
"A lyrical Kinetic Theatre work by Schneeman, who per-
forms with her troupe in a lake and on ropes rigged
through a circle of trees." -W/A/F

SCHNEIDER, ROSALIND
  *Note: package of Dream Study and Tulip, r: W/A/F.

Abstraction (1971)
8 min, c, r: FMC.   r, s: W/A/F.
"Interpretation of abstract form as found in the
combination of the nude body, landscape and objects."
-R.S.

Andrea Acting Out (1974)
12 min, c, r: W/A/F.
"Study of the filmmaker's 10-year-old daughter that
reveals the fantasy dream life of a child...the film
explores the subtle changes that have begun to take
place as she matures." -R.S.

The Butterfly
15 min, c, r, s: W/A/F.
"A poetic fantasy based on a brief encounter between
the filmmaker's 11-year-old daughter and a Monarch
butterfly. In dream-like sequences, butterfly images
superimposed in multiple layers fill the frame, until
all reality is transformed and colored by its presence."
-W/A/F

Dream Study (1972)
7 min, c, silent, r, s: W/A/F.
"Body portrait of a young woman in relation to nature and to herself, by means of superimposition.
Sensuous abstraction of a nude/nature study." -R.S.

Irvington To New York (1972)
4 min, c, r, s: W/A/F.
"Compacted imagery of a train ride that deals with
the visual onslaught of landscape and city images."
-R.S.

The Jeff Film
10 min, c, r, s: W/A/F.
"An experimental portrait of the filmmaker's 16-year-
old son, which portrays his growth to the brink of
manhood, through the abstraction and superimposition
of childhood experiences." -W/A/F

Life Notes
16 min, c, r, s: W/A/F.
"An abstract diary film, optically printed and extended sequences." -W/A/F

Moments (1974)
1 min, c, silent, r, s: W/A/F.
"The unblinding stare of a white cat half obscured
by darkness fills the screen...minimal changes in
each hair and texture in extended time. A quick
movement and an enveloping yawn climax the film."
-R.S.

On (1972)
3 min, c, r, s: W/A/F.
"Sexuality as a trip." -R.S.

Orbitas (1971)
10 min, c, r, s: W/A/F.
"Has been likened to a journey into inner/outer
space." -R.S.

Parallax (1973)
21 min, c, 3-screen projection, r: W/A/F.
"Film as a triptych. The visual extension of images
in repetition by means of a triple-screen projection.
A dance abstraction that deals with female and male
body relationships and rhythms." -R.S.

Positive/Negative Abstraction (1974)
8 min, b/w, silent, r, s: W/A/F.
"To be projected on 2 blue plexi-glass panels one
foot wide suspended in front of the screen bracket-
ing the edge of the frame. Patterns of light formed
by piercing the filmed images of body abstraction
become a rhythmic structure, bouncing off the reflective surface." -R.S.

Spring Thing (1974)
7 min, c, r, s: W/A/F.
"The tightly closed buds of dormacy and the full
flowering of peach blossoms sucked by bees, is contrasted by the slow hunting rhythms of animals."
-R.S.

Still Life (1972)
8 min, c, r, s: W/A/F.
"Voyage into red cabbage and shells. Shells transform themselves into internal orange canyons. Cabbage as the universe." -R.S.

Tulip (1973)
5 min, c, r, s: W/A/F.
"A study of the male body as an erotic abstraction
in relationship to flower forms." -W/A/F

SCHWARTZ, LILLIAN
Affinities (1972)
4 1/2 min, c, available from filmmaker.
"Beethoven's variations on Mozart's 'La ci darem la
mano' synthesized on computer...A ballet of squares
and octagons in many forms." -Whitney Museum

Alae   (1975)
5 min, c, available from filmmaker.
"The first time a sequence of birds from the real
world were optically scanned and fed into the computer to reappear as completely new images in light."
-L.S.

Apotheosis   (1972)
4 1/2 min, c, available from filmmaker.
"Pulsing variously textured and colored forms."
-Whitney Museum

Collage   (1975)
5 1/2 min, c, available from filmmaker.
"A swift assortment of moving images, filmed from a
color TV monitor that was computer controlled."   -L.S.

Enigma (1972).   Co-maker: Ken Knowlton
4 min, c, r: CFS.
"Computer film with lines and rectangles."   -Bonnie
Dawson, Women's Films In Print

Galaxies   (1974)
4 1/2 min, c, available from filmmaker.
"Computer-simulated disk galaxies that are superimposed and twirl through space in beautiful colors
at different speeds."   -L.S.

Googolplex   (1972)
5 1/2 min, b/w, available from filmmaker.
Geometric computer patterns.

Innocence   (1973)
2 1/2 min, c, available from filmmaker.
"Images and musical study of spirals rapidly moving."
-L.S.

Kinesis   (1975)
4 1/2 min, c, available from filmmaker.
"Escher-like images stepping through the frames to
the music of a jazz group."   -L.S.

Mathoms   (1970)
2 1/2 min, c, available from filmmaker.
"Playful concoction of computer produced images, a
few hand-animated scenes and shots of lab equipment."
-L.S.

Mirage (1974)
5 min, c, available from filmmaker.
"Filmed directly from color television controlled by
computer programs." -L.S.

Mis-takes (1972)
3 1/2 min, c, available from filmmaker.
"Colorful collage, with a subtle ecology theme, made
largely from footage from trial runs of programs used
for many of the other films." -L.S.

Mutations (1972)
7 1/2 min, c, available from filmmaker.
"Shot using computers and lasers to produce changing
spots and shapes." -Bonnie Dawson, Women's Films In
Print

Olympiad (1971)
3 min, c, available from filmmaker.
"Figures of computer-stylized athletes are seen in
brilliant hues chasing each other across the screen."
-Bob Lehmann, Today's Filmmaker

Papillons (1973)
2 1/2 min, c, available from filmmaker.
"Mathematical functions resembling butterflies."
-L.S.

Pictures From A Story (1975)
5 min, c, available from filmmaker.
"Picture processed photos from the artist-filmmaker's
family." -L.S.

SEVERSON, ANNE
Animals Running (1974)
23 min, b/w, r: CAN. 18 min, r: SBC.
"A continuous stream of animals from bison to splin-
ters of fishes casting a hypnotic spell." -Freude
Bartlett

I Change, I Am The Same (1969)
See KENNEDY, SHELBY (Directors, Chapter I).

Introduction To Humanities (1972)
5 min, b/w, r: CAN. r, s: SBC.
"My first year Humanities class at the San Francisco
Art Institute steps before the camera and introduces
itself one by one. This film is an appropriate compli-
ment to Near The Big Chakra and should be shown immediately
after." -A.S.

Near The Big Chakra   (1972)
17 min, c, silent, r: CAN, r, s: SBC.
"A startling and informative film presenting close-
ups of 36 vaginas ranging in age from 4 months to 64
years." -Freude Bartlett. "The impression made by
this film, its impact - has been enormous...This
film is a new approach to our femininity." -Agnes
Varda

Riverbody (1970)
See KENNEDY, SHELBY (Directors, Chapter I).

The Struggle Of The Meat   (1974)
3 min, c, r: CAN. r, s: SBC.
"A rhythmic sonnet of wildlife footage celebrating
life on Earth and conveying the struggle for sur-
vival with abstract clarity." -SBC

SHADBURNE, SUSAN
  Claymation   (1974). Co-maker: Will Vinton
  18 min, c, r, s: PYR.
  "This entertaining and informative film shows us how
  clay animation films are made...The film shows the
  mixing of colors, creation of characters who move,
  production and editing of the live action film which
  serves as an animation guide, music scoring and the
  slow, demanding process of working with the clay
  itself..." -PYR

SHAFFER, DEBORAH
  Chris And Bernie   (1974)

  How About You?   (1973)
  See FRIEDMAN, BONNIE (Directors, Chapter I).

SHAW, JEAN
  Fear   (1973)
  6 min, b/w, r, s: WMM.
  "A young typist walks to work...is harrassed by a
  construction worker, and told by her boss that she
  did not get the promotion she'd hoped for. Upset,
  she goes to the bathroom to cry and is confronted
  by a rapist who has followed her in from the street.
  We are expecting the final humiliation when..." -WMM.
  "Fear is about cowardice, and the point at which you
  say, 'I'd rather die than live like this.'" -J.S.

SHORT, MARJIE
  Kudzu (1976)
  16 min, c, r, s: PYR.
  "Kudzu is an off-beat, witty, informative documentary
  about the vine that is devouring the South. Featuring
  the Kudzu Queen, the Kudzu band, a cast of real-life
  characters and an appearance by President Jimmy Carter,
  it illustrates how Southern cultural traditions
  have quickly grown up around a botanical pest." -PYR

SILVER, JOAN MICKLIN
  Bernice Bobs Her Hair (1977)
  47 1/2 min, c, r, s: PER.
  Film based on F. Scott Fitzgerald's short story. With
  Shelley Duvall, Bud Cort, Veronica Cartwright.

  Between The Lines (1977)
  101 min, c, r: IVY.
  "Set in present day Boston, Between The Lines is
  about a group of friends who work together at the
  Back Bay Main Line, a small weekly newspaper."
  -IVY. Stars John Heard, Lindsay Crouse, Jeff Gold-
  blum, Michael J. Pollard.

  The Case Of The Elevator Duck (1974)
  The Fur Coat Club (1973)
  See GOTTLIEB, LINDA (Directors, Chapter I).

  Head Over Heels (1979)
  98 min, c, r: MGM.
  Head Over Heels is Silver's study of obsession. Film
  concerns a young man who is determined to win back
  his ex-girlfriend, even though she is now married.
  Stars John Heard, Mary Beth Hurt.

  Hester Street (1975)
  91 min, b/w, r, s: CIV.
  "Hester Street is the story of a Russian Jew who finds
  his way to America ahead of his wife. He quickly becomes assimilated and, in the process, becomes enchanted with another, more modern woman. His wife
  arrives, steeped in the manners and customs of the
  old country. How the problems of the couple are
  resolved makes for a most humourous and charming
  story..." -CIV. Stars Carol Kane, Steven Keats,
  Dorrie Kavannaugh.

The Immigrant Experience: The Long Long Journey (1973)
See GOTTLIEB, LINDA (Directors, Chapter I).

See SILVER, JOAN MICKLIN (Screenwriters).

SILVER, JODY
  Birth Of The Big Mamoo (1971-72)
  6 min, c, r: NLC.
  "Inside the Mamoo a cell is born. Struck by sperm
  it begins its metamorphosis, first into a worm. The
  Mamoo swallows an apple offered by a serpent. The
  worm bores its way into the apple and emerges a butterfly. The butterfly's flutter causes the Mamoo
  to rise and change...finally into a little Mamoo."
  -NLC

SIMON, STELLA
  Hands (1928)
  13 min, b/w, silent, r: MMA.
  "As the title implies, this is a film made of nothing
  but hand movements, all of them expressing emotion
  in a film which is the quintessence of the 1928 idea
  of expressionism." -MMA

SLOANE, PATRICIA
  A Knee Ad (1970-71)
  25 min, b/w, r: FMC.
  "...a modern reworking of Virgil's Aeneid. The
  travels take place on a movie screen, and through
  the unique spatiotemporal domain of cinematography."
  -P.S.

SNIDER, SARAH
  Maxine (1975)
  13 min, b/w, r, s: IFC.
  "A documentary portrait of a woman who is dying,
  isolated in her rural home with her husband and two
  sons - an eloquent celebration of a woman who, although her body fails her, remains strong." -IFC

SONTAG, SUSAN
  Brother Carl (1971)
  97 min, b/w, r: NYF.
  "Difficult but rewarding film of the relationships
  between two couples dealing with a young man who
  has brain damage." NYF

  Duet For Cannibals (1969)
  105 min, b/w, r, s: GRO.
  "A psychological comedy-drama of an exiled revolutionary and his wife who exercise a strange influence over a young couple..." -GRO

Promised Lands   (1974)
87 min, c, r: NYF.
"Begun just after the war ended, while the agony and
destruction still shrouded the landscape, the film
was shot in five weeks at the battle sites along
the Suez Canal, on the Golan Heights, in the Sinai
Desert, and in the villages." -Sharon Smith,
Women Who Make Movies

SPENCER, MARY ANN
Moon
2 min, b/w, silent, r: FMC.
"Images of the moon - its phases, its astronauts,
its dreams." -M.A.S.

The White Cat
1 1/2 min, c, silent, r: CAN.
"The white cat rolls and tumbles." -M.A.S.

SPHEERIS, PENELOPE
The Decline Of Western Civilization   (1981)
100 min, c and b/w, r: COR.
Alice Bag Band, X, Black Flag
Exciting film which combines concert footage with
interviews, and focuses on the punk music scene in
Los Angeles.

I Don't Know   (1971)
27 min, b/w, r, s: SBC.
"Love story between a man who wishes he were a woman
and a woman who wishes she were a man."   -Freude
Bartlett

SPIEGEL, OLGA
Alchemy Blues
10 min, c, r: W/A/F.
"Animation painted directly onto film."   -W/A/F

Psychereel   (1978)
10 min, c, r: W/A/F.
"Journey into the real and the fantastic, allowing
the subconscious to come through. We recognize it,
as the psyche is revealed through layers where the
abstract becomes the melting changing forms of association."   -W/A/F

Wings Of Thought
10 min, c, r: W/A/F.
"Mixed animation and special effects." -W/A/F

STARR, CECILE
Richter On Film (1972)
14 min, c, available from filmmaker.
Portrait of the avant-garde filmmaker.

STEIG, LAURIE
Sculpture For Children (1974)
See CHASE, DORIS (Directors, Chapter I).

STERN, JOAN KELLER
Magic Machines (1970)
14 min, c, r: VCI. r, s: PYR.
"An Academy Award-winning documentary showing how
sculptor Robert Gilbert creates fascinating, in-
genious pieces of moving sculpture with junk sal-
vaged from desert junkyards." -PYR

STERNBURG, JANET
El Teatro Campesino (1971)
See HOCHBERG, VICTORIA (Directors, Chapter I).

STRAND, CHICK
Angel Blue Sweet Wings (1966)
4 min, c, r: CAN. r, s: SBC.
"Celebration of love in animated collage." -Bonnie
Dawson, Women's Films In Print

Anselmo (1967)
4 min, c, r: CAN. r, s: SBC.
"A Mexican street musician..." -Bonnie Dawson,
Women's Films In Print

Cosas De Mi Vida (1976)
23 min, c, r: CAN. r, s: INS, SBC.
"The story of the life of Anselmo, born into poverty
and orphaned at age seven. Strand returns to the subject of her earlier film, who in the ten-year interim
has become part of Mexico's lower middle class."
-SBC

Elasticity (1975)
22 min, c, r: CAN. r, s: SBC.
"This film is autobiographical in the sense that its
elements stand for things that have been important
in my life. The Amnesia/White Light section repre-
sents those things in the past that have almost re-
treated from memory." -C.S.

Guacamole (1976)
10 min, c, r: CAN. r, s: SBC.
"A short cine-poem whose meter is in the tragic rather
than the celebratory mode. Its focus on the life/death
polarity of fiesta and bullfight, rendered in a deeply
painterly texture, where slow-motion and blue tones
give it a lyrical melancholia." -Anthony Reveaux,
Artweek

Mosori Monika (1970)
20 min, c, r: CAN, UCE. r, s: SBC.
"...a visual essay on the Mosori Indians of Venezuela
that is both anthropologically valid and aethetically
appealing...two views of the Mosori: one from the
point of view of a missionary, whoe order brought...
Christianity to the tribe twenty years earlier; the
other from an old Mosori woman, whose long life includes years before the missionaries' arrival."
-Jeanne Betancourt, Women In Focus

Mujer De Milfuegos (1976)
15 min, c, r, s: CAN.
"An expressionistic, surrealistic portrait of a
Latin American Woman." -CAN

Waterfall (1967)
3 min, c, r: CAN. r, s: SBC.
"In celebration of water, the Orient, ice skaters
and swimmers." -LA Film Coop

STROMMER, JOAN
Father (1982)
15 min, b/w, r: available from filmmaker.
"Expresses the mystery, imprecision, and the unre-
solved nature of the father-daughter bond." -J.S.

Mother (1980)
16 min, b/w, r: available from filmmaker.
"A seasonal documentation of the house reflects
the possible inwardness, isolation and contain-
ment of mother-daughter relationship." -J.S.

Twins (1979)
9 min, c, available from filmmaker.
"...both a documentary on what it means to be a twin
and a sort of villanelle, that kind of verse in which
there are frequently repeated refrains. One remembers
the voices more vividly than the solemn faces, and appro-
priately, for the twins complain that people look not
only at them but past them, and that they are not
visible as individuals..." -Edgar Daniels, American
Film

STUDIVANT, JEANETTE
No Exceptions (A Film About Rape)   (1977). Co-
maker: Christine Vasquez
24 min, c, r, s: FFC.
"...Utilizing interviews as well as dramatic situations, this film deals with three aspects of rape:
how to prevent it from happening, what to do if it
happens, and what to do afterward..." -FCC

SUTTON, SANDRA
Sittin' On Top Of The World: At The Fiddlers' Convention (1974). Co-producer: Max Kalmanowicz
24 min, sepia, r, s: PNX.
"...a documentary on the oldest and largest Blue-
grass music festival of the United States, held in
the Smokey Mountains of North Carolina." -VIE

TAYLOR, CAROL
Wild America - Who Needs It? (1978)
20 min, c, r, s: PNX.
"Shows how cities are dependent on productivity of
the land and urges city dwellers to participate in
environmental decisions." -Program, 21st Annual
American Film Festival

TESICH-SAVAGE, NADJA
Film For My Son (1975)
28 min, c, r, s: SBC.
"Film For My Son, made by the filmmaker to record
her son so that one day he might see himself as
she experiences him, is also about the intermingling
of memories which their relationship evokes from
her: principally, her childhood in rural Yugo-
slavia during World War II and her early fears of
motherhood." -Karen Cooper, Film Forum

THACHER, ANITA
Homage To Magritte (1974)
10 min, c, r, s: SBC.
"Homage To Magritte is an ambitious attempt to trans-
late a painter's vision into a series of moving images...
It consists of five brief sequences loosely connected
by their visual motifs, rather like five surrealist
paintings hanging in five different rooms. Like
Magritte, Thacher works at upsetting the viewer's pre-
conceptions by introducing the unexpected and absurd..."
-Catherine Egan, Film Library Quarterly

Manhattan Doorway (1968-80)
2 min, c, r: available from filmmaker.
"...film which explores movement and space perception turned inside out..." -A.T.

Permanent Wave (1967)
3 min, c, r: available from filmmaker.
"Optical effect film." -A.T.

Sea Travels (1978)
11 min, c, available from filmmaker.
"...visions of a pre-adolescent girl at the sea-
shore. For example, as we look at the ocean hori-
zon, an orange the size of a setting sun rolls across
it. Or in the drawing of a pyramid appears and then
fills up with water." -Edgar Daniels, American
Film

TOD, DOROTHY
Warriors' Women (1981)
27 min, c, r: available from filmmaker.
"...A sensitive and provocative portrait of veterans'
wives who are struggling with a range of physical
and emotional problems that afflict their husbands."
-D.T.

What If You Couldn't Read (1978)
28 min, c, r, s: available from filmmaker.
"A portrait of Lyle Litchfield, former Vermont
farmer now fur trader, who made his way through
10th grade and 45 years without being able to read...
It is also a portrait of a marriage undergoing change
as he gains independence and a sense of worth."
-Program, 21st Annual American Film Festival

TOYE, WENDY (British)
The Stranger Left No Card (1953)
25 min, b/w, r: KPF, VIE.
"This short story is now regarded as a classic of
its kind. Into the setting of a quiet town a
stranger brings with him all of the ingredients
of a fantastic crime." -KPF

TRICEPTS PRODUCTIONS
Woman: Who Is Me? (1977). Co-makers: Shirley
Joel, Judith Keller, Shula Wallace
11 min, c, r, s: FOC, SBC.
"Woman: Who Is Me? is a film about the persistance
of myths about women, and coincidentally men...The
film is a visually exciting montage of major art works
and popular media representations of women through
the ages. It explores biblical and mythological
themes as well as contemporary portrayals. The
Judgement Of Paris becomes today's beauty contest;
the voyeur theme of Susanna and the Elders is
brought up to date with burlesque and topless;
the odalisques of the centuries become today's
Playboy centerfold; man is Colossus and Superman,
savior and provider." -SBC

TUPPER, LOIS
Biofeedback (1973). Co-makers: Ken Boege, Alan
Kuritsky
10 min, c, r: UCE.
"Drugless, mind-over- matter treatment for medical
problems. Recommended for students of biology, psy-
chology and cybernetics." -L.T.

Our Little Munchkin Here (1975)
12 min, c, r, s: IFC.
"A painful episode in the life of an adolescent
girl who finds herself at odds with her family
environment." -IFC

TWIN CITIES WOMEN'S FILM COLLECTIVE
Continuous Woman (1973)
25 min, c, r, s: INS.
Three different types of women are examined.

My People Are My Home (1977)
45 min, c, r, s: SBC.
"My People Are My Home presents a visual narrative
of the political and poetic odyssey of Meridel
LeSueur. Born in 1900, she became the written
voice of the people's movements, whatever the
struggle happened to be. The workers, the unem-
ployed, the women, the Indians - her stories were
their stories." -SBC

VACHON, GAIL
Esmeralda And The Turkey Vulture (1978)
18 min, b/w, available from filmmaker.
"An exploration of time using pre-Columbian cave
drawings, chest x-rays, fingerprints, birds, and a
Voodoo queen." -Independent Film/Video Guide

A Strange Thing Happened (1978)
5 min, b/w, silent, available from filmmaker.
"This is a film of words; the pictures exist only
in the viewer's mind. Sentence by sentence, a sym-
metrical narrative appears on the screen." -Indepen-
dent Film/Video Guide

Te (1977)
13 min, c, available from filmmaker.
"A film about the passage of time. Its 13 minutes
are at once compressed and stretched by provocative
images which take the viewer from past to future."
-Independent Film/Video Guide

When Havoc Struck (1978)
5 min, c, silent, available from filmmaker.
"Unusual and expressive camerawork juxtaposes the
apparent calm of a breakfast table still life with
TV footage of natural disasters." -Independent
Film/Video Guide

VARDA, AGNES (French)
The Black Panthers: A Report (1969)
26 min, c, r: KPF. r, s: GRO.
"The film is composed of alternating, rhythmic,
edited passages of interviews with Huey P. Newton,
Eldridge Cleaver, Bobbie Seale, Stokeley Carmichael,
and Kathleen Cleaver, with her beautiful, expressive
hands interpolated within cinema verité shots,
taken at the August, 1968 rally to 'Free Huey Newton.'"
-KPF

Le Bonheur (1965)
85 min, c, subtitles, r: FNC.
"A poetic and sensuous hymn to the happy life,
Le Bonheur is the story of one man in love with two
women. Director Agnes Varda portrays personal happiness as a force both self-gratifying and pathetically
destructive." -JAN

Cleo From 5 To 7
90 min, b/w, subtitles, r: COR.
"Is Cleo dying? A card-reader tells her she is. So
Cleo goes to a doctor to find out for sure - but she
must wait from 6 until 7 for the results of the test,
and we wait with her." -Contemporary Catalog. With
Corinne Marchard, Antoine Bourseller, Dorothee Blanck.

Far From Vietnam (1967)
90 min, c, r: NYF.
"Impassioned cinematic collage supporting the NLF -
a coherent collaboration by leading French filmmakers
including Godard, Resnais, Varda, and Marker." -NYF

Les Creatures (1966)
102 min, c & b/w, cinemascope only, subtitles, r: NYF
"Mysterious goings-on - a writer and his wife,
reality and fantasy - on a Brittany Island: New
Wave meets Lewis Carroll." -NYF. With Catherine
Deneuve, Michel Piccoli.

Daguerreotypes (1975)
80 min, c, r: FNC.
"Daguerreotypes is Agnes Varda's homage to French
pioneer Louis Daguerre, creator of an early photographic form, and to the people who reside on the
street named after him. These are portraits in motion, just as fascinating as the frozen images which
captured the ordinary people of Daguerre's time."
-FNC

Lions Love (1969)
110 min, b/w, r: TWY.
"It is about the movies, making movies, life in
Sixties' America, being a superstar, being a woman
director, being stoned on life and participating
in a vision of the American dream as seen through
the eyes of its youth. The beauty of the film is
that it never imposes an arbitrary or logically
linear form on the events through which the prin-
cipals live...." -TWY. With Viva, Gerome Ragni,
Shirley Clarke, Max Raab.

One Sings, The Other Doesn't (1977)
105 min, c, subtitles, r, l: CIV.
"One Sings, The Other Doesn't follows the friendship of two young women over a period of fourteen
years, a time when each seeks to take control of
her destiny and eventually finds contentment...'
-CIV. With Valerie Mairesse, Therese Liotard.

Women's Answer (Reponse De Femmes) (1978)
8 min, c, r, s: SBC.
"Characterized by Varda as a 'cineleaflet,' Women's
Answer is composed of a series of visually arresting
tableaux featuring women and men engaged in dialogue
about the issues raised by the women's movement...
Our customary attitudes are jolted by the pictoral
compositions as well as by the words: People appear
in unexpected spatial arrangements, are sometimes
nude, are different ages and sizes and classes..."
-SBC

VASQUEZ, CHRISTINE
  No Exceptions (A Film About Rape) (1977)
  See STUDIVANT, JEANETTE (Directors, Chapter I).

VON DALER, JUDITH
  Afghan Women (1975)

  Women In A Changing World (1975)
  See DUPREE, NANCY (Directors, Chapter I).

WALLACE, SHULA
  Woman: Who Is Me?
  See TRICEPTS PRODUCTIONS

WALSH, ALIDA
  Happy Birthday, I'm Forty (1974)
  22 min, c, r: W/A/F.
  "Happy Birthday, I'm Forty deals with the various
  memories, fantasies, and myths that have pursued the
  filmmaker for the past forty years." - W/A/F. "Alida
  Walsh's film is brave, braver, than one is when
  watching it, braver than a woman has dared to be
  before." -Kate Millet

  The Martyrdom Of Marilyn Monroe (1973)
  30 min, c, r: W/A/F.
  "The Martyrdom Of Marilyn Monroe captures the glit-
  tery glamour of the sex symbol played by Magaly
  Alabau in a series of dramatic sketches set to music by overlapping the action with archetypal sexual
  imagery...It is an expressionistic and surreal evo-
  cation of the psycho-sexual environment Marilyn
  Monroe's myth suggests...." -Karen Cooper

  Wake Dream (1968)
  10 min, c, r: W/A/F.
  "Wake Dream is a color and sound combination of
  collages, posters, varied wall objects and live
  action that combine to make a strong anti-war statement." -W/A/F

  We Are Our Own Myth (1978)
  10 min, c, r: W/A/F.
  "Film/dance celebrating the natural potency of the
  female psyche, through which Woman, in her role as
  shaman, sibyl, priestess and wise woman, has influenced the world." -W/A/F

WALSH, DIERDRE
  Sykes
  13 min, c, r, s: PER.
  Portrait of Sykes Williams, a man who leads a full
  life though he is blind.

WARDWELL, JUDITH
Calfeteria Or How Are You Going To Keep Her Down On
The Farm After She's Seen Paris Twice?
1 min, c & b/w, r: CAN.
"Diana feeds calves imagination and granola to see
life's possibilities from many viewpoints while
tap dancing with a marble bear." -CAN

Flimfly
1 min, c, r: CAN.
"A lyrical song to the joys of childhood." -Freude
Bartlett

Pastel Pussies (1972)
3 min, c, r: CAN. r, s: SBC.
"Cats walking, playing, rolling, jumping - warped
through wonderful printing techniques..." Programme
"Women and Film Festival," Toronto

WARRENBRAND, JANE
Cat, A Woman Who Fought Back (1978)
27 min, c, r, s: FNC.
"Undefeated with 14 K.O.'s, the 24-year-old boxer
takes on the New York State Athletic Commission,
Joe Frazier and Muhammed Ali who all insist the
ring is no place for a lady." -WMM

Healthcaring From Our End Of The Speculum (1976)
See BOSTROM, DENISE (Directors, Chapter I).

WARSHAW, MIMI
Smoke Screen (1970). Co-maker: Michael Warshaw
5 min, c, r, s: PYR.
Cigarette advertising contrasted with reality.

WEAVER, SHEELAH
Livia Makes Some Changes (1974)
See MALANAPHY, KATHLEEN (Directors, Chapter I).

WEILL, CLAUDIA
*Note: Big Town package, total 25 min, c & b/w,
r: UCE. r, s: TEX. Includes Weill's Commuters,
Lost And Found, Marriage, Yoga and Michael Bortman's
Mannequin.

Commuters. Co-maker: Eliot Noyes, Jr.
5 min, c, r: NLC.
A look at two types of commuters in New York City.

Girl Friends (1978)
88 min, c, r: SWA.
"Girl Friends examines the relationship of two former
roommates: Anne, an aspiring poet who chooses to marry,
and Susan, an aspiring photographer who chooses to
live alone and to pursue her career. We see the women's
shifting loyalties and priorities, and sense the mu-
tuality of their successes and their jealousies as they
grow apart from each other. The female characters are
uniformly appealing and well-realized, with Melanie
Mayron in a particularly likable performance." -A. Gambrell. Edited by Suzanne Pettit.

It's My Turn (1980)
91 min, c, r: SWA.
Jill Clayburgh, Michael Douglas, Charles Grodin.
Clayburgh is a college professor, and Douglas is a
baseball player, who meet when her father and his
mother get married to each other.
See FOWLER, MARJORIE (Editors).

Joyce At 34
See CHOPRA, JOYCE (Directors, Chapter I).

Lost And Found. Co-maker: Eliot Noyes, Jr.
5 min, c, r: UCE.
"A vew from the other side of the counter - an old
man looking for a briefcase full of mandolin music,
a woman looking for her umbrella..." -Programme,
"Women And Film Festival," Toronto

Marriage (1972). Co-maker: Eliot Noyes, Jr.
5 min, c, r: UCE.
"Documentary about a day at the marriage license
bureau in NYC which manages to be funny without con-
descension." -Programme, "Women And Film Festival,"
Toronto

The Other Half Of The Sky: A China Memoir (1974)
See MACLAINE, SHIRLEY (Directors, Chapter I).

This Is The Home of Mrs. Levant Graham (1970). Co-
makers: Topper Carew, Eliot Noyes, Jr.
15 min, b/w, r, s: PYR.
Film portrait of a Black family living in Washington,
D.C.

Yoga (1972). Co-maker: Eliot Noyes, Jr.
5 min, c, r: UCE.
"Rich suburban wives 'thinking beautiful thoughts.'"
-Programme, "Women And Film Festival," Toronto

WEINSTEIN, MIRIAM
Access (1978)
23 min, c, r, s: POY.
"Two individuals - Mildred, with three grown children raised while she was in a wheelchair and re-
cently starting a new career, and Roy, a mechanical
engineer suddenly afflicted by a crippling nerve
disease and returning to work after a two and a
half year struggle - are the basis of this personal
look at the life of the handicapped." -POY

Call Me Mama (1977)
14 min, c, r, s: POY.
"In this frank autobiography, Miriam Weinstein, a
30-year-old woman with an 18-month-old son, talks
of herself as a mother." -POY

Last Summer (1979)
17 min, c, r, s: PRE.
"Three women, at the end of pregnancy, pass some time
together being silly, hopeful, happy, and scared. They
meet again that fall with their babies to see how their
lives have changed. A funny/serious fictional film."
-Program, 21st Annual American Film Festival

Living With Peter
22 min, c, r, s: SBC.
Weinstein's thoughts concerning her husband-to-be
are examined.

Not Me Alone (1970)
30 min, c, r, s: POY.
Film concerning natural childbirth.

Not Together Now (1974)
25 min, c, r: UCE. r, s: POY.
"In Not Together Now a couple who are separated speak
with unusual candor of why they were first attracted
to each other, why they chose to marry, and what
happened during their lives together. We learn about
their children, their gradually diverging interests
and needs, their inability to resolve their differ-
ences, and their eventual decision to separate."
-POY

We Get Married Twice
25 min, c, r, s: SBC.
Peter and Miriam have two wedding ceremonies.

WENGRAF, SUSAN
Love It Like A Fool   (1978)
28 min, c, r, s: NDF.
Documentary about the 76-year-old folksinger Malvina Reynolds.

WHEELER, ANNE
Great Grand Mother   (1978)
See Rasmussen, Lorna   (Directors, Chapter I).

WIAN, DEBORAH
It's Not Me   (1975)
26 min, c, r, s: PNX.
"Nancy Holman is a survivor. The story of her
efforts to reclaim her own sense of purpose following an intense emotional crisis reveals a person immersed in humanitarian causes to the point of
almost losing her own identity." -PNX

WILEY, DOROTY
Cabbage
9 min, c, r: CAN.
"I like to film ordinary things I do and see everyday because film makes it so easy to see the immense
cosmic fearsomeness and beauty of everything."-D.W.

Five Artists Billbobbillbillbob   (1970-71)
Fog Pumas   (1967)
See NELSON, GUNVOR   (Directors, Chapter I).

Letters
11 min, c, r: CAN.
Film concerning four letters.

Miss Jesus Fries On Grill
12 min, c, r: CAN.
"Transition from grief to peace, pain to curiosity,
life to death, etc..."   -D.W.

Schmeerguntz   (1966)
See NELSON, GUNVOR   (Directors, Chapter I).

WOHL, RACHEL
Rosi   (1976)
9 min, c, r, s: SBC.
"A young woman speaks frankly about trying to inte-
trate her public and private lives giving most of
her attention to satisfying her creative and sexual
needs."   -SBC

WOLFF, PEGGY
Waterwheel Village (1977)
14 min, c, r, s: FFC.
"Two brothers find a miniature village...(but)
when they find that a girl has built it, their
eagerness to play vanishes..." -FFC. A film
about prejudice and sex bias.

WOOD, ELIZABETH
Sculpture For Children (1974)
See CHASE, DORIS (Directors, Chapter I).

WOZNIAK, VICTORIA
Loose Ends (1975). Co-maker: David Burton Morris
100 min, b/w, r: TWY.
"...Loose Ends is a stunning narrative study of
Billy, an unmanageable smart-ass and his mechanic
buddy, Eddie. Billy, a restless bachelor, self-
ishly uses Eddie as a foil for his wanton and care-
less attitude; and after continually pestering
the weak, married Eddie, succeeds in enticing him
on a tragic and senseless journey to Denver."
-TWY. With Chris Mulkey, John Jenkins, Linda
Jenkins.

ZWERIN, CHARLOTTE
Gimme Shelter (1970). Co-makers: David and Albert
Maysles
90 min, c, r, l: CIV.
"...300,000 people came to celebrate a Woodstock
West. The Jefferson Airplane, Ike and Tina Turner
and the Stones performed. But something went wrong,
and Altamont became a milestone in the history of
a generation." -CIV

Meet Marlon Brando (1966). Co-makers: David and
Albert Maysles
28 min, b/w, r: MAY.
"A record of the actor's thorny, ironic confronta-
tion with the press during a promotional tour." -MAY

Running Fence (1978). Co-makers: David and Albert
Maysles
57 min, c, r: MAY.
Documentary which follows artist Christo's attempt
at building a 24-mile, 18-foot high, nylon fence
across California.

Salesman (1969). Co-makers: David and Albert Maysles
90 min, b/w, r: MAY.
"A comic and poignant documentary of four representatives of the Mid-American Bible Company." -Bonnie Dawson, Women's Films In Print

<u>A Visit With Truman Capote</u> (1967). Co-makers: David
and Albert Maysles
29 min, b/w, r: MAY.
A visit with Truman Capote.

CHAPTER 2:

DIRECTORS

DIRECTORS

While Chapter 1 is concerned with the independent filmmakers, Chapter 2 includes those women who have worked within the motion picture industry. Though there were several women directors during the silent era of films, Dorothy Arzner was virtually the only American woman director in Hollywood during the 1930's and early 1940's. Later, in 1949, Ida Lupino took over this dubious honor. In Europe, meanwhile, aside from Leni Riefenstahl, women directors were very scarce. Today, however, America boasts such promising directors as Elaine May, Joan Darling, Claudia Weill, and Joan Micklin Silver*, who are working within the motion picture industry. And Europe offers audiences directors such as Jeanne Moreau, Mai Zetterling, Margarethe Von Trotta, and Lina Wertmuller.

Note: These films are in chronological order and are available for rental and/or sale. Filmographies of some of the directors are listed in the back of the book.

*Both Weill and Silver are included in Chapter 1.

AHRNE, MARIANNE (Swedish) .
Near And Far Away (1978)
98 min, c, subtitles, r: CIV.
Lilga Kovanko, Robert Farrant
"Near And Far Away, Swedish director Marianne Ahrne's
first feature film, is a moving film about a woman
training to be a therapist and a male patient she
comes to love. Her humanistic attempt to provide
therapy is seen in direct contrast to the hospital's
detached, scientific approach." -CIV

ARMSTRONG, GILLIAN (Australian)
My Brilliant Career (1980)
101 min, c, r: CIV.
Judy Davis, Sam Neill
Autobiographical film, which is set in Australia
during the 1860's, about a strong-minded young woman
who is determined to become a writer despite economic
and social pressures on her.

ARZNER, DOROTHY
The Wild Party (1929)
76 min, b/w, r: SWA.
Clara Bow
"Clara Bow plays Stella, a headstrong college girl
who forms a society called the 'hardboiled maidens,'
which is regarded with considerable distrust by the
college authorities. Activities include arranging
all-night parties and raiding nearby men's colleges
and speak-easies." -Program, "Women's Cinema Festival, London

Paramount On Parade (1930)
77 min, b/w, r: SWA.
All-star film showcasing Paramount players and directors, which is divided into vignettes. Arzner directed
the 'Gallows Song' sequence.

Christopher Strong (1933)
77 min, b/w, r: FNC.
Katharine Hepburn, Colin Clive, Billie Burke, Helen Chandler
In her second film, Hepburn stars as an aviatrix who becomes involved with a married man in a doomed relationship.

Nana (1934)
87 min, b/w, r: FNC.
Anna Sten, Lionel Atwill
"Sten plays the brash coquette in a free adaptation of
the Zola novel transplanted to the Paris of 1868 who
climbs from the streets to center stage at the legendary
Apollo Theatre, where she reigns as the queen of Parisian
society, until her notorious fall as a courtesan."
-Macmillan catalog

Craig's Wife   (1936)
75 min, b/w, r: KPF, TWY.
Rosalind Russell, John Boles, Thomas Mitchell, Billie
Burke
Russell gives a strong performance as a woman whose
only concern is obtaining material wealth and keeping
it, even if it means losing her husband and all those
around her.
See LAWRENCE, VIOLA (Editors).

The Bride Wore Red   (1937)
100 min, b/w, r: MGM.
Joan Crawford, Franchot Tone, Robert Young, Billie
Burke
Crawford stars as a young woman who poses as a socialite
in this comedy.
See FAZAN, ADRIENNE (Editors).

Dance, Girl, Dance   (1940)
89 min, b/w, r: FNC.
Lucille Ball, Maureen O'Hara, Ralph Bellamy, Louis
Hayward
Ball and O'Hara are dance hall girls in this musical
comedy. Arzner based Ball's characterization on
"Texas" Guinan.

First Comes Courage   (1943)
86 min, b/w, r: TWY.
Merle Oberon, Brian Aherne
"The film is a stirring and well-made tale of heroism...
Merle Oberon, a secret member of the Norwegian under-
ground pretends to be the secret lover of the local
Nazi colonel as she feeds military secrets to her
compatriots." -TWY
See LAWRENCE, VIOLA (Editors).

See ARZNER, DOROTHY (Editors).

BALDWIN, RUTH ANN
   49-'17 (1917)
   79 min, at 16 fps, 53 min at 24 fps, b/w, silent,
   r: KPF.
   The film's title is derived from its being the 49th
   Universal production in 1917. "Longing for the 'old
   west'...(a) judge sends his male secretary to buy...
   a western semi-ghost town...and populate it with
   authentic types. The secretary hires the members
   of a 'down-on-their-luck' wild west show." -KPF

BANCROFT, ANNE
  Fatso (1980)
  94 min, c, r: FNC.
  Don DeLuise, Anne Bancroft
  Bancroft directed, wrote, and starred in this comedy
  concerning a fat man determined to lose weight when
  he falls in love.

BATCHELOR, JOY (British)
  Animal Farm (1954). Co-maker: John Halas
  73 min, c, r: KPF, FNC.
  "The first full-length animated film to tell a serious story, based on George Orwell's famous political
  fable. It's a remarkable achievement, comprising
  some 300,000 drawings, and vividly characterising
  many of the animals who create a revolution only
  to be crushed by a new kind of tyranny." -Michael
  Webb, American Film Institute

BIRCH, PATRICIA
  Grease 2 (1982)
  114 min, c, available in cinemascope, r: FNC.
  Maxwell Cauldfield, Michelle Pfeiffer
  Birch, the choreographer for Grease, directed this
  sequel. This time the new boy at Rydell High mas-
  querades as a motorcycle racer to win the girl with
  whom he's in love.

BOX, MURIEL (British)
  The Truth About Women (1958)
  106 min, c, r: KPF.
  Laurence Harvey, Mai Zetterling, Julie Harris
  Harvey is a playboy who has several romantic flings
  and lives to tell about it in this comedy.
  See COATES, ANNE V. (Editors).

CAVANI, LILIANA (Italian)
  Beyond Good And Evil (1977)
  127 min, c, r: FNC.
  Dominique Sanda, Erland Josephson
  Drama based loosely on Friedrich Nietzsche's life which
  concerns the personal struggles of three people who wish
  to live their beliefs, politically and spiritually.

DARLING, JOAN
  First Love (1977)
  92 min, c, r: FNC.
  William Katt, Susan Dey, John Heard, Beverly D'Angelo
  Darling's first film is an honest and emotional view of
  a college student's first intense experience with love.

DULAC, GERMAINE (French)
  The Smiling Madame Beudet (La Souriante Madame Beudet)(1922)
  27 min. at 24 fps, b/w, musical score, subtitles, r,s: KPF.
  A woman struggles with her growing hatred of her husband.
  "Madame Dulac's direction, both sensitive and bold, raises
  this story of domestic conflict (bourgeois husband, artistic
  wife) to a further level - one which pictorially expresses
  the atmosphere and the implications of the story."-Museum of
  Modern Art

  The Seashell And The Clergyman (La Coquille Et Le Clergyman)
  (1928)
  Allix Allen
  43 min, b/w, silent, subtitles, r: KPF.
  "Dulac employed slow motion, split images, and optical dis-
  tortions in this drama of a priest's displaced lust for his
  confessee."-Macmillan catalog

GENEE, HEIDI (German)
  1 + 1 = 3 (1981)
  85 min, c, subtitles, r: CIV.
  Adelheid Arndt, Dominik Graf
  Warm-hearted drama about a young woman who, when she discovers
  that she is pregnant, decides to have the baby, though it will
  be illegitimate.

GRAYSON, HELEN
  The Cummington Story (1944-45)
  20 min, b/w, r: KPF.
  Rare example of World War II propaganda film directed by Helen
  Grayson, a woman who worked as a film director for the U.S.
  Government during the war. "This pastoral and..'heartwarming'
  film was made for overseas distribution to our allies as the
  war years wound down...story of European refugees finding home
  in New England until the end of WWII."-KPF

GUY-BLANCHE, ALICE (French)
  A House Divided (1913)
  13 min, b/w, silent, r: MMA.
  Directed by one of the first women directors in the motion
  picture industry, A House Divided is a comedy concerning
  marriage.

HERKERLING, AMY
Fast Times At Ridgemont High (1982)
92 min, c, r: SWA.
Sean Penn, Jennifer Jason Leigh, Judge Reinhold
Based on Cameron Crowe's book, which was researched by his
returning to high school for a year as a student, this comedy
deals with the good, bad, and high times of high school.

KERNOCHAN, SARAH
Marjoe (1972). Co-director: Howard Smith
88 min, c, r,l: CIV.
Excellent documentary portrait of Marjoe (his name is a
contraction of the names Mary and Joseph) Gortner, an
evangelist who was preaching and saving souls at the age
of 3. The film shows the viewer Marjoe at the age of 28 as
he talks about his experiences as a child evangelist and
why he decided to stop preaching.

LINDBLOM, GUNNEL (Swedish)
Summer Paradise (1977)
113 min, c, subtitles, r, l: CIV
"This is the story of four generations of one family, who
gather for the summer at Paradise Place, their idyllic
seaside retreat..."-CIV. "In this contemporary story...,
Gunnel Lindblom makes as awesome debut as a film director:
intuitive and tenderly incisive about the loneliness and
needs of every member of the family and the lives they
touch..."-Judy Stone, San Francisco Chronicle

LUPINO, IDA
Not Wanted (1949)
94 min, b/w, s: SFM.
Sally Forrest, Keefe Brasselle
"Not Wanted is the story of a young unwed mother who during
her pregnancy commits her baby to adoption, then attempts
to kidnap the child and is sent to jail. For all its melo-
drama, the film deals incisively with the poverty of a
woman's fantasy life."-Sharon Smith, Women Who Make Movies
This was Lupino's debut as a director.

Never Fear (also known as Young Lovers) (1950)
75 min, b/w, r: ICS
Sally Forrest, Keefe Brasselle, Hugh O'Brian
"Sally Forrest and Keefe Brasselle are a dance team that
is broken up when the young woman is stricken with polio.
Although the picture devotes scrupulous attention to medical
detail and treats forcefully the anguish of the disease, it
is an upbeat film that celebrates a woman's determination to
fight back."-Program, 2nd Int'l Festival of Women's Films,
New York

Outrage(1950)
75 min, c, r: IVY
Malà Powers, Tod Andrews, Robert Clarke

"A young woman is raped and the trauma drives her from her home and fiance to seek anonymity in a small town. Filled with anguish and guilt for her 'crime', she finds solace with a minister who tries to lead her back to normality. This dramatic film reflects the unenlightened attitude that was prevalent at the time the film was made."-Program, 2nd Int'l Festival Of Women's Films, New York

Hard, Fast And Beautiful (1951)
76 min, b/w, r: IVY.
Claire Trevor, Sally Forrest, Robert Clarke
"...The fragile relationship between a driving, ambitious mother and her tennis-playing daughter."-Sharon Smith, Women Who Make Movies. The daughter must ultimately make the choice between living for her mother or living for herself.

The Bigamist (1953)
80 min, b/w, r: IVY.
Ida Lupino, Edmund O'Brien, Joan Fontaine
"The Bigamist is the story of a traveling salesman, sympathetically depicted, who is in love with two women, and wed to both...it gives Lupino an opportunity...to manipulate her favorite cinematic situation - people trying to find their own way out of a bewilderment induced by their own psychogenic conflicts or the accident of outside events."-Sharon Smith, Women Who Make Movies

The Trouble With Angels (1965)
112 min, c, r: FNC.
Rosalind Russell, Hayley Mills, June Harding, Gypsy Rose Lee
Rosalind Russell is superb as the Mother Superior in this comedy about a convent school. Her two biggest problems are Hayley Mills and June Harding who are never out of trouble. Lupino's direction encompasses well-timed comedy situations, the sensitivity of friendship, and the pain of growing up.

MADISON, CLEO
Her Defiance (1916). Co-director: Joe King
23 min, b/w, silent, r: MMA.
Willis Marks, Edward Hearn
"Her Defiance is noteworthy for its own defiance of thematic taboos and its avoidance of a stereotypical portrayal of women. It concerns a young girl (played by Madison) who becomes pregnant and believes herself abandoned by her lover. She refuses...to marry a rich old man, and...she bears her illegitimate child and goes to work as a cleaning lady in order to support it."-MMA

MAY, ELAINE
A New Leaf (1971)
102 min, c, r: FNC.
Walter Matthau, Elaine May
May directed, wrote, and starred in this comedy about a rich playboy who, after losing all of his money, attempts to marry a rich, but eccentric botanist for her fortune.

MOREAU, JEANNE (French)
Lumiere (1976)
95 min, c, r: FNC.
"Jeanne Moreau's directorial debut is a woman's frank,
personal vision of herself, other women, and their
relationship to the world at large." -FNC

NAZIMOVA, ALLA
Salome (1922). Co-director: Charles Bryant
30 min, b/w, silent, r: BUD, KPF. s: REE.
Alla Nazimova, Mitchell Lewis
Film concerning the story of Salome from the Bible.
"Costumes and set designs are based on drawings by
Aubrey Beardsley." -Macmillan catalog

PEETERS, BARBARA
Summer School Teachers (1977)
86 min, c, r: FNC.
Candice Rialson, Pat Anderson
Young women teachers give students "extra help."

Humanoids From The Deep (1980)
82 min, c, r: FNC.
Vic Morrow, Doug McClure
Science fiction film concerning aliens who come
out of the sea for one purpose: to mate with
Earthwomen!

REID, DOROTHY DAVENPORT (MRS. WALLACE REID)
The Red Kimono (1925)
75 min, b/w, silent with music soundtrack, r: BUD.
Tyrone Power, Priscilla Bonner, Theodore Von Etts
Story of a young girl who becomes a hardened prostitute. A rare example of one of America's early women
director's work. Reid also stars in the film.

RIEFENSTAHL, LENI (German)
The Blue Light (Das Blaue Licht) (1932)
60 min, b/w, silent with English translation, r: FNC.
Leni Riefenstahl's first feature film which she directed,
produced, wrote, edited, and starred in was The Blue
Light, a poignant film concerning a traveler who
stops at a small village, and becomes enchanted with
a strange peasant girl who lives high in the mountains.

Triumph Of The Will (Triumph Des Willens) (1934-36)
107 min, b/w, subtitles, r: FNC. 110 min, in German, r: KPF.
"The most disturbing product of one of the cinema's most
controversial figures, Triumph Of The Will is a 'record'
of the Party rally in Nuremberg in 1934, an event meant to
reassure the German public of the solidarity of the Nazi
Party after the notorious Rohm purges and to introduce the
Party leaders, hitherto relatively unknown. Set in the
medieval town of Nuremberg, the rally was filmed with a
grand touch deliberately modelled on the Wagnerian music-

drama, with Hitler as its hero...A two-minute over-
ture and credits precede the arrival of Hitler's
airplane, soaring through massive cloud banks and
swooping down to the cheering crowds who will accom-
pany him to the Party rally in Nuremberg." -Macmillan
Catalog

Day Of Freedom (Tag Der Freigeit) (1935)
21 min, b/w, r: KPF.
"A remarkable rare film made immediately following
'Triumph Of The Will' upon a request granted by
Hitler to the ill-fated General Von Blomberg...
The war games photographed in this short were shot
in one day by six cameramen." -KPF

Olympia (Olympiad) (1936-38)
212 min, r: FNC. r, s: PNX.
"Ostensibly a 'record' of the 1936 Berlin Olympics,
Olympia goes far byond documentation in its utili-
zation of music, camera and editing to convey the
prowess and beauty of the athlete in motion. Mem-
orable sequences include the opening (the carrying
of the Olympic torch), the high dive and the marathon; an added bonus is the presence of the American runner, Jesse Owens, whose brilliant performance
dismayed Hitler." -MAC. Olympia was directed, produced, and edited by Riefenstahl.
"Olympia is divided into two parts, each complete in
itself. Part I (Festival Of The People) (Fest Der
Volker) consists of an abstract introduction, the
carrying of the flame plus the track and field events.
Part II (Festival Of Beauty) (Fest Der Schonheit)
includes the gymnastic and aquatic events, sailing and
rowing, equestrian events, bicycling and the decath-
lon events." -Macmillan Catalog
The diving and marathon sequences are also available
for rental and sale from Budget Films.

Tiefland (1954)
98 min, b/w, subtitles, f: FNC.
Leni Riefenstahl, Franz Eichberger, Luise Rainer
Tiefland, based on Eugen D'Albert's operetta, was
started in Spain in 1942 by Riefenstahl, but because
of World War II, lack of support, and illness, the
film was not completed until 1954.

RIVERS, JOAN
  Rabbit Test (1977)
  86 min, c, r: FNC
  Billy Crystal, Imogene Coca, Fannie Flagg, Jimmie
  Walker, Paul Lynde
  Comedy about the world's first pregnant man. "Rabbit
  Test is an energetic, intelligent spoof of traditional
  roles and mores, pulled off with originality and flair..."
  -FNC

ROTHMAN, STEPHANIE
  The Student Nurses (1970)
  85 min, c, r: FMC
  Elaine Giftos, Karen Carlson, Brioni Farrell, Barbara
  Leigh
  The adventures of four student nurses in learning and
  loving.

  The Working Girls (1974)
  81 min, c, r: FNC.
  Sarah Kennedy, Laurie Rose, Lynne Guthrie
  Four young women who will do almost anything to earn
  a living!

SAGAN, LEONTINE (German)
  Maedchen In Uniform (1931)
  89 min, b/w, subtitles, r: FNC.
  "This legendary film, temporarily obstructed by U.S.
  censors...(concerns]...A sensitive young girl in a
  fashionable school (who) is unhappy under the harsh,
  Prussian discipline; she flowers when a sympathetic
  teacher gives her special consideration. This consideration is ambiguous and certainly sensual." -Janus
  Films

SILVER, JOAN MICKLIN
  See SILVER, JOAN MICKLIN (Directors, Chapter I).

TEWKESBURY, JOAN
  Old Boyfriends (1979)
  103 min, c, r: FNC.
  Talia Shire, John Belushi, Keith Carradine
  Shire plays a young psychologist who searches for a
  meaningful life by reliving past love affairs. She
  travels across the country to visit her three most
  important lovers, hoping to answer questions about her
  past and her future.

  See TEWKESBURY, JOAN (Screenwriters).

VON TROTTA, MARGARETHE (German)
The Lost Honor Of Katharina Blum (1975). Co-director:
Volker Schlondorff
102 min, c, subtitles, r: FNC.
Angela Winkler, Mario Adorf
"This political thriller examines the abrasive power and
unrelenting pressure of 'yellow' exploitative journalism.
A young woman's chance affair with a fugitive terrorist
results in a reign of terror characterized by a pervasive
sexism that victimizes and destroys the heroine." -FNC

The Second Awakening Of Christa Klages (Das Zweite Er-
wachen Der Christa Klages) (1978)
93 min, c, r: NLC.
Tina Engel, Silvia Reize, Katharine Thalbach
"The second effort of actress and screenwriter von Trotta
is based on a true story of a kindergarten teacher at a
financially troubled school who robs a bank with her
boyfriend. The story of her flight is that of three
women and their isolation." -Paul Page

Sisters Or The Balance Of Happiness (1981)
95 min, c, r: CIV.
Jutta Lampe, Gudrun Gabriel
Drama concerning the growing conflict between two
sisters: one, who is content to fit into society's
restrictions, and the other, who realizes that she is
just the opposite.

WAGNER, JANE
Moment By Moment (1978)
105 min, c, r: CLE.
Lily Tomlin, John Travolta
Film concerning an older woman's romance with (of
course) a younger man. The film's uniqueness lies in
the role reversal: Tomlin's character is aggressive while
Travolta is shy and sensitive.

WALKER, NANCY
Can't Stop The Music (1980)
122 min, c, r: SWA.
Valerie Perrine, Steve Guttenberg, The Village People
Disco musical showcasing the Village People about an
ex-model who helps a friend by finding a disco group for
his record company.

WEBER, LOIS
  The Blot (1921)
  110 min, b/w, silent, r: BUD, MMA.
  Phillip Hubbard, Louis Calhern, Claire Windsor
  "Lois Weber was one of the most important woman directors
  of the silent era, having made some 400 films between the
  years of 1908 and 1934...Characteristic of Weber's films,
  The Blot deals with a social issue - the plight of intel-
  lectuals (college professors, ministers) in American
  society whose work is underpaid and accorded minimal
  status...Significantly, she focuses on women and emphasizes
  how their economic destinies are determined by marriage..."-MMA
  The Blot was produced and written by Weber.

  A Chapter In Her Life (1923)
  60 min, b/w, s: REE.
  "One of the incredibly rare features by the talented and pro-
  lific female director of the 20's. A family's relationships
  are transformed when a young girl enters the household."-REE

WEILL, CLAUDIA
  See WEILL, CLAUDIA (Directors, Chapter 1).

WERTMULLER, LINA (Italian)
  Love And Anarchy (1974)
  108 min, c, subtitles, r,l:CIV.
  Lina Polito, Giancarlo Giannini, Mariangela Melato
  "Turin, a shy and awkward peasant, arrives in Rome from the
  countryside in the early 1930's...determined...to kill Benito
  Mussolini...But when Turin falls in love with a young prostitute, the conflict between 'love and anarchy' sparks an ex-
  plosion of passions that is felt far beyond the bordello."-CIV

  The Seduction Of Mimi (1974)
  92 min, c, r: NLC.
  Giancarlo Giannini, Mariangela Melato
  "The Seduction Of Mimi tells the story of an ambitious factory
  worker (Mimi) whose chauvinistic values - both social and
  sexual - lead to his 'seduction' into the Mafia-controlled
  fascist establishment. Wertmuller's penetrating view of Mimi's
  obsessive pursuit of 'machismo' found appreciative audiences
  throughout the world."-NLC

  Swept Away (1975)
  116 min, c, subtitles, r,l: CIV.
  Giancarlo Giannini
  "Raffaella, a rich, beautiful, acid-tongued Milanese who has
  chartered a yacht and Gennarino, a swarthy Sicilian deckhand,
  are marooned on an isolated island in the Mediterranean. She
  is a capitalist for whom the System has paid off: he is a dedicated communist. Swept Away is the story of their tumultuous cour-
  ship." -CIV

All Screwed Up (1976)
100 min, c, r: NLC.
Luigi Diberti, Lina Polito
"All Screwed Up completes Ms. Wertmuller's trilogy (with
Love and Anarchy and The Seduction Of Mimi) on class, work
and sex in industrial society. But her vision here is more
powerful and ruthlessly honest..."-NLC

Let's Talk About Men (1976)
93 min, b/w, subtitles, r: HUR.
Nino Manfredi, Luciana Paluzzi, Margaret Lee
Four stories by Wertmuller concerning chauvinistic men
and the women in love with them. Available in 35mm only.

Seven Beauties (1976)
116 min, c, subtitles, r,l: CIV.
Giancarlo Giannini
"Pasqualino...is a great loser, an imitation bandit, bread-
winner, lover, soldier, whose only grip on selfhood is his
macho code...But Pasqualino has real feeling, especially for
women, and Wertmuller uses this to achieve some of the most
astonishing and profound comedy since the blackest absurdities
in Dostoevski..."-Jack Kroll, Newsweek

The End Of The World In Our Usual Bed In A Night Full Of Rain
(1978)
104 min, c, r: FNC.
Candice Bergen, Giancarlo Giannini
"A romantic comedy about the courtship and marriage of an
American photographer, Candice Bergen, and an Italian
Communist-journalist, played by Giancarlo Giannini. After
ten years of marriage bliss he experiences a delayed case
of the seven-year-itch and subsequently, becomes disillusioned
with the Party. She wants to have him and branch out on her
own - all of which make for a constant rain of romantic
comedy trysts."-SWA

WINSLOW, SUSAN
All This And World War II (1976)
99 min, b/w, r: FNC.
"For this spunky, irreverent film, director Susan Winslow
selected documentary footage of World War II and scenes
from American films of the same period. This panorama of
history is cleverly paired with Lennon-McCartney Beatle
tunes performed by top recording artists like Elton John,
Rod Stewart, Tina Turner, Leo Sayer, David Essex, Keith
Moon, and Helen Reddy. The result is a highly entertaining
kaleidoscopic vision of history seen in a contemporary
context."-FNC

ZETTERLING, MAI (Danish)
Loving Couples (1965)
113 min, b/w, subtitles, r: FNC.
Harriet Andersson, Gunnel Lindblom
"...a study of female inferiority in an exclusively masculine
society. The three von Pahlen sisters are in a hospital expecting babies. Through a flashback technique,...the women
recall their lives up to that point."-MAC

Doctor Glas (1969)
83 min, b/w, subtitles, r: FNC.
Per Oscarsson, Ulf Palme, Lone Hertz
"an alienated old man aimlessly wanders through Stockholm
and bitterly recollects his youth and the crucial moments
of his life. Filtering the story entirely from the hero's
point of view, Zetterling...powerfully dramatizes Glas's
multifold consciousness in rapid flashes of memory, dream
and daydream."-FNC

The Girls (1970)
100 min, c, r: NLC.
Harriet Andersson, Bibi Andersson, Gunnel Lindblom
"A strong feminist statement, Mai Zetterling's The Girls
lucidly articulates the dissatisfaction of three unhappy
women whose identities have always been defined in terms
of their men. On tour with Lysistrata, (Aristophanes' comedy
about women who refuse their husbands sexual favors until
the men put an end to war), the actresses find that the play
is a catalyst, and, as they become immersed in their roles,
they confront the truths about their own personal oppression..."-
NLC

Visions Of Eight (1973)
105 min, c, r,l: CIV.
"For the Games at Munich, eight of the world's most
accomplished film directors decided to make a film which
would reveal aspects of the Olympics few of us have ever
seen...(Zetterling) contributed a very witty and unorthodox
view of the strongest men in the world - the weight-lifters."-
CIV
See ALLEN, DEDE (Editors).

CHAPTER 3

EDITORS

EDITORS

The editor of a motion picture is not just a person who splices close-ups into the right places or who cuts a film to an acceptable running time. The editor is as important as the director, for at times, a good editor can save a motion picture from a bad director by shaping seemingly useless footage into a simple, powerful and visual story. Even a good director depends heavily on his or her editor to mold the film into a completed work which carries the thoughts and action which the director wishes to convey to a viewer. For example, Cecil B. DeMille worked with editor Anne Bauchens on quite a few of the silent pictures which he directed. In 1936, Barbara McLean began a long association with director Henry King which lasted off and on until 1955. Marguerite Renoir is credited with editing several of Jean Renoir's classics, including Grand Illusion and Rules Of The Game (La Regle Du Jeu). The enigmatic Ingmar Bergman works almost exclusively with Ulla Ryghe on the films which he writes and directs. Dede Allen's professional alliance with director Arthur Penn has given audiences Bonnie And Clyde, Night Moves, and Little Big Man.

There have been women editors from the beginning of motion pictures to the present time, for editing is a job area in which women have had very good opportunities. This chapter lists only a few of these many women who have edited film.

Note: These films are in chronological order and are available for rental and/or sale. Filmographies of some editors are listed in the back of the book.

ALLEN, DEDE
Terror From The Year 5000   (1958)
74 min, b/w, r: FNC.
Joyce Holden, Ward Costello
d: Robert J. Gurney
Horror film about a woman monster.

Odds Against Tomorrow   (1959)
95 min, b/w, r: MGM.
Harry Belafonte, Robert Ryan, Shelley Winters
d: Robert Wise
Drama concerning three bank robbers planning the perfect robbery.

The Hustler   (1961)
135 min, b/w, available in cinemascope, r: FNC.
Paul Newman, George C. Scott, Piper Laurie, Jackie Gleason
d: Robert Rossen
Intense drama involving Newman as a pool hustler who challenges
champion Minnesota Fats to a "winner take all" game of pool.

Bonnie And Clyde   (1967)
111 min, c, r: BUD, FNC, SWA.
Warren Beatty, Faye Dunaway, Gene Hackman, Estelle Parsons
d: Arthur Penn
Dunaway and Beatty star in this exciting and violent film
based on the lives of the infamous bankrobbers Bonnie Parker
and Clyde Barrow.

Rachel, Rachel   (1968)
104 min, c, r: FNC.
Joanne Woodward, Estelle Parsons
d: Paul Newman
Excellent drama which features Woodward as a lonely spinster
working as a teacher in a small town.

Alice's Restaurant   (1969)
110 min, c, r: MGM.
Arlo Guthrie, Pat Quinn, James Broderick
d: Arthur Penn
Based on Guthrie's hit song "Alice's Restaurant," this film is
a realistic look at a commune of young adults during the 1960's.

Little Big Man   (1971)
139 min, c, available in cinemascope, r: SWA.
Dustin Hoffman, Faye Dunaway, Martin Balsam
d: Arthur Penn
Superbly edited film composed mostly of flashbacks, which stars
Hoffman as a 120-year-old man who recalls events from his long
life in the Wild West.

Slaughterhouse-Five   (1972)
104 min, c, r: SWA.
Michael Sacks, Valerie Perrine, Ron Liebman
d: George Roy Hill
Faithful adaptation of Kurt Vonnegut's novel about Billy Pilgrim,
a man who is able to "time travel" from his present to his past
and future.

Visions Of Eight (1973)
105 min, c, r: CIV
Allen edited the polevault sequence which was directed
by Arthur Penn.
See ZETTERLING, MAI (Directors, Chapter 2).

Serpico (1974). Co-editor: Richard Marks
140 min, c, r: FNC.
Al Pacino, John Randolph, Jack Kehoe
d: Sidney Lumet
True story of a New York policeman who blew the whistle
on corruption among his co-workers.

Dog Day Afternoon (1975)
129 min, c, r: SWA.
Al Pacino, John Cazale, Charles Durning
d: Sidney Lumet
Fascinating film based on a true incident in New York in
which a married man attempts to rob a bank in order to
pay for a sex change for his male lover.

Night Moves (1975)
100 min, c, r: SWA.
Gene Hackman, Susan Clark, Jennifer Warren
d: Arthur Penn
Perceptive film which stars Hackman as a detective sent to
find a runaway girl in Florida.

The Missouri Breaks (1976). Co-editors: Gerald Greenberg,
Steve Rotter
126 min, c, r: FNC.
Marlon Brando, Jack Nicholson, Kathleen Lloyd
d: Arthur Penn
Off-beat, beautifully photographed western which stars Brando
as an eccentric hired killer and Nicholson as the horse thief
he has been paid to kill.

Slap Shot (1977)
123 min, c, r: SWA.
Paul Newman, Strother Martin, Michael Ontkean, Jennifer Warren
d: George Roy Hill
Newman is coach of a third-rate hockey team which must
improve or face bankruptcy in this well-paced, funny, and
sometimes brutal story written by Nancy Dowd.

The Wiz (1978)
133 min, c, r: SWA.
Diana Ross, Lena Horne, Michael Jackson
d: Sidney Lumet
Film based on the Broadway musical with an all-star Black cast.

Reds (1982). Co-editor: Craig McKay
200 min, c, r: FNC.
Warren Beatty, Diane Keaton, Jack Nicholson
d: Warren Beatty
Beatty directed, wrote, and starred in this film based on
Communist John Reed and his life with Louise Bryant.

ARZNER, DOROTHY
Blood And Sand (1922)
93 min, b/w, silent, r: BUD, KPF, MMA.
Rudolph Valentino, Nita Naldi
d: Fred Niblo
Valentino is featured as a bullfighter in this excellent
silent drama.

The Covered Wagon (1923)
83 min, b/w, silent, r: KPF, FNC.
Ernest Torrence, Lois Wilson, J. Warren Kerrigan
d: James Cruze
Western which takes place in a wagon train concerning two
men who are in love with the same woman.

Old Ironsides (1926)
111 min, b/w, silent, r: FNC.
George Bancroft, Esther Ralston
d: James Cruze
Adventure film, which is a tribute to the ship Constitution,
also combines comedy and romance.

See ARZNER, DOROTHY (Directors, Chapter 2).

BAUCHENS, ANNE
The Squaw Man (1918)
60 min, b/w, silent, r: FNC.
Elliot Dexter, Ann Little, Katherine MacDonald
d: Cecil B. DeMille
Drama concerning a man, who, due to circumstances, leaves
his home, moves out west, and marries an Indian.
See MACPHERSON, JEANIE (Screenwriters).

Male And Female (1919)
145 min, b/w, silent, r: MMA.
Gloria Swanson, Thomas Meighan
d: Cecil B. DeMille
Moralistic drama which points out the similarities of the
wealthy of today with the rich of Biblical times.
See MACPHERSON, JEANIE (Screenwriters).

Manslaughter (1922)
101 min, b/w, silent, r: FNC.
Leatrice Joy, Thomas Meighan
d: Cecil B. DeMille
Drama concerning a society girl accused of manslaughter and
the district attorney who falls in love with her.
See MACPHERSON, JEANIE (Screenwriters).

The Ten Commandments (1923)
146 min, b/w, silent, r: FNC.
Richard Dix, Leatrice Joy, Rod La Rocque
d: Cecil B. DeMille
Moralistic drama which compares contemporary society and its
evils with those of Biblical times.
See MACPHERSON, JEANIE (Screenwriters).

The Road To Yesterday (1925)
105 min, b/w, silent, r: BUD, KPF.
William Boyd, Jetta Goudal, Joseph Schildkraut
d: Cecil B. DeMille
DeMille transports his modern-day characters back in time
to 17th-century England to help two confused couples solve
their problems.
See MACPHERSON, JEANIE (Screenwriters).

The King Of Kings (1927). Co-editor: Harold McLernon
115 min, b/w, silent with music, r: BUD. Part color
version available from KPF.
H. B. Warner, Ernest Torrence, Joseph Schildkraut
d: Cecil B. DeMille
Biblical epic telling the story of Jesus Christ with a
cast of thousands.
See MACPHERSON, JEANIE (Screenwriters).

Dynamite (1929)
127 min, b/w, r: MGM.
Conrad Nagel, Kay Johnson, Charles Bickford
d: Cecil B. DeMille
A young woman has to find a husband in order to obtain an
inheritance in this comedy/drama.
See MACPHERSON, JEANIE (Screenwriters).

Madam Satan (1930)
116 min, b/w, r: MGM.
Lillian Roth, Roland Young, Kay Johnson
d: Cecil B. DeMille
Story of a wife who realizes that she is losing her husband
to another woman, and what she does about it.
See MACPHERSON, JEANIE (Screenwriters).

The Sign Of The Cross (1932)
120 min, b/w, r: SWA.
Fredric March, Claudette Colbert, Charles Laughton
d: Cecil B. DeMille
Drama set during Nero's reign involving the forbidden
relationship between a Roman soldier and a Christian maid.

This Day And Age (1933)
85 min, b/w, r: SWA.
Charles Bickford, Richard Cromwell
d: Cecil B. DeMille
Drama involving a group of students who capture a wealthy
criminal and force him to confess his crimes.

Cleopatra (1934)
102 min, b/w, r: SWA.
Claudette Colbert, Warren William
d: Cecil B. DeMille
Spectacular film version of Cleopatra's history made in the
DeMille epic style.

Four Frightened People (1934)
78 min, b/w, r: SWA.
Claudette Colbert, Herbert Marshall
d: Cecil B. DeMille
Four very civilized people must make their way through the
jungle of Malaya after abandoning their ship which is infested
with the bubonic plague.

The Crusades (1935)
127 min, b/w, r: SWA.
Loretta Young, Henry Wilcoxon, Joseph Schildkraut
d: Cecil B. DeMille
Adventure epic concerning the exploits of Richard the Lion-
Hearted.

The Plainsman (1936)
113 min, b/w, r: CLE.
Gary Cooper, Jean Arthur, Charles Bickford
d: Cecil B. DeMille
Historical western featuring Cooper as Wild Bill Hickök
and Arthur as Calamity Jane.

Union Pacific (1939)
135 min, b/w, r: CLE.
Barbara Stanwyck, Joel McCrea
d: Cecil B. DeMille
Well-paced drama (with a love story thrown in) which tells
the story of the first transcontinental railroad.

Northwest Mounted Police (1940)
126 min, c, r: TWY, SWA.
Gary Cooper, Madeleine, Carroll, Paulette Goddard
d: Cecil B. DeMille
DeMille combines action and romance in his exciting tribute
to the Royal Canadian Mounted Police.

Reap The Wild Wind (1942)
124 min, c, r: CLE.
John Wayne, Susan Hayward, Paulette Goddard
d: Cecil B. DeMille
Goddard and Wayne investigate a pirate ring which wrecks
ships in order to salvage them in this adventure film.

The Story Of Dr. Wassell (1944)
136 min, c, r: SWA.
Gary Cooper, Paulette Goddard
d: Cecil B. DeMille
True story of Dr. Corydon M. Wassell, a country doctor who
become a World War II hero.

Unconquered (1947)
148 min, c, r: TWY, CLE.
Gary Cooper, Paulette Goddard
d: Cecil B. DeMille
Adventure film concerning America in the 18th century and the
uneasy relations between Indians and the white people.

Samson And Delilah (1949)
120 min, c, r: FNC.
Hedy Lamarr, Victor Mature, George Sanders, Angela Lansbury
d: Cecil B. DeMille
Sensuous version of the legend of Samson, the man whose hair
gave him strength, and Delilah, the woman who cut his hair.

The Greatest Show On Earth (1952)
153 min, c, r: FNC.
Betty Hutton, Charlton Heston, Dorothy Lamour, James Stewart
d: Cecil B. DeMille
A solid screenplay and excellent acting from an all-star cat
make this picture more than another circus story.

The Ten Commandments (1956)
220 min, c, r: FNC.
Charlton Heston, Yul Brynner, Anne Baxter, Edward G. Robinson
d: Cecil B. DeMille
DeMille outdid all of his other spectacles with this remake of
his own 1923 Ten Commandments, the story of Moses and his
struggle to lead his people to the "Promised Land".

BOOTH, MARGARET
  The Mysterious Lady (1928)
  90 min, b/w, r: MGM.
  Greta Garbo, Conrad Nagel
  d: Fred Niblo
  Garbo is a Russian spy in this film.

  Wise Girls (1929)
  78 min, b/w, r: MGM.
  Roland Young, Norma Lee
  d: E. Mason Hopper
  This cute domestic comedy was based on the play "Kempy"
  and was one of MGM's first talkies.

  The Lady Of Scandal (1930)
  80 min, b/w, r: MGM.
  Basil Rathbore, Ruth Chatterton
  d: Sidney Franklin
  Chatterton plays an actress who must decide between love and
  a career.

A Lady's Morals (1930)
75 min, b/w, r: MGM.
Grace Moore, Reginald Denny, Wallace Beery
d: Sidney Franklin
Film biography of Jenny Lind.

Redemption (1930)
75 min, b/w, r: MGM.
John Gilbert, Conrad Nagel, Renee Adoree
d: Fred Niblo
Drama based on Tolstoy's The Living Corpse was Gilbert's
second sound film.

The Rogue Song (1930)
108 min, c, r: MGM.
Lawrence Tibbett, Stan Laurel, Oliver Hardy
d: Lionel Barrymore
A stylish comic operetta, The Rogue Song was MGM's first
technicolor feature.

Strictly Unconventional (1930)
56 min, b/w, r: MGM.
Mary Forbes, Tyrrell Davis, Paul Cavanagh
d: David Burton
Drama based on Somerset Maugham's "The Circle."

The Cuban Love Song (1931)
82 min, b/w, r: MGM.
Lawrence Tibbett, Lupe Velez, Jimmy Durante
d: W. S. Van Dyke
Musical about man with two loves: an American socialite and
a hot-blooded Cuban peanut vendor.

Five And Ten (1931)
93 min, b/w, r: MGM.
Marion Davies, Leslie Howard
d: Robert Z. Leonard
Davies is a poor little rich girl who owns a chain of "five
and ten cent" stores.

It's A Wise Child (1931)
83 min, b/w, r: MGM.
Marion Davies, Sidney Blackmer
d: Robert Z. Leonard
Comedy based on Laurence Johnson's play.

New Moon (1931)
105 min, b/w, r: MGM.
Grace Moore, Lawrence Tibbett
d: Jack Conway
Musical based on the operetta New Moon.

Susan Lenox - Her Fall And Rise (1931)
75 min, b/w, r: MGM.
Greta Garbo, Clark Gable, Jean Hersholt
d: Robert Z. Leonard
Garbo plays the title role in this film about a young woman
who is forced to run away from home and make her way in the
world despite abuse by several men.

Lovers Courageous (1932)
78 min, b/w, r: MGM.
Robert Montgomery, Madge Evans
d: Robert Z. Leonard
Romance concerning a poor man who falls in love with a rich
woman in London.

Smilin' Through (1932)
96 min, b/w, r: MGM.
Norma Shearer, Leslie Howard, Fredric March
d: Sidney Franklin
Intensely romantic film starring Shearer in a dual role as
a woman who is killed on her wedding day, and as the bride's
niece who falls in love with the murderer's son.

The Son-Daughter (1932)
79 min, b/w, r: MGM.
Helen Hayes, Ramon Navarro
d: Clarence Brown
Hayes is sold into slavery in this drama set in Chinatown.

The Strange Interlude (1932)
112 min, b/w, r: MGM.
Norma Shearer, Clark Gable, Robert Young
d: Robert Z. Leonard
Film involving Shearer, a married woman, and Gable, as
lovers in a time period that spans twenty years.

Bombshell (1933)
91 min, b/w, r: MGM.
Jean Harlow, Frank Morgan
d: Victor Fleming
Harlow stars as Lola Burns, a sexy movie star who decides that
she wants to get married and settle down.

Dancing Lady (1933)
82 min, b/w, r: MGM.
Joan Crawford, Clark Gable, Franchot Tone, Fred Astaire
d: Robert Z. Leonard
Joan Crawford stars as a young dancer who starts in burlesque
determined to become a big star without comprising her morals.

The White Sister (1933)
101 min, b/w, r: MGM.
Helen Hayes, Clark Gable
d: Victor Fleming
Tragic story of a woman who becomes a nun because she thinks
that her lover has been killed in the Italian Air Service.

Storm At Daybreak (1933)
80 min, b/w, r: MGM.
Kay Francis, Nils Asther, Jean Parker
d: Richard Boleslawsky
Francis is torn between two men in Serbia in this drama.

Peg O' My Heart (1933)
86 min, b/w, r: MGM.
Marion Davies, Onslow Stevens
d: Robert Z Leonard
A young free-spirited Irish woman inherits a sum of money
and is sent to England for her education in this comedy.
See MARION, FRANCIS (Screenwriters).

The Barretts Of Wimpole Street (Forbidden Alliance)(1934)
111 min, b/w, r: MGM.
Norma Shearer, Fredric March, Charles Laughton, Maureen O'Sullivan
d: Sidney Franklin
Film version of the romance of poets Robert Browning and
Elizabeth Barrett.

Reckless (1935)
96 min, b/w, r: MGM.
Jean Harlow, William Powell, Franchot Tone
d: Victor Fleming
Musical concerning an actress and her agent who become involved in a scandal when a wealthy man commits suicide.

Mutiny On The Bounty (1935)
132 min, b/w, MGM.
Clark Gable, Charles Laughton, Franchot Tone
d: Frank Lloyd
Excellent adventure film based on a true story of the ship
Bounty, whose crew took over command from an unreasonable
captain.

Camille (1936)
108 min, b/w, r: MGM.
Greta Garbo, Robert Taylor
d: George Cukor
Often called Garbo's best film, Camille is the story of a
young man desperately in love with a woman who is dying.
See MARION, FRANCIS (Screenwriters).

Romeo And Juliet (1936)
127 min, b/w, r: MGM.
Leslie Howard, Norma Shearer, John Barrymore
d: George Cukor
Beautifully acted film version of Shakespeare's tragic play
about the doomed romance of two young lovers.

A Yank At Oxford (1937)
110 min, b/w, r: MGM.
Robert Taylor, Vivien Leigh, Maureen O'Sullivan
d: Jack Conway
Robert Taylor is the American studying at the famous university
in this film.

The Owl And The Pussycat (1970)
97 min, c, available in cinemascope, r: FNC.
Barbra Streisand, George Segal
d: Herbert Ross
Comedy involving the misadventures of a prostitute and a
bookstore clerk.

Fat City (1972)
96 min, c, r: FNC.
Stacy Keach, Jeff Bridges, Susan Tyrrell
d: John Huston
Keach is a down and out boxer and Tyrrell is his sometimes
lover in this engrossing drama about losers.

To Find A Man (1972). Co-editor: Rita Roland
94 min, c, r: SWA.
Pamela Sue Martin, Lloyd Bridges
d: Buzz Kulik
Drama concerning a young woman's search for an abortionist.
See ROLAND, RITA (Editors).

The Way We Were (1973)
118 min, c, available in cinemascope, r: FNC.
Barbra Streisand, Robert Redford, Bradford Dillman
d: Sydney Pollack
Streisand and Redford both give strong characterizations in
this motion picture about the bumpy courtship and marriage
of two willful people.

Funny Lady (1975)
140 min, c, available in cinemascope, r: FNC.
Barbra Streisand, James Caan, Omar Sharif
d: Herbert Ross
Musical sequel to Funny Girl which continues the biography
of Fanny Brice.
See ALLEN, JAY PRESSON (Screenwriters).

The Sunshine Boys (1975)
111 min, c, r: MGM.
Walter Matthau, George Burns, Richard Benjamin
d: Herbert Ross
Based on Neil Simon's play, this comedy/drama concerns two
vaudeville comedians who unwillingly reunite for a television
show.

Murder By Death (1976)
94 min, c, r: SWA.
Eileen Brennan, Truman Capote, Peter Falk
d: Robert Moore
Wonderful spoof which utilizes every plot twist and suspicious
character ever used in mystery stories.

The Goodbye Girl (1977). Co-editor: John F. Burnett
110 min, c, r: SWA.
Richard Dreyfuss, Marsha Mason
d: Herbert Ross
Comedy by Neil Simon about a woman and her daughter who find
that their apartment has been sublet to an actor.

California Suite (1978) Co-editor: Michael A. Stevenson
103 min, c, r: FNC, SWA.
Michael Caine, Jane Fonda, Maggie Smith
d: Herbert Ross
From Neil Simon's play comes this film about the misadventures
of four couples staying at the Beverly Hills Hotel.

Chapter Two (1979)
124 min, c, r: SWA.
Marsha Mason, James Caan, Valerie Harper
d: Robert Moore
A newly widowed man and a divorcee find themselves having doubts
after getting married in this film based on Neil Simon's play.

Annie (1982). Co-editor: Michael A. Stevenson
128 min, c, r: SWA.
Albert Finney, Carol Burnett, Aileen Quinn
d: John Huston
Film version of Broadway musical about Little Orphan Annie,
a little girl given an opportunity to live with a wealthy
man for a week.

COATES, ANNE V. (British)
The Truth About Women (1958)
See BOX, MURIEL (Directors, Chapter 2).

The Horse's Mouth (1959)
96 min, c, r: FNC.
Alec Guinness, Kay Walsh
d: Ronald Neame
Guinness gives an outstanding performance as a seemingly
untalented artist in this comedy.

Tunes Of Glory (1960)
106 min, c, r: FNC.
Alec Guinness, John Mills
d: Ronald Neame
Drama about the relationship between a casual colonel and his
exemplary officer.

Lawrence Of Arabia (1962)
221 min, c, available in cinemascope, r: FNC, SWA.
Peter O'Toole, Omar Sharif, Claude Rains, Jose Ferrer
d: David Lean
True story based on the life of the hero T. E. Lawrence and
his incredible struggle to help the Arabs against Turkey.

Becket (1964)
148 min, c, available in cinemascope, r: TWY.
Richard Burton, Peter O'Toole
d: Peter Glenville
Historical drama about the relationship between Thomas
Becket and King Henry II.

Young Cassidy (1965)
110 min, c, r: MGM.
Rod Taylor, Maggie Smith, Julie Christie
d: Jack Cardiff/John Ford
Drama set in Dublin based on the life of Sean O'Casey,
who struggled from poverty to become a famous playwright.

Hotel Paradiso (1966)
100 min, c, r: MGM.
Alec Guinness, Gina Lollobrigida, Robert Morley
d: Peter Glenville
Comedy about the sexual adventures and misadventures of several
people in a hotel in Paris in the 1900's.

The Bofors Gun (1968)
107 min, c, r: SWA.
Nicol Williamson, David Warner, Ian Holm
d: Jack Gold
Intense drama which takes place at a British army camp
after World War II about two men put in charge of guarding
a Bofors gun.

Great Catherine (1968)
99 min, c, r: BUD.
Jeanne Moreau, Peter O'Toole, Zero Mostel
d: Gordon Flemyng
Moreau stars as Catherine the Great in this film based on
George Bernard Shaw's farce.

The Adventurers (1970)
171 min, c, r: FNC.
Bekim Fehmin, Charles Aznavour, Candice Bergen
d: Lewis Gilbert
Involved film taken from Harold Robbins' novel about a young
man who becomes a revolutionary in South America.

Friends (1971)
102 min, c, r: FNC.
Susan Bury, Anice Alviha
d: Lewis Gilbert
Sensitive film concerning a teenage boy and girl's struggle
to lead their own lives without adult interference.

Murder On The Orient Express (1974)
128 min, c, r: FNC.
Albert Finney, Lauren Bacall, Ingrid Bergman
d: Sidney Lumet
Beautifully filmed and acted mystery based on a story by
Agatha Christie which takes place aboard the famous train.

Catholics (1974)
82 min, c, r: TWY.
Martin Sheen, Trevor Howard
d: Jack Gold
A fable which takes place in the future, and raises questions
about God, politics, and mankind.

11 Harrowhouse (1974)
95 min, c, cinemascope only, r: FNC.
Charles Grodin, Candice Bergen, James Mason
d: Aram Avakian
Grodin starred in and scripted this comedy about an attempt
to rob a huge diamond exchange.

The Eagle Has Landed (1977)
123 nin, c, r: TWY.
Michael Caine, Donald Sutherland
d: John Sturges
Film based on the novel by Jack Higgins concerning a plot
to kidnap Sir Winston Churchill.

The Medusa Touch (1978)
110 min, c, r: TWY.
Richard Burton, Lee Remick
d: Jack Gold
Tightly constructed mystery about a man who is able to will
disasters and murders.

The Legacy (1979)
100 min, c, r: SWA.
Katharine Ross, Sam Elliott
d: Richard Marquand
Horror film concerning a group of people who must attempt a
series of tests to inherit the "legacy" and immortality.

The Elephant Man (1980)
123 min, b/w, available in cinemascope, r: FNC.
John Hurt, Anthony Hopkins, Anne Bancroft
d: David Lynch
Superb drama based on a true story about John Merrick, a
hideously deformed man, and the doctor who attempts to help
him lead a normal life in Victorian England.

Ragtime (1982). Co-editors: Antony Gibbs, Stanley Warnow
155 min, c, available in cinemascope, r: FNC.
Elizabeth McGovern, Howard E. Rollins, Mary Steenburgen
d: Milos Forman
Film based on E. L. Doctorow's best selling novel which combines
history and fiction about events around the turn of the century.

DECUGIS, CECILE (French)
A Bout De Souffle (Breathless)(1959)
89 min, b/w, subtitles, r: IMA.
Jean-Paul Belmondo, Jean Seberg
d: Jean-Luc Godard
Intense film which concerns a young man wanted by the police,
and the girl who betrays him.

Les Quatre Cents Coups (The Four Hundred Blows)(1959)
98 min, b/w, subtitles, available in cinemascope, r: FNC.
Jean-Pierre Leaud, Patrick Auffay
d: Francois Truffaut
Realistic drama about a young boy who rebels against his
terrible family life by stealing.

Le Genou De Claire (Claire's Knee)(1970)
105 min, c, subtitles, r: COR, SWA.
Jean-Claude Brialy
d: Eric Rohmer
Young man becomes obsessed with, of all things, Claire's knee.

L'Amour, L'Apres-Midi (Chloe In The Afternoon) (1972)
95 min, c, subtitles, r: SWA.
Bernard Verley, Zouzou
d: Eric Rohmer
Film involving a married man's reaquaintance and fascination with
a free-spirited girl from his past.

La Marquise D'O (The Marquise Of O) (1975)
102 min, c, subtitles, r: NLC.
Bruno Genz, Edith Clever, Peter Luhr
d: Eric Rohmer
A short story by Heinrich von Kleist is the basis for this
drama set in Germany at the end of the 18th century.

DEMETRAKAS, JOHANNA
  Nunzio (1978)
  87 min, c, r: SWA.
  David Proval, James Andronica
  d: Paul Williams
  Film about a young retarded man growing up in New York City.

  See DEMETRAKAS, JOHANNA (Directors, Chapter I).

FAZAN, ADRIENNE
  Day Of Reckoning (1933)
  82 min, b/w, r: MGM.
  Richard Dix, Madge Evans, Clarence Wison
  d: Charles Brabin
  Early prison drama with Dix as prisoner.

  The Bride Wore Red (1937)
  See ARZNER, DOROTHY (Directors, Chapter 2).

  You're Only Young Once (1937)
  78 min, b/w, r: MGM.
  Mickey Rooney, Lewis Stone, Ann Rutherford
  d: George B. Seitz
  This comedy was the second of the popular Andy Hardy film series.

  Barbary Coast Gent (1944)
  87 min, b/w, r: MGM.
  Wallace Beery, Binnie Barnes, John Carradine
  d: Roy Del Ruth
  Beery is the "gent" who decides to give up his life of crime.

  Between Two Women (1944)
  83 min, b/w, r: MGM.
  Van Johnson, Lionel Barrymore
  d: Willis Goldbeck
  Barrymore stars as Dr. Gillespie in this continuation of the
  Dr. Kildare series.

Anchors Aweigh   (1945)
103 min, c, r: MGM.
Frank Sinatra, Gene Kelly, Kathryn Grayson
d: George Sidney
Great musical featuring Sinatra and Kelly as two sailors on leave
in Hollywood.
See LENNART, ISOBEL (Screenwriters).

She Went To The Races   (1945)
86 min, b/w, r: MGM.
James Craig, Frances Gifford, Ava Gardner
d: Willis Goldbeck
A woman figures out a method to win at horse racing in this comedy.

Holiday In Mexico   (1946)
127 min, c, r: MGM.
Walter Pidgeon, Jane Powell, Xavier Cugat
d: George Sidney
Great musical numbers highlight this comedy about a widowed am-
bassador's daughter who attempts to find her dad a new wife.
See LENNART, ISOBEL (Screenwriters).

The Secret Heart   (1946)
97 min, b/w, r: MGM.
Claudette Colbert, Walter Pidgeon, June Allyson
d: Robert Z. Leonard
Psychological drama involving Allyson's struggle with hatred
for her stepmother and her obsessive love for her dead father.

The Kissing Bandit   (1948). Co-writer: John Briard Harding
102 min, b/w, r: MGM.
Frank Sinatra, Kathryn Grayson
d: Laslo Benedek
Musical about a young man who decides to become what his father
was - a bandit.
See LENNART, ISOBEL (Screenwriters).

Three Daring Daughters   (1947)
115 min, c, r: MGM.
Jeanette MacDonald, Ann Todd
d: Fred Wilcox
Drama with music concerning three daughters and their reactions
to their mother's new husband.
See LEVIEN, SONYA (Screenwriters)

In The Good Old Summertime   (1949)
102 min, c, r: MGM.
Judy Garland, Van Johnson, S.Z. Sakall
d: Robert Z. Leonard
Romantic comedy about a couple who work together in the same
shop, not knowing that each is the other's pen pal.
See GOODRICH, FRANCES (Screenwriters).

The Duchess Of Idaho   (1950)
98 min, c, r: MGM.
Esther Williams, Van Johnson, John Lund
d: Robert Z. Leonard
Williams is a swimming star involved with two men at the same time

Nancy Goes To Rio   (1950)
99 min, c, r: MGM.
Ann Sothern, Jane Powell
d: Robert Z. Leonard
Musical involving a mother and daughter who want the same man
and the same singing job.

The Pagan Love Song   (1950)
76 min, c, r: MGM.
Esther Williams, Howard Keel
d: Robert Alton
Esther stars as a Tahitian diver in this musical.

Texas Carnival   (1951)
76 min, c, r: MGM.
Esther Williams, Red Skelton, Howard Keel, Ann Miller
d: Charles Walters
Musical comedy involving a bum who is mistaken for a Texas
millionaire at a resort.

An American In Paris   (1951)
113 min, c, r: MGM.
Gene Kelly, Leslie Caron
d: Vincente Minnelli
Incredible musical celebrating Paris which combines Ira and
George Gershwin's music with Kelly's choreography.

Singin' In The Rain   (1952)
103 min, c, r: MGM.
Gene Kelly, Debbie Reynolds, Jean Hagen
d: Gene Kelly/Stanley Donen
One of MGM's best-loved musicals, this film is set in Hollywood
during the late 1920's when "talkies" began to appear, and
features Kelly and Reynolds at their finest.
See COMDEN, BETTY (Screenwriters).

Everything I Have Is Yours   (1952)
92 min, c, r: MGM.
Marge and Gower Champion
d: Robert Z. Leonard
Musical starring the Champions as a dance team working to get
their first big chance on Broadway.

Give A Girl A Break   (1953)
82 min, c, r: MGM.
Debbie Reynolds, Marge and Gower Champion
d: Stanley Donen
Musical about three girls anxious to get parts in a Broadway show
See GOODRICH, FRANCES (Screenwriters).

I Love Melvin   (1953)
79 min, c, r: MGM.
Debbie Reynolds, Donald O'Connor
d: Don Weis
Reynolds is a football in one of the musical sequences which
highlight this comedy about a photographer and his girlfriend.

Deep In My Heart (1954)
132 min, c, r: MGM.
Jose Ferrer, Merle Oberon
d: Stanley Donen
Musical based on songwriter Sigmund Romberg's life.

It's Always Fair Weather (1955)
101 min, c, available in cinemascope, r: MGM.
Gene Kelly, Cyd Charisse
d: Gene Kelley/Stanley Donen
Musical involving the ten-year reunion of three men who fought
together in World War II.
See COMDEN, BETTY (Screenwriters).

Kismet (1955)
113 min, c, available in cinemascope, r: MGM.
Howard Keel, Ann Blyth
d: Vincente Minnelli
Colorful musical taken from a fable about a poet with magical
powers.

Invitation To The Dance (1956). Co-editors: Raymond Poulton,
Robert Watts
93 min, c, r: MGM.
Gene Kelly, Claire Sombert
d: Gene Kelly
Kelly painstakingly constructed an ambitious film divided
into three parts - each with a story interpreted by dance.

Lust For Life (1956)
122 min, c, available in cinemascope, r: MGM.
Kirk Douglas, Anthony Quinn
d: Vincente Minnelli
Film based on the life of artist Vincent Van Gogh.

Designing Woman (1957)
117 min, c, available in cinemascope, r: MGM.
Gregory Peck, Lauren Bacall
d: Vincente Minnelli
Romantic comedy starring Bacall as a fashion designer and
Peck as a sportswriter.

Don't Go Near The Water (1957)
102 min, c, r: MGM.
Glenn Ford, Gia Scala
d: Charles Walters
Hilarious comedy about a South Pacific naval base during World
War II where the main preoccupation is building an officer's
club.

Gigi (1958)
116 min, c, available in cinemascope, r: MGM.
Leslie Caron, Louis Jourdan, Maurice Chevalier
d: Vincente Minnelli
Musical comedy concerning the education of a young French
girl in social and romantic issues.

The Reluctant Debutante (1958)
96 min, c, available in cinemascope, r: MGM.
Rex Harrison, Kay Kendall, Sandra Dee
d: Vincente Minnelli
Witty film about a husband and wife's efforts to find the
right husband for their daughter.

Some Came Running (1958)
137 min, c, available in cinemascope, r: MGM.
Frank Sinatra, Shirley MacLaine, Dean Martin, Martha Hyer
d: Vincente Minnelli
Tragic and moving film about an author who returns to his
hometown and becomes involved with a gambler, a lonely young
woman, and a school teacher.

The Big Circus (1959)
109 min, c, r: HUR.
Victor Mature, Peter Lorre, Rhonda Fleming
d: Joseph Newman
Life under the "big top" is explored in this story about the
problems of a circus troupe.

The Gazebo (1959)
102 min, b/w, available in cinemascope, r: MGM.
Glenn Ford, Debbie Reynolds
d: George Marshall
Black comedy involving Ford as a man who is afraid that
someone will stumble onto the body that he has buried under
the new gazebo.

Bells Are Ringing (1960)
127 min, c, available in cinemascope, r: MGM.
Judy Holliday, Dean Martin
d: Vincente Minnelli
Musical about an answering service operator who becomes
involved in her customers' lives.
See COMDEN, BETTY (Screenwriters).

Four Horsemen Of The Apocalypse (1962). Co-editor: Ben Lewis
153 min, c, r: MGM.
Glenn Ford, Charles Boyer, Ingrid Thulin
d: Vincente Minnelli
Drama remade from silent version of family on opposite sides
during World War II.

Two Weeks In Another Town (1962)
107 min, c, available in cinemascope, r: MGM.
Kirk Douglas, Cyd Charisse
d: Vincente Minnelli
Drama about the trials and tribulations of a group of filmmakers in Rome on location.

The Courtship Of Eddie's Father (1963)
117 min, c, available in cinemascope, r: MGM.
Glenn Ford, Shirley Jones
d: Vincente Minnelli
Gentle film about a widower's son's search for the perfect
wife for his father.

The Prize (1963)
136 min, c, r: MGM.
Paul Newman, Elke Sommer, Edward G. Robinson
d: Mark Robson
Newman becomes involved in intrigue when he travels to
Stockholm to receive the Noble Peace Prize.

Looking For Love (1964)
83 min, c, r: MGM.
Jim Hutton, Connie Francis, Susan Oliver
d: Don Weis
Musical comedy involving Francis as an operator with designs
on Hutton.

Billie (1965)
87 min, c, r: MGM.
Patty Duke, Jim Backus, Warren Berlinger
d: Don Weis
Duke is an athlete who faces problems when her parents and
boyfriend expect her to become less involved in sports and
be more "ladylike".

This Property Is Condemned (1966)
110 min, c, r: FNC.
Natalie Wood, Robert Redford, Charles Bronson
d: Sydney Pollack
Based on Tennessee Williams' play, this drama tells the story
of Alva Starr and her unhappy relationships with her mother
and various lovers.

Who's Minding The Mint (1967)
97 min, c, r: FNC.
Jim Hutton, Dorothy Provine, Milton Berle
d: Howard Morris
Comedy with an all-star cast concerning a Mint employee who
hires thieves to help him print money to replace the amount
he threw away by accident.

Where Angels Go, Trouble Follows (1968)
95 min, c, r: FNC.
Susan Saint James, Rosalind Russell, Stella Stevens
d: James Neilson
Sequel to The Trouble With Angels, with a whole new class
of students tormenting Mother Superior.

With Six You Get Eggroll (1968)
95 min, c, r: SWA.
Brian Keith, Doris Day
d: Howard Morris
Comedy about a widower and widow who fall in love and marry,
only to find that their children refuse to get along with
each other.

The Comic (1969)
94 min, c, r: BUD.
Dick Van Dyke, Mickey Rooney
d: Carl Reiner
Van Dyke stars as a silent film comedian.

The Cheyenne Social Club (1970)
103 min, c, r: SWA.
James Stewart, Henry Fonda, Shirley Jones
d: Gene Kelly
Stewart plays a cowboy who inherits a whorehouse in this
comedy.

FIELDS, VERNA
Studs Lonigan (1960)
103 min, c, r: MGM.
Christopher Knight, Jack Nicholson
d: Irving Lerner
Knight stars as Studs in this drama set in 1920's Chicago.

Nothing But A Man (1964)
92 min, b/w, r: FNC.
Abbey Lincoln, Ivan Dixon
d: Michael Roemer
Excellent drama about a Southern black man and his family,
and the suffering they must endure during the 1960's.

Medium Cool (1969)
110 min, c, r: FNC.
Robert Forster, Peter Boyle
d: Haskell Wexler
Forster is a cameraman during the turbulent 1968 Chicago
Democratic National Convention in this semi-documentary.

What's Up Doc? (1972)
94 min, c, r: SWA.
Barbra Steisand, Ryan O'Neal, Madeline Kahn
d: Peter Bogdanovich
Streisand makes things difficult for O'Neal and his fiancee
in this farce, which is the director's tribute to screwball
comedy.

American Graffiti (1973). Co-editor: Marcia Lucas
109 min, c, available in cinemascope, r: SWA.
Richard Dreyfuss, Ron Howard, Candy Clark, Paul Le Mat
d: George Lucas
Excellent comedy highlighted by music from the early 1960's
which concerns the adventures of several teenagers as they
"cruise" down Main Street on a Saturday night in a California
town.

Paper Moon (1973)
102 min, b/w, r: FNC.
Tatum O'Neal, Ryan O'Neal, Madeline Kahn
d: Peter Bogdanovich
Delightful comedy about a con man and his daughter traveling
through the dustbowl during the Depression.

Daisy Miller (1974)
91 min, c, r: FNC.
Cybill Shepherd, Barry Brown, Cloris Leachman
d: Peter Bogdanovich
Shepherd stars in the title role in this film based on Henry
James' short story.

<u>Sugarland Express</u> (1974). Co-editor: Edward Abroms
109 min, c, available in cinemascope, r: SWA, TWY.
Goldie Hawn, Ben Johnson, William Atherton
d: Steven Spielberg
True story involving a husband and wife fresh from jail, and
their attempts to kidnap their child, who is being put up
for adoption.

<u>Jaws</u> (1975)
124 min, c, r: SWA.
Robert Shaw, Richard Dreyfuss, Roy Scheider
d: Steven Spielberg
Intense film about three men and their attempts to kill a
huge shark that is terrorizing a small coastal town in New
England.

FOWLER, MARJORIE
<u>The Woman In The Window</u> (1944)
99 min, b/w, r: MGM.
Joan Bennett, Edward G. Robinson
d: Fritz Lang
Wonderful drama concerning a man who becomes involved with
a beautiful woman and murder while his wife is on vacation.

<u>The Three Faces Of Eve</u> (1957)
95 min, b/w, available in cinemascope, r: FNC.
Joanne Woodward, David Wayne, Lee J. Cobb
d: Nunnally Johnson
True story taken from notes made by a psychiatrist about
Eve, a patient who had developed two distinct personalities.

<u>Separate Tables</u> (1958)
98 min, b/w, r: MGM.
David Niven, Deborah Kerr, Rita Hayworth
d: Delbert Mann
Excellent film version of Terence Rattigan's play about a
group of guests staying at an inn.

<u>Elmer Gantry</u> (1960)
146 min, c, r: MGM.
Burt Lancaster, Jean Simmons, Shirley Jones
d: Richard Brooks
Powerful film taken fron Sinclair Lewis' novel about evangelists
with strong performances by Lancaster, Jones, and Simmons.

<u>The Outsider</u> (1961)
108 min, b/w, r: SWA.
Tony Curtis, James Franciscus
d: Delbert Mann
Film based on the life of Ira Hayes, an American Indian who
helped raise the flag at Iwo Jima.

What A Way To Go! (1964)
111 min, c, cinemascope only, r: FNC.
Shirley MacLaine, Paul Newman, Dean Martin
d: J. Lee Thompson
Comedy which features MacLaine as a woman whose husbands keep
dying and leaving her fortunes.
See COMDEN, BETTY (Screenwriters).

Dear Brigitte (1965)
100 min, c, available in cinemascope, r: FNC.
James Stewart, Glynis Johns, Billy Mumy
d: Henry Koster
Comedy about a boy's wish to meet Brigitte Bardot.

Doctor Dolittle (1967)
152 min, c, available in cinemascope, r: FNC.
Rex Harrison, Anthony Newley
d: Richard Fleischer
Musical about Dr. Dolittle, a man with the ability to
communicate with animals.

The Strawberry Statement (1970)
107 min, c, r: MGM.
Bruce Davison, Kim Darby
d: Stuart Hagmann
Film about the late 1960's Columbia University riots and
"sit-ins" from a student's point of view.

Conquest Of The Planet Of The Apes (1972)
87 min, c, cinemascope only, r: FNC.
Roddy MacDowall, Don Murray
d: J. Lee Thompson
Film which continues in the vein of Planet Of The Apes
about the stuggle between man and apes.

It's My Turn (1980) Co-editors: Byron Brandt, James Coblenz
See WEILL, CLAUDIA (Directors, Chapter 1).

GUILLEMOT, AGNES (French)
RoGoPag (1962). Co-editor: Lila Lakshmanan
124 min, b/w, subtitles, r: FNC.
Episode: Le Noveau Monde (20 min).
d: Jean-Luc Godard
Guillemot's section of the film concerns a man who tries to
come to terms with his feelings of isolation.

Les Carabiniers (The Riflemen)(1963). Co-editor: Lila Lakshmanan
75 min, b/w, subtitles, r: FAC.
Marino Mase, Albert Juross
d: Jean-Luc Godard
Two farmers leave home to fight for their king.

Le Mepris (Contempt)(1963). Co-editor: Lila Lakshmanan
103 min, c, subtitles, r: FNC.
Brigitte Bardot, Jack Palance, Fritz Lang
d: Jean-Luc Godard
Director Fritz Lang plays himself in this motion picture about
filmmakers in Rome.

Bande A Part (Band Of Outsiders) (1964). Co-editor: Francoise
Collin
95 min, b/w, subtitles, r: COR.
Anna Karina, Claude Brasseur
d: Jean-Luc Godard
Two young men attempt a robbery in this film.

Une Femme Mariee (A Married Woman) (1964). Co-editor: Francoise
Collin
94 min, c, subtitles, r: SWA, TWY.
Macha Meril, Phillipe LeRoy
d: Jean-Luc Godard
Effective film about a woman and her relationship with both her
husband and her lover.

Alphaville (1965)
100 min, b/w, subtitles, r: IMA.
Eddie Constantine, Anna Karina, Akim Tamiroff
d: Jean-Luc Godard
Great film with detective Lemmy Caution attempting to rescue "the
girl."

Masculin-Feminin (Masculine-Feminine)(1966)
103 min, b/w, subtitles, r: SWA.
Jean-Pierre Leaud, Chantal Goya
d: Jean-Luc Godard
A young man attempts to find happiness after coming home from
serving in the military.

La Chinoise (1967). Co-editor: Delphine Desfons
95 min, c, subtitles, r: LEA.
Jean-Pierre Leaud, Anne Wiazemsky
d: Jean-Luc Godard
Film about five people and their attempts to live a
Marxist-Lenninist lifestyle.

Week-End (1968)
105 min, c, subtitles, r: NYF.
Mireille Darc, Jean Yanne
d: Jean-Luc Godard
Bizarre film about a wealthy Parisian couple's weekend
adventure and ultimate encounter with terrorists.

La Sirene Du Mississippi (Mississippi Mermaid)(1969)
109 min, c, cinemascope only, subtitles, r: MGM.
Jean-Paul Belmondo, Catherine Deneuve
d: Francois Truffaut
Deneuve stars as a mail order bride sent to marry a farmer.

L'Enfant Sauvage (The Wild Child)(1969)
109 min, b/w, subtitles, r: MGM.
Francois Truffaut, Jean-Pierre Cargol
d: Francois Truffaut
Truffaut stars as Dr. Jean Itard, a doctor who attempted to
educate a young boy found abandoned and living among animals.

Domicile Conjugal (Bed And Board)(1970)
95 min, c, subtitles, r: TWY, SWA.
Jean-Pierre Leaud, Claude Jade
d: Francois Truffaut
Young couple's marriage develops problems when they move
into a small apartment building where everybody knows everything that everybody does.

KLINGMAN, LYNZEE
One Flew Over The Cuckoo's Nest (1975). Co-editors: Richard
Chew, Sheldon Kahn
129 min, c, r: MGM.
Jack Nicholson, Louise Fletcher
d: Milos Forman
Wonderful film based on Ken Kesey's bizarre novel of a
free-spirited rebel who has himself committed to an insane
asylum.

Almost Summer (1978)
89 min, c, r: SWA.
Didi Conn, Bruno Kirby
d: Martin Davidson
High school kids learn the experiences and pain of growing up.

Hair (1979)
118 min, c, r: MGM.
Treat Williams, Beverly D'Angelo, John Savage
d: Milos Forman
Energetic screen version of the long-running Broadway musical.

Gilda Live (1980). Co-editors: Ellen Hovde, Muffie Meyer
95 min, c, r: SWA.
Gilda Radner
d: Mike Nichols
Film version of Gilda Radner's one-woman show on Broadway,
"Gilda - Live From New York."
See MEYER, MUFFIE (Editors).

True Confessions (1981)
107 min, c, r: MGM.
Robert Duvall, Robert De Niro, Charles Durning
d: Martin Scorsese
Two brothers, one a Catholic priest, the other, a homicide
investigator, become involved in political corruption following
the murder of the mysterious "Black Dahlia".

LAWRENCE, VIOLA
Man's Castle (1933)
78 min, b/w, r: KPF.
Spencer Tracy, Loretta Young
d: Frank Borzage
Film concerning young couple who try to find happiness though
they do not have much money.

The Whole Town's Talking (1935)
86 min, b/w, r: FNC.
Edward G. Robinson, Jean Arthur

d: John Ford
Comedy about a mild-mannered man mistaken for a ruthless
criminal.

Craig's Wife (1936)
See ARZNER, DOROTHY (Directors, Chapter 2).

The King Steps Out (1936)
86 min, b/w, r: SWA.
Grace Moore, Franchot Tone
d: Josef von Sternberg
Musical with Tone as a young king in love with Moore.

Only Angels Have Wings (1939)
121 min, b/w, r: FNC.
Cary Grant, Jean Arthur, Thomas Mitchell
d: Howard Hawks
Two woman disrupt the pattern of dare-devil mail pilots in
South America in this wonderful drama.

Here Comes Mr. Jordan (1941)
93 min, b/w, r: FNC.
Robert Montgomery, Claude Rains
d: Alexander Hall
Fantasy about a prizefighter, who, after he is killed in an
accident, is sent back to earth for a chance to win the champ-
ionsip fight.

My Sister Eileen (1942)
96 min, b/w, r: FNC, KPF.
Rosalind Russell, Janet Blair
d: Alexander Hall
Two sisters move to "The Big Apple" from Ohio to make it in
the big city.

First Comes Courage (1943)
See ARZNER, DOROTHY (Directors, Chapter 2).

Cover Girl (1944)
107 min, c, r: BUD, FNC, KPF.
Rita Hayworth, Gene Kelly, Phil Silvers
d: Charles Vidor
Great musical about a dancer who becomes a cover girl for a
fashion magazine and gets carried away by fame and success.

Tonight And Every Night (1945)
92 min, c, r: KPF.
Rita Hayworth, Janet Blair
d: Victor Saville
Wonderful musical drama about an acting troupe in London that believes "the show must go on" even in the midst of World War II.

Down To Earth   (1947)
101 min, c, r: TWY.
Rita Hayworth, Larry Parks
d: Alexander Hall
Hayworth stars as a Greek goddess who comes to earth to stop the
production of a musical based on the Muses.

The Lady From Shanghai   (1948)
87 min, b/w, r: FNC.
Rita Hayworth, Orson Welles, Everett Sloane
d: Orson Welles
Underrated drama about a sailor and his encounter with a
beautiful woman and her husband.

Knock On Any Door   (1949)
100 min, b/w, r: FNC.
Humphrey Bogart, John Derek
d: Nicholas Ray
Bogart defends a young man charged with murder in this intense
courtroom drama.

In A Lonely Place   (1950)
94 min, b/w, r: FNC.
Humphrey Bogart, Gloria Grahame
d: Nicholas Ray
Brooding film and a great example of "film noir" about a man
accused of murder, and his relationship with the woman who can
prove his innocence.

Harriet Craig (1950)
98 min, b/w, r: KPF.
Joan Crawford, Wendell Corey
d: Vincent Sherman
Remake of Craig's Wife about a woman interested only in material
possessions.

Affair In Trinidad (1952)
98 min, b/w, r: FNC.
Rita Hayworth, Glenn Ford
d: Vincent Sherman
Ford and Hayworth become involved in intrigue as they search
for her husband's murderer.

Miss Sadie Thompson (1953)
91 min, c, r: FNC.
Rita Hayworth, Jose Ferrer, Aldo Ray
d: Curtis Bernhardt
Rita is Sadie in this remake of Rain about a prostitute who
becomes involved with a preacher when they and others are
trapped on an island together.

Salome (1953)
103 min, c, r: FNC.
Rita Hayworth, Charles Laughton, Judith Anderson
d: William Dieterle
Hayworth stars in the title role in this drama about the dancer.

Tight Spot (1955)
97 min, b/w, r: KPF.
Ginger Rogers, Edward G. Robinson
d: Phil Karlson
Drama involving the police force using a woman as bait for
a dangerous criminal.

Three For The Show (1955)
91 min, c, r: FNC.
Betty Grable, Marge and Gower Champion, Jack Lemmon
d: H. C. Potter
Musical involving Grable as a Broadway performer who remarries,
thinking that her first husband is dead.

The Eddy Duchin Story (1956). Co-editor: Jack Ogilvie
123 min, c, r: FNC.
Tyrone Power, Kim Novak
d: George Sidney
Power is Duchin is this film about the pianist's life and
early death of leukemia.

Pal Joey (1957). Co-editor: Jerome Thoms
111 min, c, r: FNC.
Frank Sinatra, Rita Hayworth, Kim Novak
d: George Sidney
Great songs highlight this musical about an attractive
singer who becomes involved with two women.

Pepe (1960). Co-editor: Al Clark
157 min, c, r: FNC.
Cantinflas, Dan Dailey, Shirley Jones
d: George Sidney
Comedy concerning a man who goes to Hollywood to retrieve his
favorite horse.
See LEVIEN, SONYA (Screenwriters).

LITTLETON, CAROL
French Postcards (1979)
95 min, c, r: FNC.
Marie-France Pisier, Jean Rochefort, Debra Winger
d: Willard Huyck
The experiences of several American students in living and
loving on their year abroad in France.

Roadie (1980). Co-editor: Tom Walls
106 min, c, r: MGM.
Meat Loaf, Art Carney, Deborah Harry
d: Alan Rudolph
Comedy about the trials and tribulations of a rock and roll
band's stagehand.

Body Heat (1981)
118 min, c, r: SWA.
William Hurt, Kathleen Turner, Richard Crenna
d: Lawrence Kasdan
This stylish film, which involves a naive lawyer and a beautiful
married woman, is a throwback to the 1940's film noir tradition.

E. T., The Extra-Terrestrial (1982)
115 min, c, r: SWA.
Dee Wallace, Henry Thomas, Drew Barrymore
d: Steven Spielberg
Box office smash about an alien, who is left on earth when his
expedition's spaceship leaves without him, and the boy who
befriends him.

MACRORIE, ALMA RUTH
Road To Zanzibar (1941)
92 min, b/w, r: CLE.
Bing Crosby, Bob Hope, Dorothy Lamour
d: Victor Schertzinger
This time Crosby and Hope go on a safari in Africa.

Lady In The Dark (1944)
100 min, c, r: SWA.
Ginger Rogers, Ray Milland
d: Mitchell Leisen
Unconventional film with Rogers as troubled lady executive who
seeks treatment for her psychological problems.
See GOODRICH, FRANCES (Screenwriters).

To Each His Own (1946)
122 min, b/w, r: SWA.
Olivia de Havilland, John Lund
d: Mitchell Leisen
Sensitive film involving de Havilland as a unwed mother.

Golden Earrings (1947)
95 min, b/w, r: TWY.
Ray Milland, Marlene Dietrich
d: Mitchell Leisen
Comedy involving Milland as a spy and Dietrich as a gypsy who
hides him.

Rhubarb (1951)
94 min, b/w, r: FNC.
Ray Milland, Jan Sterling
d: Arthur Lubin
A cat plays the lead in this comedy about a millionaire who
leaves his baseball team to his pet when he dies. Written by
DOROTHY DAVENPORT REID (Directors, Chapter 2).

Dear Brat (1951)
82 min, b/w, r: FNC.
Mona Freeman, Billy De Wolfe
d: William A. Seiter
Comedy concerning Freeman as a young woman who hires a man as
the gardener, not knowing that her father once sent him to jail.

Little Boy Lost (1953)
95 min, b/w, r: FNC.
Bing Crosby, Claude Dauphin
d: George Seaton
Drama with Crosby as a man who returns to Europe after World
War II to find his son, whom he has never seen.

Botany Bay (1953)
94 min, c, r: FNC.
Alan Ladd, James Mason
d: John Farrow
Drama about the conflict between a wrongly accused man and an
evil captain aboard a prison ship.

Knock On Wood (1954)
103 min, c, r: FNC.
Danny Kaye, Mai Zetterling
d: Norman Panama/Melvin Frank
Comedy about the misadventures of a puppeteer.

The Bridges At Toko-Ri (1955)
103 min, c, r: FNC.
William Holden, Grace Kelly, Fredric March
d: Mark Robson
Film which features Kelly as a wife at home while her husband
is a pilot in the Korean war.

Three Violent People (1956)
100 min, c, r: FNC.
Charlton Heston, Anne Baxter
d: Rudolph Mate
Western which features Baxter and Heston as husband and wife
in conflict with carpetbaggers after the Civil War.

The Proud And The Profane (1956)
111 min, b/w, r: FNC.
William Holden, Deborah Kerr
d: George Seaton
Holden is an officer and Kerr is a widow who meet and fall in
love during World War II.

The Tin Star (1957)
93 min, b/w, r: FNC.
Henry Fonda, Anthony Perkins
d: Anthony Mann
Good western about a sheriff's attempt to rid a town of villains.

Geisha Boy (1958)
98 min, c, r: FNC.
Jerry Lewis
d: Frank Tashlin
Lewis is a magician on a U.S.O. tour in this comedy.

Rock-A-Bye Baby (1958)
103 min, c, r: FNC.
Jerry Lewis, Marilyn Maxwell
d: Frank Tashlin
This time Lewis is a babysitter.

Teacher's Pet (1958)
120 min, b/w, r: FNC.
Clark Gable, Doris Day, Gig Young
d: George Seaton
Comedy and romance combine in this film about a journalism
teacher and a newspaper editor in her class.
See KANIN, FAY (Screenwriters).

But Not For Me (1959)
105 min, b/w, r: FNC.
Clark Gable, Carroll Baker, Lilli Palmer
d: Walter Lang
Gable is involved in a May-December romance with Baker in this
comedy.

The Rat Race (1960)
105 min, c, r: FNC.
Tony Curtis, Debbie Reynolds
d: Robert Mulligan
Gentle film about a young woman and man, who out of necessity,
share an apartment in New York City.

The Pleasure Of His Company (1961)
114 min, c, r: FNC.
Fred Astaire, Debbie Reynolds
d: George Seaton
Comedy with Astaire as a father who suddenly returns home for
his daughter's wedding after being away for years.

The Counterfeit Traitor (1962)
147 min, c, r: FNC.
William Holden, Lilli Palmer
d: George Seaton
Espionage film about a double agent believed to be a traitor.

MCLEAN, BARBARA
The Bowery (1933)
90 min, b/w, r: FNC.
Wallace Beery, George Raft, Jackie Cooper
d: Raoul Walsh
Raft stars as Steve Brodie, the man who jumped off of the
Brooklyn Bridge in the 1880's.

The House Of Rothschild (1934). Co-editor: Allen McNeil
87 min, b/w, r: FNC.
George Arliss, Boris Karloff, Loretta Young
d: Alfred Werker
Biographical film about the famous bank.

Clive Of India (1935)
90 min, b/w, r: FNC.
Ronald Colman, Loretta Young, Colin Clive
d: Richard Boleslawski
Biography of British adventurer Robert Clive.

Les Miserables (1935)
120 min, b/w, r: FNC.
Fredric March, Charles Laughton
d: Richard Boeslawski
Drama taken from Victor Hugo's novel about a thief who is
hounded by policemen.

The Country Doctor (1936)
110 min, b/w, r: FNC.
Jean Hersholt, June Lang, Dionne Quintuplets
Hersholt stars as Dr. Dafoe, the Dionne Quintuplets' doctor.
See LEVIEN, SONYA (Screenwriters).

Lloyds Of London (1936)
115 min, b/w, r: FNC.
Tyrone Power, Madeleine Carroll, Freddie Bartholomew
d: Henry King
Adventure film loosely based on the origins of the English in-
surance firm which features Power as a young man who grows up
along with the company.

Sing, Baby, Sing (1936)
87 min, b/w, r: SEL.
Alice Faye, Adolphe Menjou
d: Sidney Lanfield
Musical with Faye as a nightclub singer and Menjou as a drunken actor.

Seventh Heaven (1937)
102 min, b/w, r: FNC.
James Stewart, Simone Simon
d: Henry King
Remake of the silent film about a couple falling in love in Paris.

Alexander's Ragtime Band (1938)
106 min, b/w, r: FNC.
Tyrone Power, Alice Faye, Don Ameche, Ethel Merman
d: Henry King
Composer Ameche and bandleader Power are both in love with
singer Faye in this musical which features Irving Berlin tunes.

In Old Chicago (1938)
111 min, b/w, r: FNC.
Tyrone Power, Alice Faye, Don Ameche
d: Henry King
This drama about the famous Chicago fire and the O'Leary
family features Power and Ameche, who are both still in love
with Faye.
See LEVIEN, SONYA (Screenwriters).

Suez (1938)
104 min, b/w, r: FNC.
Tyrone Power, Loretta Young
d: Allan Dwan
Historical film based loosely on the life of canal builder
Ferdinand de Lesseps.

Jesse James (1939)
105 min, c, r: FNC.
d: Henry King
Excellent western about the outlaw and his brother Frank.

The Rains Came (1939)
104 min, b/w, r: FNC.
Myrna Loy, Tyrone Power, George Brent
d: Clarence Brown
Drama concerning a British woman who falls in love with an
Indian doctor despite the fact that society will not accept
the romance.

Stanley And Livingstone (1939)
98 min, b/w, r: FNC.
Spencer Tracy, Nancy Kelly, Walter Brennan
d: Henry King
Adventure film concerning Henry Stanley's search for the
missionary Dr. Livingstone, who was believed missing in
Africa.

Down Argentine Way (1940)
88 min, c, r: FNC.
Betty Grable, Don Ameche, Carmen Miranda
d: Irving Cummings
Grable stars as a rich woman who falls for Ameche in this
musical.

Little Old New York (1940)
100 min, b/w, r: BUD.
Alice Faye, Fred MacMurray
d: Henry King
Film concerning one of the first steamboats on the Hudson river.

Maryland (1940)
91 min, c, r: FNC.
John Payne, Walter Brennan
d: Henry King
Film about a horse-racing family set in Maryland.

Remember The Day (1941)
86 min, b/w, r: FNC.
Claudette Colbert, John Payne
d: Henry King
Payne and Colbert are lovers in this romantic look at
America before World War I.

Tobacco Road (1941)
84 min, b/w, r: FNC.
Gene Tierney, Charley Grapewin, Dana Andrews
d: John Ford
Film based on Erskine Caldwell's novel about a poor Georgia
family.

A Yank In The R.A.F. (1941)
99 min, b/w, r: FNC.
Tyrone Power, Betty Grable
d: Henry King
Power plays an American in the Royal Air Force during the
second World War who ultimately helps in the Dunkirk rescue.

The Black Swan (1942)
85 min, c, r: FNC.
Tyrone Power, Maureen O'Hara, George Sanders
d: Henry King
Good adventure film about a pirate who falls in love with
the daughter of the governor of Jamaica.

The Magnificent Dope (1942)
83 min, b/w, r: FNC.
Henry Fonda, Don Ameche
d: Walter Lang
Fonda is the dope, a man from the country who is sent to
success school in the big city.

Rings On Her Fingers (1942)
85 min, b/w, r: FNC.
Henry Fonda, Gene Tierney, Laird Cregar
d: Rouben Mamoulian
Tierney is a thief who intends to con Fonda but falls in love
with him instead.

Hello, Frisco, Hello (1943)
90 min, c, r, FNC.
Alice Faye, John Payne
d: Bruce Humberstone
Musical set in San Francisco during the 1900's concerning
four people in show business who want to become famous.

The Song Of Bernadette (1943)
157 min, b/w, r: FNC.
Jennifer Jones, Charles Bickford, Anne Revere
d: Henry King
Jones gives an excellent performance as a young girl who sees
a religious vision and is disbelieved and scorned because of
it.

Wilson (1944)
120 min, c, r: FNC.
Alexander Knox, Geraldine Fitzgerald
d: Henry King
Excellent film biography of President Woodrow Wilson.

A Bell For Adano (1945)
104 min, b/w, r: FNC.
John Hodiak, Gene Tierney, William Bendix
d: Henry King
Wartime story of the American occupation of an Italian town.

The Dolly Sisters (1945)
114 min, c, r: FNC.
Betty Grable, John Payne, June Haver
d: Irving Cummings
Musical about sister team during vaudeville days.

Margie (1946)
94 min, c, r: FNC.
Jeanne Crain, Glenn Langan, Alan Young
d: Henry King
Comedy about a girl's high school days.

Three Little Girls In Blue (1946)
90 min, c, r: FNC.
June Haver, George Montgomery, Vivian Blaine
d: Bruce Humberstone
Three sisters go to the big city to snare wealthy husbands
in this musical.

Captain From Castile (1947)
140 min, c, r: FNC.
Tyrone Power, Jean Peters
d: Henry King
Beautiful adventure film set during the Inquisition about
young nobleman and his wife who are trying to escape their
past and start a new life in the New World.

Nightmare Alley (1947)
111 min, b/w, r: FNC.
Tyrone Power, Joan Blondell
d: Edmund Goulding
Powerful drama about a circus performer who becomes famous
by using everyone around him.

Deep Waters (1948)
86 min, b/w, r: FNC.
Dana Andrews, Jean Peters
d: Henry King
Film set in Maine concerning a lobsterman whose relationship
with a troubled boy gives him a chance at happiness.

The Prince Of Foxes (1949)
107 min, b/w, r: FNC.
Tyrone Power, Orson Welles
d: Henry King
Power is the assistant of the notorious Cesare Borgia in this
film.

All About Eve (1950)
130 min, b/w, r: FNC.
Bette Davis, George Sanders, Anne Baxter, Celeste Holm
d: Joseph L. Mankiewicz
Superb drama about a young actress who uses actors, playwrights, and critics to get to the top of her profession.

The Gunfighter (1950)
85 min, b/w, r: FNC.
Gregory Peck, Karl Malden
d: Henry King
Excellent western concerning a retired gunfighter who must constantly defend himself against younger gunfighters who want to become famous by killing him.

No Way Out (1950)
106 min, b/w, r: FNC.
Sidney Poitier, Richard Widmark, Linda Darnell
d: Joseph L. Mankiewicz
Drama concerning racism with Poitier as a young doctor and Widmark as a bigot who wants to kill him.

Twelve O'Clock High (1950)
133 min, b/w, r: FNC.
Gregory Peck, Gary Merrill, Dean Jagger
d: Henry King
Good wartime drama about bomber pilots in England, and the new officer sent to command them.

David And Bathsheba (1951)
116 min, c, available in cinemascope, r: FNC.
Gregory Peck, Susan Hayward
d: Henry King
Good film version of the Bible story.

Follow The Sun (1951)
93 min, b/w, r: FNC.
Glenn Ford, Anne Baxter
d: Sidney Lanfield
Film biography of golfer Ben Hogan.

I'd Climb The Highest Mountain (1951)
88 min, c, r: FNC.
William Lundigan, Susan Hayward
d: Henry King
Lovely drama concerning the wife of a parson in Georgia.

People Will Talk (1951)
110 min, b/w, r: FNC.
Cary Grant, Jeanne Crain
d: Joseph L Mankiewicz
Film which features Grant as a mysterious doctor who offers
to marry a single woman who is pregnant.

Lure Of The Wilderness (1952)
92 min, c, r: FNC.
Jean Peters, Jeffrey Hunter, Walter Brennan
d: Jean Negulesco
Remake of Swamp Water which involves a young hunter who finds
a suspected killer and his daughter deep in a Georgia swamp
and attempts to clear the man's name.

O'Henry's Full House (1952)
117 min, b/w, r: FNC.
Collection of five O'Henry's short stories. McLean edited two
sequences.
Sequence: "The Ransom Of Red Chief."
Fred Allen, Oscar Levant
d: Howard Hawks
Two kidnappers get more that they bargained for when the boy
they are holding for ransom begins to drive them crazy.
Sequence: "The Gift Of The Magi."
Farley Granger, Jeanne Crain
d: Henry King
A husband and wife both sell their most precious possessions
to buy each other expensive Christmas gifts.

Viva Zapata (1952)
113 min, b/w, r: FNC.
Marlon Brando, Jean Peters, Anthony Quinn
d: Elia Kazan
Brando stars as Zapata in this film based on the life of the
Mexican revolutionary.

Wait Till The Sun Shines Nellie (1952)
109 min, c, r: FNC.
David Wayne, Jean Peters
d: Henry King
Drama concerning a barber and his life in a small town.

The Desert Rats (1953)
88 min, b/w, r: FNC.
Richard Burton, James Mason, Robert Newton
d: Robert Wise
Drama set during World War II concerning the battle at Tobruk
with Mason featured as Rommel.

King Of The Khyber Rifles (1953)
99 min, c, r: FNC.
Tyrone Power, Terry Moore
d: Henry King
Because he is a half-caste, a British officer finds that he
has problems with his fellow officers and his love life.

Niagara (1953)
89 min, c, r: FNC.
Joseph Cotten, Marilyn Monroe, Jean Peters
d: Henry Hathaway
Murder mystery which takes place at Niagara Falls has Monroe
plotting to kill husband Cotten.

The Robe (1953)
135 min, c, available in cinemascope, r: FNC.
Richard Burton, Jean Simmons
d: Henry Koster
Burton is a Roman officer who converts to Christianity after
obtaining Christ's robe at the Crucifixion.

The Egyptian (1954)
140 min, c, available in cinemascope, r: FNC.
Edmond Purdom, Victor Mature, Jean Simmons, Gene Tierney
d: Michael Curtiz
Biblical spectacle about a young Egyptian doctor who comes to
believe in God.

Untamed (1955)
111 min, c, r: FNC.
Tyrone Power, Susan Hayward
d: Henry King
Hayward is in love with Power in this adventure film set in
Africa.

MEYER, MUFFIE
The Lords Of Flatbush (1974)
86 min, c, r: FNC.
Perry King, Henry Winkler, Sylvester Stallone
d: Stephen F. Verona
Comedy concerning three high school students growing up
during the 1950's.

The Groove Tube (1974)
73 min, c, r: FNC.
Ken Shapiro, Chevy Chase, Richard Belzer
d: Ken Shapiro
A satirical look at television involving short sketches.

Gilda Live (1980). Co-editors: Ellen Hovde, Lynzee Klingman
See KLINGMAN, LYNZEE (Editors).

See MEYER, MUFFIE (Directors, Chapter 1).

MORRA, IRENE
<u>Sunny Side Up</u> (1929)
123 min, b/w, r: KIL.
Janet Gaynor, Charles Farrell
d: David Butler
First talkie for the famous romantic team is a musical in which
a poor girl falls in love with a wealthy playboy.

<u>Bright Eyes</u> (1934)
83 min, b/w, r: FNC.
Shirley Temple, James Dunn, Jane Withers
d: David Butler
In this film Temple is an orphan who is adopted by a pilot.

<u>The Little Colonel</u> (1935)
80 min, b/w, r: FNC.
Shirley Temple, Bill "Bojangles" Robinson, Lionel Barrymore
d: David Butler
Temple survives the Civil War and keeps her family together.

<u>Kentucky</u> (1938)
96 min, b/w, r: FNC.
Loretta Young, Richard Greene, Walter Brennan
d: David Butler
Gentle film about a Kentucky family who has complete faith
in a race horse to win back their fortune.

<u>Caught In The Draft</u> (1941)
82 min, b/w, r: CLE.
Bob Hope, Dorothy Lamour
d: David Butler
A movie actor goes into the Army so that his girlfriend will
marry him.

<u>Road To Morocco</u> (1942)
81 min, b/w, r: CLE.
Bing Crosby, Bob Hope, Dorothy Lamour
d: David Butler
One of Hope and Crosby's hilarious "Road" pictures - this
time they're in Morocco.

<u>Thank Your Lucky Stars</u> (1943)
127 min, b/w, r: MGM.
Dennis Morgan, Joan Leslie, Bette Davis
d: David Butler
All-star variety film featuring Warner Brothers talents.

<u>The Horn Blows At Midnight</u> (1945)
80 min, b/w, r: MGM.
Jack Benny, Alexis Smith
d: Raoul Walsh
Benny is superb as a radio musician in this comedy with a
surprise ending.

The Time, The Place, And The Girl (1946)
105 min, b/w, r: MGM.
Dennis Morgan, Jack Carson
d: David Butler
Musical comedy concerning some show people who attempt to find
money in order that they can finance their musical productions.

Look For The Silver Lining (1949)
105 min, b/w, r: MGM.
June Haver, Ray Bolger
d: David Butler
Musical biography starring Haver as Marilyn Miller.

It's A Great Feeling (1949)
85 min, b/w, r: MGM.
Doris Day, Jack Carson, Dennis Morgan
d: David Butler
Cameo appearances abound in this comedy set in Hollywood
which features Day as an aspiring singer and Carson as
a ham actor.

Calamity Jane (1953)
101 min, c, r: FNC.
Doris Day, Howard Keel
d: David Butler
Day is Jane and Keel is Wild Bill Hickok in this rowdy
musical set in the Wild West.

MORSE, SUSAN E.
Manhattan (1979)
96 min, b/w, available in cinemascope, r: MGM.
Woody Allen, Diane Keaton, Mariel Hemingway
d: Woody Allen
Set in New York City, Manhattan is about Allen's relationships
with a teenager, his ex-wife, and a confused intellectual.

Stardust Memories (1980)
88 min, b/w, r: MGM.
Woody Allen, Charlotte Rampling, Jessica Harper
d: Woody Allen
Allen's view of fame - how the public reacts to it, and how
his relationships are effected by it - is the subject of this
film.

Arthur (1981)
100 min, c, r: FNC.
Dudley Moore, Sir John Gielgud, Liza Minnelli
d: Steve Gordon
Wonderful comedy about a wealthy drunk who wants to rebel
against family tradition and marry the poor girl that he
loves, even though he would lose his inheritance.

A Midsummer Night's Sex Comedy (1982)
88 min, c, r: FNC.
Woody Allen, Mia Farrow, Jose Ferrer, Mary Steenburgen
d: Woody Allen
Comedy which takes place over one weekend around the turn of
the century about three couples on holiday in the country.

NEWMAN, EVE

Let's Live A Little (1948)
85 min, b/w, r: IVY.
Hedy Lamarr, Bob Cummings
d: Richard Wallace
Comedy concerning a man who is neurotic about a woman doctor.

Bikini Beach (1964)
100 min, c, available in cinemascope, r: FNC.
Frankie Avalon, Annette Funicello
d: William Asher
Frankie and Annette are in danger of having their beach taken
over by a man who wants to use it for a retirement community.

Muscle Beach Party (1964)
96 min, c, available in cinemascope, r: FNC.
Frankie Avalon, Annette Funicello
d: William Asher
Musclemen threaten to take over Frankie and Annette's strip
of the beach.

Pajama Party (1964). Co-editor: Fred Feitschans
85 min, c, r: FNC.
Tommy Kirk, Annette Funicello
d: Don Weis
A martian comes to earth and falls in love with a young
woman.

Sergeant Deadhead (1965). Co-editors: Fred Feitschans, Ronald
Sinclair
89 min, c, r: FNC.
Frankie Avalon, Deborah Walley
d: Norman Taurog
An Air Force sergeant becomes a girl chaser after he comes
back to earth from a space orbit.

Dr. Goldfoot And The Bikini Machine (1965). Co-editors: Fred
Feitschans, Ronald Sinclair
90 min, c, r: FNC.
Vincent Price, Frankie Avalon
d: Norman Taurog
Price is a crazy scientist who manufactures beautiful robots
dressed in bikinis to lure wealthy men in order to obtain
their money.

Fireball 500 (1966). Co-editor: Fred Feitschans
92 min, c, r: FNC.
Frankie Avalon, Annette Funicello, Fabian
d: William Asher
Fabian and Frankie play racecar drivers in competition in
this motion picture.

Three In The Attic (1968). Co-editor: Richard C. Meyer
90 min, c, r: FNC.
Yvette Mimieux, Christopher Jones
d: Richard Wilson
A college student attempts to handle more than one woman
at one time.

Wild In The Streets (1968). Co-editor: Fred Feitschans
96 min, c, r: FNC.
Hal Holbrook, Shelley Winters, Christopher Jones, Diane Varsi
d: Barry Shear
A young superstar runs for president on the platform that he
will put everyone over 35 in retirement camps.

Angel, Angel, Down We Go (Cult Of The Damnèd)(1969)
96 min, c, r: FNC.
Jennifer Jones, Jordan Christopher, Roddy McDowall
d: Richard Thom
Bizarre film about a young man who first has an affair with
a young woman, next her mother, and finally her father.

Bloody Mama (1970)
70 min, c, r: FNC.
Shelley Winters, Pat Hingle, Bruce Dern, Robert De Niro
d: Roger Corman
Exaggerated but fun view of Ma Barker and her sons based on
the real life outlaws.

The Other Side Of The Mountain - Part 2 (1978)
99 min, c, r: SWA.
Marilyn Hassett, Timothy Bottoms
d: Larry Peerce
Sequel of Other Side Of The Mountain which concerns Jill
Kinmont, an Olympic skier made a quadraplegic by a skiing
accident.

Paradise Alley (1978)
107 min, c, r: SWA.
Sylvester Stallone, Armand Assante, Lee Canalito
d: Sylvester Stallone
Stallone's first film as a director is about three brothers
growing up in a New York ghetto and how each makes his way
out.

Little Miss Marker (1980)
103 min, c, r: SWA.
Julie Andrews, Walter Matthau
d: Walter Bernstein
A gambler uses a little girl as collateral in this comedy
remake.

Silence Of The North (1981). Co-editor: Arla Saare
94 min, c, available in cinemascope, r: SWA.
Ellen Burstyn, Tom Skerrit
d: Allan Winton King
Film based on the book by Olive Frederickson about her
experiences in the Canadian wilderness.

RENOIR, MARGUERITE (French)
  La Chienne (1931)
100 min, b/w, subtitles, r: FNC.
Michel Simon, Janie Mareze
d: Jean Renoir
A lonely painter becomes attracted to a loose woman.

Boudu Sauve Des Eaux (Boudu Saved From Drowning)(1932)
Co-editor: Suzanne de Troyes
87 min, b/w, subtitles, r: FNC. r,s: KPF.
Michel Simon, Charles Granval
d: Jean Renoir
A man saves a tramp (who does not want to be saved) from
drowning in the Seine.

Madame Bovary (1934)
102 min, b/w, subtitles, r: FNC.
Pierre Renoir, Valentine Tessier
d: Jean Renoir
Film taken from Flaubert's novel concerning a woman who
lives through her imagination.

Toni (1935)
90 min, b/w, subtitles, r: IMA.
Charles Blavette
d: Jean Renoir
Film concerning an Italian immigrant and his relationship
with two women.

La Crime De Monsieur Lange (The Crime Of Monsieur Lange)(1936)
90 min, b/w, subtitles, r: FNC.
Rene Lafevre, Jules Berry
d: Jean Renoir
Story of a group of workers led by Monsieur Lange, who take
over a publishing company when the owner goes bankrupt.

Les Bas Fonds (The Lower Depths)(1936)
91 min, b/w, subtitles, r: FNC.
Jean Gabin, Louis Jouvet
d: Jean Renoir
A disgraced baron becomes part of a group of bums and social
outcasts who live in Russia's underground.

La Grande Illusion (The Grand Illusion)(1937)
111 min, b/w, subtitles, r: FNC. s: IMA.
Erich von Stroheim, Jean Gabin, Pierre Fresnay
d: Jean Renoir
Excellent film set during World War I involving the lives
and thoughts of French prisoners who are imprisoned in a
castle owned and inhabited by a German nobleman.

La Marseillaise (1938)
137 min, b/w, subtitles, r: COR, KPF.
Louis Jouvet, Lise Delamare
d: Jean Renoir
Set during the French Revolution, this historical film
shows the conflict from both the side of the peasants and the
side of the aristocrats.

La Bete Humaine (Human Desire)(1938)
90 min, b/w, subtitles, r: FNC. r,s: KPF.
Jean Gabin, Simone Simon
d: Jean Renoir
A railroad engineer becomes involved with a married woman
and is driven to commit murder in this intense and sensuous
drama.

La Regle Du Jeu (The Rules Of The Game) (1939)
110 min, b/w, subtitles, r: FNC.
Carl Koch, Jean Renoir
d: Jean Renoir
Excellent film which includes both comedy and drama about the
actions of several people who are spending a weekend at an
elegant French chateau.

ROLAND, RITA
Girl Happy (1965)
96 min, c, r: MGM.
Elvis Presley, Shelley Fabares
d: Boris Sagal
Presley promises to keep an eye on the attractive daughter of
a nightclub owner, but he soon finds that she is more than
he can handle.

A Patch Of Blue (1965)
105 min, b/w, available in cinemascope, r: MGM.
Sidney Poitier, Shelley Winters, Elizabeth Hartman
d: Guy Green
Excellent drama with Hartman as blind girl, Winters as her
dominating mother, and Poitier as the man who befriends the
girl.

The Singing Nun (1966)
98 min, c, available in cinemascope, r: MGM.
Debbie Reynolds, Ricardo Montalban, Greer Garson
d: Henry Koster
Reynolds brightens up her convent with her songs until one
of the songs becomes famous worldwide in this film based
on a true story.

Penelope (1966)
125 min, c, available in cinemascope, r: FNC.
Natalie Wood, Dick Shawn
d: Arthur Hiller
Comedy which features Wood in the title role as a woman
who robs her husband's bank to get his attention.

Spinout (1966)
90 min, c, available in cinemascope, r: MGM.
Elvis Presley, Shelley Fabares
d: Norman Taurog
Presley is pursued by three girls who want to marry him.

Where Were You When The Lights Went Out? (1968)
94 min, c, available in cinemascope, r: MGM.
Doris Day, Robert Morse
d: Hy Averback
Film about the comic trials and tribulations of people
caught during the 1967 New York blackout.

Justine (1969)
115 min, c, cinemascope only, r: FNC.
Anouk Aimee, Dirk Bogarde. Michael York
d: George Cukor
The story of a resourceful woman who helps her husband
smuggle guns into Palestine.

Move (1970)
90 min, c, cinemascope only, r: FNC.
Elliott Gould, Paula Prentiss
d: Stuart Rosenberg
Gould is the author of pornographic books and Prentiss is
his wife in this comedy concerning the couple's problems
after moving to New York.

To Find A Man (1972)
See BOOTH, MARGARET (Editors).

The Betsy (1978)
125 min, c, r: HUR.
Laurence Olivier, Robert Duvall, Katharine Ross
d: Daniel Petrie
Film based on Harold Robbins' novel about an auto tycoon
and his struggle with power.

Resurrection (1980)
103 min, c, r: SWA.
Ellen Burstyn, Sam Shepard, Eva La Gallienne
d: Daniel Petrie
Woman finds that after a near fatal car accident, she has
the ability to heal others.

Fort Apache, The Bronx (1981)
124 min, c, r: MGM.
Paul Newman, Edward Asner, Ken Wahl, Pam Grier
d: Daniel Petrie
Excellent drama set in The Bronx about the daily risks of
police officers and the hate that sometimes develops between the residents and the police.

Six Pack (1982)
110 min, c, r: FNC.
Kenny Rogers, Diane Lane
d: Daniel Petrie
Rogers attempts a comeback to the race car circuit with
the help of a group of kids who act as his pit crew.

ROTHMAN, MARION
The Boston Strangler (1968)
120 min, c, available in cinemascope, r: FNC.
Tony Curtis, Henry Fonda
d: Richard Fleischer
Startling film based on the notorious murderer with Curtis
in the title role.

Beneath The Planet Of The Apes (1970)
95 min, c, cinemascope only, r: FNC.
Charlton Heston, James Franciscus, Kim Hunter, Roddy McDowall
d: Ted Post
Sequel to Planet Of The Apes starring many of the original
stars.

Escape From The Planet Of The Apes (1971)
97 min, c, cinemascope only, r: FNC.
Kim Hunter, Roddy McDowall
d: Don Taylor
Sequel to the sequel.

Play It Again, Sam (1972)
86 min, c, r: FNC.
Woody Allen, Diane Keaton
d: Herbert Ross
Delightful comedy with Allen getting advice on his love life
from Humphrey Bogart.

Tom Sawyer (1973)
99 min, c, available in cinemascope, r: MGM.
Johnny Whitaker, Celeste Holm
d: Don Taylor
Musical version of Mark Twain's book.

Comes A Horseman (1978)
118 min, c, available in cinemascope, r: SWA.
Jane Fonda, James Caan, Jason Robards
d: Alan J. Pakula
Good film about two cattle ranchers who must join together
to save their land from oil businessmen.

Starting Over (1979)
105 min, c, r: FNC.
Burt Reynolds, Jill Clayburgh, Candice Bergen
d: Alan J. Pakula
Film with good mix of comedy and drama about a man trying
to get over a divorce and begin dating again.

All Night Long (1981)
88 min, c, r: SWA.
Barbra Streisand, Gene Hackman, Diane Ladd
d: Jean-Claude Tramont
A man gives up his job and wife, and becomes involved with
another woman, not knowing that his son is dating her.

RYGHE, ULLA (Swedish)
Sasom i en Spegel (Through A Glass Darkly)(1961)
91 min, b/w, subtitles, r: FNC.
Harriet Andersson
d: Ingmar Bergman
A writer attempts to cope with his son and daughter's
emotional crisis during a stay at a summer house.

Nattvargsgästerna (Winter Light)(1962)
80 min, b/w, subtitles, r: FNC.
Ingrid Thulin, Gunnar Bjornstrand
d: Ingmar Bergman
A minister struggles with his faith and the problems of
the people around him.

Tystnaden (The Silence)(1963)
95 min, b/w, subtitles, r: FNC.
Ingrid Thulin, Gunnel Lindblom
d: Ingmar Bergman
Film concerning the stopover in a town by two sisters and
one of the women's little boy, and the events which occur
during the stay.

For Att Inte Tala Om Alla Desse Kvinnor (Not To Mention All
These Women)(1964)
80 min, subtitles, r: FNC.
Eva Dahlbeck, Harriet Andersson, Bibi Andersson
d: Ingmar Bergman
Beginning with the funeral of a musician who mourned by his
wife and several mistresses, this film uses flashback to
give the viewer more information about the dead man.

Persona (1966)
81 min, b/w, subtitles, r: FNC.
Bibi Andersson, Liv Ullman
d: Ingmar Bergman
Excellent study of two women: an actress who refuses to talk
because of an emotional breakdown, and her nurse, who slowly
becomes the patient of the actress as she comes to know more
about her.

Vargtimmen (Hour Of The Wolf)(1968)
88 min, b/w, subtitles, r: MGM..
Max von Sydow, Liv Ullman
d: Ingmar Bergman
The story of a painter's descent into insanity as observed by
him and his wife.

Skämmen (Shame)(1969)
103 min, b/w, subtitles, r: MGM.
Max von Sydow, Liv Ullman
d: Ingmar Bergman
Ullman and von Sydon are musicians who must live on an island
in the midst of a war in this film, which is Bergman's view
of war as God's shame.

SCHOONMAKER, THELMA
Passages From Finnegan's Wake (1965)
See BUTE, MARY ELLEN (Directors, Chapter 1).

Woodstock! (1970)
160 min, c, available in cinemascope, r: SWA.
d: Michael Wadleigh
Documentary filmed during the famous Woodstock rock festival
featuring some of the most influential rock performers of
the 1960's and 70's, including The Who and Joe Cocker.

Raging Bull (1980)
129 min, b/w, r: MGM.
Robert De Niro, Cathy Moriarty, Joe Pesci
d: Martin Scorsese
Film based on the life of Jake La Motta, the infamous New
York boxer.

The King Of Comedy (1983)
101 min, c, r: FNC.
Robert De Niro, Jerry Lewis, Diahnne Abbott
d: Martin Scorsese
De Niro stars as a man who kidnaps his favorite talk show
host in an attempt to get a chance to be on his television
show.

SEWELL, BLANCHE
The Big House (1930)
84 min, b/w, r: MGM.
Chester Morris, Wallace Beery
d: George Hill
Drama which has Beery causing problems for the guards in a
jail.
See MARION, FRANCES (Screenwriters).

The Secret Six (1931)
83 min, b/w, r: MGM.
Clark Gable, Wallace Beery, Jean Harlow
d: George Hill
Gable, in an early role as a reporter, investigates mysterious
deaths connected with a bootleg liquor operation.
See MARION, FRANCES (Screenwriters).

Hell Divers (1931)
113 min, b/w, r: MGM.
Wallace Beery, Clark Gable
d: George Hill
Adventure film about two rival Navy pilots.

Grand Hotel (1932)
115 min, b/w, r: MGM.
John Barrymore, Greta Garbo, Joan Crawford, Wallace Beery
d: Edmund Goulding
Involving drama about the occupants of a hotel with an all-star
cast and great performances.

Red-Headed Woman (1932)
74 min, b/w, r: MGM.
Jean Harlow, Chester Morris
d: Jack Conway
Film about a young woman without much money who becomes
wealthy by way of her various lovers.
See LOOS, ANITA (Screenwriters).

Red Dust (1932)
83 min, b/w, r: MGM.
Jean Harlow, Clark Gable, Mary Astor
d: Victor Fleming

Sensual film about a rubber plantation manager involved with
two women: a sexy, good-humored prostitute and a prim and proper
married woman.

Queen Christina (1933)
100 min, b/w, r: MGM.
Greta Garbo, John Gilbert
d: Rouben Mamoulian
Garbo gives a wonderful performance as a woman who is
mistaken at first for a young man by Gilbert because of
her masculine disguise.

Tugboat Annie (1933)
85 min, b/w, r: MGM.
Marie Dressler, Wallace Beery
d: Mervyn LeRoy
Comedy featuring Dressler and Beery as rival tugboat
pilots.

Broadway Melody Of 1936 (1935)
110 min, b/w, r: MGM.
Jack Benny, Eleanor Powell
d: Roy Del Ruth
Powell shows off her incredible tap dancing in this
musical featuring Metro-Goldwyn-Mayer talent.

Naughty Marietta (1935)
80 min, b/w, r: MGM.
Jeanette MacDonald, Nelson Eddy
d: W.S. Van Dyke
Based on Victor Herbert's operetta, this film was
the first screen teaming of MacDonald and Eddy.
See GOODRICH, FRANCES (Screenwriters).

Born To Dance (1936)
106 min, b/w, r: MGM.
Eleanor Powell, James Stewart
d: Roy Del Ruth
Musical with songs by Cole Porter which features
Powell as a dancer and Stewart as a sailor in love
with her.

Rose Marie (1936)
110 min, b/w, r: MGM.
Jeanette MacDonald, Nelson Eddy
d: W.S. Van Dyke
MacDonald stars as Rose Marie, and Eddy as the
mountie who loves her in this musical.
See GOODRICH, FRANCES (Screenwriters).

The Gorgeous Hussy (1936)
105 min, b/w, r: MGM.
Joan Crawford, Robert Taylor
d: Clarence Brown
Based loosely on fact, this film concerns Peggy Eaton,
the woman for whom President Andrew Jackson fired his
cabinet.

Broadway Melody Of 1938 (1937)
105 min, b/w, r: MGM.
Judy Garland, George Murphy
d: Roy Del Ruth
Another musical showcase for MGM talent, featuring
15-year-old Judy Garland.

Rosalie (1937)
123 min, b/w, r: MGM.
Eleanor Powell, Nelson Eddy
d: W.S. Van Dyke
Extravagant musical with a score by Cole Porter featuring
Powell and Eddy as co-stars.

The Wizard Of Oz (1939)
100 min, b/w & c, r: MGM.
Judy Garland, Ray Bolger, Jack Haley
d: Victor Fleming
Superb fantasy with Garland as a young girl who learns
about courage, knowledge, and love from a scarecrow, a
tin man, and a lion.

Broadway Melody Of 1940 (1940)
102 min, b/w, r: MGM.
Fred Astaire, Eleanor Powell
d: Norman Taurog
The last of the MGM Broadway Melody films features
the dancing talents of Astaire and Powell.

Boom Town (1940)
120 min, b/w, r: MGM.
Clark Gable, Spencer Tracy, Claudette Colbert, Hedy Lamarr
d: Jack Conway
Action-packed film which follows the exploits and friendship of two oil "wildcatters."

Honky Tonk (1941)
105 min, b/w, r: MGM.
Lana Turner, Clark Gable
d: Jack Conway
Western which features Gable as a con-man with a heart
of gold and Turner as his wife.

Ziegfeld Girl (1941)
130 min, b/w, r: MGM.
Judy Garland, Hedy Lamarr, Lana Turner
d: Robert Z. Leonard
Musical/drama with the Ziegfeld Follies as a backdrop
for the careers of three young starlets.
See LEVIEN, SONYA (Screenwriters).

It Happened In Brooklyn (1947)
103 min, b/w, r: MGM.
Frank Sinatra, Kathryn Grayson
d: Richard Whorf
Musical which features Sinatra as a young man determined to make it in show business.
See LENNART, ISOBEL (Screenwriters).

The Pirate (1948)
102 min, c, r: MGM.
Judy Garland, Gene Kelly
d: Vincente Minnelli
Wonderful musical with an incredible dream sequence
about an actor who pretends to be a pirate to attract
the woman that he loves.
See FRANCES, GOODRICH (Screenwriters).

Take Me Out To The Ball Game (1949)
93 min, c, r: MGM.
Frank Sinatra, Esther Williams, Gene Kelly
d: Busby Berkeley
Kelly and Sinatra are surprised to find that the
baseball team on which they play is owned by a woman
in this musical.
See COMDEN, BETTY (Screenwriters).

SPENCER, DOROTHY
  Stand-In (1937). Co-editor: Otho Lovering
  93 min, b/w, r: BUD. FNC.
  Leslie Howard, Joan Blondell, Humphrey Bogart
  d: Tay Garnett
  Blondell is the stand-in in this comedy spoof of
  the movie industry.

Blockade (1938). Co-editor: Otho Lovering
84 min, b/w, r: FNC. r, s: LCA.
Henry Fonda, Madeleine Carroll
d: William Dieterle
Love story which is set during the Spanish Civil War.

Trade Winds (1938). Co-editor: Otho Lovering
94 min, b/w, r: FNC. r, s: LCA.
Joan Bennett,Fredric March
d: Tay Garnett
Bennett is a murder suspect and March the investigating
detective in this mystery.

Stagecoach (1939). Co-editor: Otho Lovering
96 min, b/w, r: FNC.
John Wayne, Claire Trevor, Thomas Mitchell
d: John Ford
Excellent western which involves several passengers
aboard a stagecoach, and the dangers that they face
throughout the trip.

Winter Carnival (1939). Co-editor: Otho Lovering
91 min, b/w, r: FNC.
Ann Sheridan, Virginia Gilmore
d: Charles Reisner
Musical comedy which concerns the annual Winter Carnival at Dartmouth College.

The House Across The Bay (1940). Co-editor: Otho
Lovering
72 min, b/w, r: FNC.
Joan Bennet, George Raft, Adolphe Menjou
d: Archie Mayo
Bennett stars as a woman who falls in love with another
man while her husband is in jail.

Foreign Correspondent (1940). Co-editor: Otho Lovering
82 min, b/w, r: FNC, KPF.
Joel McCrea, Laraine Day
d: Alfred Hitchcock
Intrigue and romance are involved in this film about
a reporter who is trying to track down enemy spies.
See HARRISON, JOAN (Screenwriters).

Slightly Honorable (1940). Co-editor: Otho Lovering
85 min, b/w, r: FNC.
Edward Arnold, Pat O'Brien, Eve Arden
d: Tay Garnett
Murder mystery which stars Arnold as a dishonest poli-
tician and O'Brien as a lawyer out to get him.

Sundown (1941)
92 min, b/w, r: FNC.
Gene Tierney, George Sanders, Joseph Calleia
d: Henry Hathaway
Set in Africa during World War II, this film concerns a young
native woman who decides to aid the British against the Nazis.

To Be Or Not To Be (1942)
90 min, b/w, r: FNC.
Carole Lombard, Jack Benny, Robert Stack
d: Ernst Lubitsch
Superb comedy about a group of actors who must impersonate
Nazi officers, including Hitler, during World War II.

Happy Land (1943)
75 min, b/w, r: FNC.
Don Ameche, Frances Dee, Henry Morgan
d: Irving Pichel
Drama about a man who learns that his son has been killed in
World War II, and how he comes to terms with the death.

Heaven Can Wait (1943)
112 min, c, r: FNC.
Don Ameche, Gene Tierney, Charles Coburn
d: Ernst Lubitsch
A man's experiences and romances are shown in flashback as he
argues with the Devil why he should be allowed to go to Hell.

Lifeboat (1943)
97 min, b/w, r: FNC.
Tallulah Bankhead, John Hodiak, William Bendix
d: Alfred Hitchcock
Drama concerning passengers aboard a lifeboat waiting to be
rescued after their ship is attacked by Germans during World
War II.

A Royal Scandal (1945)
94 min, b/w, r: FNC.
d: Otto Preminger/Ernst Lubitsch
Comedy based on Catherine the Great of Russia.

A Tree Grows In Brooklyn (1945)
128 min, b/w, r: FNC.
Dorothy McGuire, James Dunn, Peggy Ann Garner, Joan Blondell
d: Elia Kazan
Gentle film seen from a little girl's point of view about
a family who must learn to survive after the father's death.

Cluny Brown (1946)
100 min, b/w, r: FNC.
Jennifer Jones, Charles Boyer, Peter Lawford
d: Ernst Lubitsch
Enchanting comedy about a woman plumber and the older man
who falls in love with her.

Dragonwyck   (1946)
103 min, b/w, r: FNC.
Gene Tierney, Vincent Price, Walter Huston
d: Joseph L. Mankiewicz
Unsuspecting Tierney comes to live at a depressing mansion
in this period murder mystery.

My Darling Clementine   (1946)
97 min, b/w, r: FNC.
Henry Fonda, Victor Mature, Linda Darnell
d: John Ford
Fine western about the life of Wyatt Earp with excellent characterizations by Mature as Doc Holliday and Fonda as Earp.

The Ghost And Mrs. Muir   (1947)
104 min, b/w, r: FNC.
Rex Harrison, Gene Tierney
d: Joseph L. Mankiewicz
Tierney is a widow who moves into an old house inhabited by
a sea captain's ghost.

The Snake Pit   (1948)
108 min, b/w, r: FNC.
Olivia de Havilland, Mark Stevens
d: Anatole Litvak
Drama concerning a disturbed young woman and her fight back
to sanity despite being placed in an overcrowded mental institution.

Down To The Sea In Ships   (1949)
120 min, b/w, r: FNC.
Lionel Barrymore, Richard Widmark
d: Henry Hathaway
Adventure film about whale hunters.

It Happens Every Spring   (1949)
87 min, b/w, r: FNC.
Ray Milland, Jean Peters
d: Lloyd Bacon
Romantic comedy involving a chemistry teacher who becomes a
baseball pitcher after he discovers a method to control the
direction of baseballs.

Three Came Home   (1950)
106 min, b/w, r: FNC.
Claudette Colbert, Sessue Hayakawa, Patric Knowles
d: Jean Negulesco
Superb film based on a true story concerning a woman's day to
day life in a Japanese prison camp and her mental anguish
over the safety of her family.

Under My Skin   (1950)
86 min, b/w, r: FNC.
John Garfield, Micheline Prelle
d: Jean Negulesco
Drama based on Ernest Hemingway's My Old Man, a story about a
jockey who wants to become honest for his son.

Decision Before Dawn (1951)
120 min, b/w, r: FNC.
Oskar Werner, Richard Basehart, Gary Merrill, Hildegarde Neff
d: Anatole Litvak
Drama set during World War II.

14 Hours (1951)
91 min, b/w, r: FNC.
Barbara Bel Geddes, Paul Douglas, Richard Basehart
d: Henry Hathaway
Drama concerning a man who climbs onto a window ledge and
threatens to kill himself.

Man On A Tightrope (1953)
105 min, b/w, r: FNC.
Fredric March, Adolphe Menjou, Gloria Grahame
d: Elia Kazan
Drama concerning Czech circus performers and their attempts
to get to the West from the Iron Curtain.

Tonight We Sing (1953)
109 min, c, r: FNC.
David Wayne, Ezio Pinza
d: Mitchell Leisen
Musical biography of Sol Hurok.

Vicki (1953)
85 min, b/w, r: FNC.
Jean Peters, Jeanne Crain, Richard Boone
d: Harry Horner
Boone is a cop investigating a woman's murder in this
thriller.

Black Widow (1954)
95 min, c, cinemascope only, r: FNC.
Ginger Rogers, Gene Tierney, Van Heflin
d: Nunnally Johnson
Fine murder mystery about young aspiring actress who is murdered
and the detective who must find the killer.

Broken Lance (1954)
96 min, c, available in cinemascope, r: FNC.
Spencer Tracy, Robert Wagner, Jean Peters
d: Edward Dmytryk
Tracy is a dishonest ranch owner with four sons in this drama.

Demetrius And The Gladiators (1954). Co-editor: Robert Fritsch
101 min, c, available in cinemascope, r: FNC.
Susan Hayward, Victor Mature, Anne Bancroft
d: Delmer Daves
Dramatic sequel to The Robe stars Mature as Demetrius.

Night People (1954)
93 min, c, r: FNC.
Gregory Peck, Broderick Crawford
d: Nunnally Johnson
Espionage story involving the attempt to rescue a kidnapped
American soldier from Berlin.

The Left Hand Of God (1955)
87 min, c, available in cinemascope, r: FNC.
Gene Tierney, Humphrey Bogart, Agnes Moorehead
d: Edward Dmytryk
Good action film set in China with Bogart posing as a priest.

Prince Of Players (1955)
105 min, c, r: FNC.
Richard Burton, John Derek, Maggie McNamara
d: Philip Dunne
Biographical study of John Wilkes Booth's brother, Edwin.

The Rains Of Ranchipur (1955)
104 min, c, r: FNC.
Richard Burton, Lana Turner, Fred MacMurray
d: Jean Negulesco
Remake of The Rains Came about a proper woman who falls in
love with a half-caste.

Soldier Of Fortune (1955)
96 min, c, cinemascope only, r: FNC.
Clark Gable, Susan Hayward, Gene Barry
d: Edward Dmytryk
Adventure film involving Gable as a "soldier of fortune"
investigating the disappearance of Hayward's husband.

The Best Things In Life Are Free (1956)
104 min, c, r: FNC.
Gordon MacRae, Dan Dailey
d: Michael Curtiz
Musical biography of 1920's songwriters DeSylva, Brown, and
Henderson.

The Man In The Gray Flannel Suit (1956)
152 min, c, available in cinemascope, r: FNC.
Gregory Peck, Jennifer Jones, Fredric March
d: Nunnally Johnson
Drama based on the best seller by Sloan Wilson about an
advertising man who must decide between his career and
his family.

A Hatful Of Rain (1957)
107 min, b/w, available in cinemascope, r: FNC.
Don Murray, Eva Marie Saint
d: Fred Zinnemann
Drama concerning a drug addict and his struggle to rehabilitate.

The Young Lions (1958)
167 min, b/w, available in cinemascope, r: FNC.
Marlon Brando, Montgomery Clift, Dean Martin
d: Edward Dmytryk
Drama concerning three soldiers - two Americans, and one
German during World War II.

The Journey (1959). Co-editor: Bert Bates
122 min, c, r: MGM.
Yul Brynner, Deborah Kerr, Jason Robards
d: Anatole Litvak
Drama with an all-star cast about a group of people trying
to escape from Hungary during the 1950's.

From The Terrace (1960)
144 min, c, available in cinemascope, r: FNC.
Paul Newman, Joanne Woodward
d: Mark Robson
A young man becomes too involved in his career and money, and
finds that he is ruining his life and destroying his marriage.

North To Alaska (1960)
122 min, c, available in cinemascope, r: FNC.
John Wayne, Stewart Granger, Ernie Kovacs
d: Henry Hathaway
Fast moving comedy/adventure about the trials of two rowdy
prospectors.

Seven Thieves (1960)
102 min, b/w, cinemascope only, r: FNC.
Edward G. Robinson, Eli Wallach, Rod Steiger
d: Henry Hathaway
Seven people plan a robbery in Monte Carlo in this well-timed
drama.

Cleopatra (1963)
186 min, c, available in cinemascope, r: FNC.
Elizabeth Taylor, Richard Burton, Rex Harrison
d: Joseph L. Mankiewicz
Elaborate "historical" drama about the Egyptian ruler
and her various relationships.

Circus World (1964)
135 min, c, r: FNC.
John Wayne, Rita Hayworth, Claudia Cardinale
d: Henry Hathaway
Film involving a circus in financial trouble and the problems
of its performers.

Von Ryan's Express (1965)
117 min, c, available in cinemascope, r: FNC.
Frank Sinatra, Trevor Howard
d: Mark Robson
Adventure story set during World War II in an Italian prison
camp which features Sinatra as a soldier who plans an escape
for his men and himself.

A Guide For The Married Man (1967)
91 min, c, available in cinemascope, r: FNC.
Walter Matthau, Robert Morse, Inger Stevens
d: Gene Kelly
Comedy about husbands trying their best to keep their
extramarital affairs from their wives.

Valley Of The Dolls   (1967)
120 min, c, available in cinemascope, r: FNC.
Patty Duke, Sharon Tate, Barbara Parkins
d: Mark Robson
Drama based on Jacqueline Susann's novel about three women in
Hollywood and how each copes with problems in her life and
show business career.

Daddy's Gone A-Hunting   (1969)
108 min, c, r: SWA.
Carol White, Scott Hylands
d: Mark Robson
Horror film in which a crazy man stalks his first wife and her son.

Happy Birthday, Wanda June   (1971)
105 min, c, r: FNC.
Rod Steiger, Susannah York, Don Murray, George Grizzard
d: Mark Robson
Based on Kurt Vonnegut's satirical play, this film concerns
a man who returns to his wife unexpectedly after an eight
year absence.

Limbo   (1972)
112 min, c, r: SWA.
Kate Jackson, Kathleen Nolan
d: Mark Robson
Excellent drama concerning three women whose husbands are believed
to be missing or dead in Vietnam.
See SILVER, JOAN MICKLIN   (Screenwriters).

Earthquake   (1974)
129 min, c, r: CLE.
Charlton Heston, Ava Gardner, George Kennedy
d: Mark Robson
All-star cast attempts to survive a massive earthquake in
Los Angeles in this "disaster" film.

The Concorde - Airport '79   (1979)
123 min, c, r: SWA.
Robert Wagner, Alain Delon, Susan Blakely
d: David Lowell Rich
Fourth film in the Airport series has all-star cast aboard the
Concorde.

TURNER, HELEN
Undersea Kingdom   (1936)
Serial, 12 chapters, b/w, r: IVY.
Ray Corrigan, Monte Blue, William Farnum, Lois Wilde
d: B. Reeves Eason/Joseph Kane
Adventure serial about explorers in a submarine who find the
lost continent of Atlantis.

The Vigilantes Are Coming   (1936)
Serial, 12 chapters, b/w, r: IVY.
Bob Livingston, Kay Hughes, Raymond Hatton
d: Mack V. Wright/Ray Taylor
The mysterious Eagle must stop General Burr from stealing his
family's land and becoming dictator of the country.

Robinson Crusoe Of Clipper Island (1936)
Serial, 14 chapters, 253 min, b/w, r: IVY.
Mala, Rex Buck, Herbert Rawlinson
d: Mack V. Wright/Ray Taylor
Mala finds a group of international spies on Clipper Island
who have sabotaged a dirigible.

The Painted Stallion (1937)
Serial, 12 chapters, b/w, r: IVY.
Ray Corrigan, Hoot Gibson
d: William Witney/Ray Taylor
An American agent fights criminals in the west who are
trying to disrupt a trade agreement with Mexico.

Zorro Rides Again (1937)
Serial, 12 chapters, 217 min, b/w, r: IVY.
John Carroll, Reed Howes, Duncan Renaldo
d: William Witney/John English
Zorro must fight criminals trying to take control of a
railroad company.

S.O.S. Coast Guard (1937)
Serial, 12 chapters, b/w, r: IVY.
Ralph Byrd, Bela Lugosi, Maxine Doyle
d: William Witney/Alan James
Lugosi is a mad scientist using deadly gas in warfare in
this serial.

Hawk Of The Wilderness (1938)
Serial, 12 chapters, b/w, r: IVY.
Herman Brix (Bruce Bennett)
d: William Witney/John English
A scientist and his family search for a lost tribe on a
volcanic island and find themselves lost.

Fighting Devil Dogs (1938)
Serial, 12 chapters, 100 min, b/w, r: IVY.
Lee Powell, Herman Brix (Bruce Bennett)
d: William Witney/John English/Robert Beche
Two marines try to find out what kind of weapon causes
a huge thunderbolt.

WARREN, EDA
Dangerous Curves (1929)
79 min, b/w, r: SWA.
Clara Bow, Richard Arlen
d: Lothar Mendes
Bow is a bareback rider and Arlen is a tightrope walker in
this drama about life and love in the circus.

The Big Broadcast (1932)
97 min, b/w, r: SWA.
George Burns, Gracie Allen, Bing Crosby
d: Frank Tuttle
Music of the big bands and comedy from Burns and Allen make
this a very entertaining film.

So Red The Rose (1935)
83 min, b/w, r: SWA.
Margaret Sullavan, Walter Connolly
d: King Vidor
Drama concerning a proud Louisiana family destroyed by
the Civil War.

Anything Goes (1936)
95 min, b/w, r: FNC.
Bing Crosby, Ethel Merman
d: Lewis Milestone
Musical starring Crosby and Merman singing some of Cole Porter's
greatest songs.

The General Died At Dawn (1936)
93 min, b/w, r: SWA.
Gary Cooper, Madeleine Carroll
d: Lewis Milestone
Cooper stars as O'Hara, an American who attempts to help the
peasants against the cruel General Yang.

Swing High, Swing Low (1937)
96 min, b/w, r: BUD.
Carole Lombard, Fred MacMurray
d: Mitchell Leisen
Lombard and MacMurray are entertainers in a club in Panama
in this beautifully photographed motion picture.

The Big Broadcast Of 1938 (1938)
91 min, b/w, r: SWA.
W. C. Fields, Bob Hope, Dorothy Lamour
d: Mitchell Leisen
Variety film showcasing Paramount's biggest talents of 1938.

Virginia (1941)
109 min, b/w, r: SWA.
Madeleine Carroll, Fred MacMurray
d: Edward H. Griffith
Carroll goes home to Virginia to sell the family mansion
but decides to remain there instead.

I Married A Witch (1942)
80 min, b/w, r: FNC, KPF. s: LCA.
Fredric March, Veronica Lake, Susan Hayward
d: Rene Clair
Lake is a witch who comes back to haunt March on his wedding
day in this comedy.

And The Angels Sing (1944)
96 min, b/w, r: SWA.
Betty Hutton, Dorothy Lamour
d: George Marshall
Good music and comedy are featured in this film about sisters
trying to get their first big break in show business.

Two Years Before The Mast (1946)
98 min, b/w, r: SWA.
Alan Ladd, Brian Donlevy
d: John Farrow
This drama concerns the sailors on a ship run by a cruel
and sadistic captain.

Submarine Command (1951)
87 min, b/w, r: FNC.
William Holden, Nancy Olsen
d: John Farrow
Holden is excellent in this story of a Navy officer after
World War II who is still haunted by actions that he took
during wartime.

Son Of Paleface (1952)
95 min, c, r: FNC.
Bob Hope, Jane Russell
d: Frank Tashlin
Hope and Russell take care of business in the Wild West in
this comedy.

Pony Express (1953)
101 min, c, r: FNC.
Charlton Heston, Rhonda Fleming
d: Jerry Hopper
Western which tells the story of Wild Bill Hickok and Buffalo
Bill Cody.

Secret Of The Incas (1954)
101 min, c, r: FNC.
Charlton Heston, Robert Young
d: Jerry Hopper
Adventure film about a group of archaelogists in Peru.

Strategic Air Command (1955)
114 min, c, r: FNC.
James Stewart, June Allyson
d: Anthony Mann
Excellent tribute to the Air Force stars Stewart as a baseball
player called back into the service, and Allyson as his wife
who helps him through his career problems.

At Gunpoint (1956)
81 min, c, r: HUR.
Fred MacMurray, Dorothy Malone
d: Alfred Werker
Sheriff MacMurray faces a dangerous shootout with gunmen in
this western.

Back From Eternity (1956)
98 min, b/w, r: KPF.
Robert Ryan, Rod Steiger
d: John Farrow
Drama concerning the passengers on an airplane which has
crashed in South America.

World Without End (1956)
80 min, c, r: HUR.
Hugh Marlowe, Nancy Gates
d: Edward Bernds
Surprised earthlings headed for Mars go through the time
barrier and land on Earth in a future time.

The Unholy Wife (1957)
94 min, c, r: BUD.
Diana Dors, Rod Steiger
d: John Farrow
Drama about a woman convicted of murder who is waiting to
go to the gas chamber.

St. Louis Blues (1958)
93 min, b/w, r: FNC.
Nat "King" Cole, Eartha Kitt
d: Allen Reisner
Film biography of the Black composer W.C. Handy.

Wreck Of The Mary Deare (1959)
105 min, c, available in cinemascope, r: FNC.
Gary Cooper, Charlton Heston
d: Michael Anderson
Cooper is the only survivor of the wreck of a ship which he
suspects was sabotaged.

John Paul Jones (1959)
126 min, c, r: FNC.
Robert Stack, Bette Davis
d: John Farrow
Film biography of John Paul Jones.

One Foot In Hell (1960)
90 min, c, cinemascope only, r: FNC.
Alan Ladd, Don Murray
d: James B. Clark
Ladd stars as a man determined to kill three men who he thinks
caused his wife's death in this drama, set after the Civil
War.

The Young Savages (1961)
100 min, b/w, r: FNC.
Burt Lancaster, Shelley Winters
d: John Frankenheimer
Drama concerning juvenile delinquents and their parents.

CHAPTER 4

SCREENWRITERS

SCREENWRITERS

The women listed in this chapter wrote almost exclusively for motion pictures, unlike many authors who had one or two literary successes which they adapted for the screen, and in so doing, became "screenwriters." The writers included here are only a small percentage of the many women who have been involved in writing for the screen, for women have been scriptwriting since the beginning of motion pictures. Before sound movies existed, women such as Frances Marion and Anita Loos were writing the title cards for silent films.

There are several women who wrote screenplays with their husbands, and these collaborations yielded successful motion pictures, both artistically and financially. Ruth Gordon and Garson Kanin, Edna and Edward Anhalt, Harriet Frank, Jr. and Irving Ravetch, Frances Goodrich and Albert Hackett, and Fay and Michael Kanin are all examples of wife-husband collaboration. There are also instances of husbands directing their wives' screenplays, as in the case of Alma Reville and Alfred Hitchcock, Anita Loos and John Emerson, and Eleanor and Frank Perry.

Of course, not all of these women wrote only with their husbands. Several, such as Ruth Gordon, Anita Loos, and Edna Anhalt have had enormously successful screenplays which they wrote either with other writers or alone. And, as significant as collaborations may be, they should never overshadow the extraordinary contributions by women who worked alone.

The films in this chapter are in chronological order and are available for rental and/or sale. Filmographies of some of the screenwriters are listed in the back of the book.

ALLEN, JAY PRESSON
  Marnie (1964)
  130 min, c, r: CLE.
  Sean Connery, Tippi Hedren, Diane Baker
  d: Alfred Hitchcock
  Drama about a woman who is a kleptomaniac, terrified of men
  and the color red. Connery is the man who tries to cure her
  of all three manias.

  The Prime Of Miss Jean Brodie (1969)
  116 min, c, r: FNC.
  Maggie Smith, Robert Stephens, Pamela Franklin
  d: Ronald Neame
  Smith won an Academy Award for her performance as Miss Brodie,
  a strong-minded and romantic teacher who offers her students
  "her prime".

  Travels With My Aunt (1972)
  110 min, c, r: MGM.
  Maggie Smith, Alex McCowen, Lou Gossett
  d: George Cukor
  McCowen is the befuddled nephew who is taken on a tour of Europe
  by his crazy and uninhibited aunt.

  Cabaret (1972)
  123 min, c, r: HUR.
  Liza Minnelli, Michael York, Joel Grey
  d: Bob Fosse
  Superb musical based on Christopher Isherwood's stories about
  a cabaret in Germany during the years before World War II.

  Funny Lady (1975)
  See BOOTH, MARGARET (Editors).

  Just Tell Me What You Want (1979)
  135 min, c, r: SWA.
  Ali McGraw, Alan King, Myrna Loy
  d: Sidney Lumet
  King is a crooked tycoon and McGraw his straying mistress in this
  comedy drama.

  Deathtrap (1982)
  115 min, c, r: SWA.
  Michael Caine, Christopher Reeve, Dyan Cannon
  d: Sidney Lumet
  Film version of Ira Levin's Broadway comedy thriller about a
  writer who is desperate enough to murder for a successful play.

  Prince Of The City (1981). Co-writer: Sidney Lumet
  167 min, c, r: FNC.
  Treat Williams, Lindsay Crouse, Jerry Orbach
  d: Sidney Lumet
  Excellent drama based on a true story about a New York policeman who cooperates with authorities concerning police corruption, and the consequences that he faces.

ANHALT, EDNA

Embraceable You (1948)
80 min, b/w, r: MGM.
Dane Clark, Geraldine Brooks
d: Felix Jacoves
Romance involving a man who begins to fall in love with a girl
that he has injured.

Sierra (1950)
83 min, c, r: SWA.
Audie Murphy, Wanda Hendrix
d: Alfred E. Green
Drama concerning a man and his son who attempt to escape the
police and prove their innocence.

Panic In The Streets (1950). Co-writer: Edward Anhalt
96 min, b/w, r: FNC.
Richard Widmark, Barbara Bel Geddes
d: Elia Kazan
Good drama involving a doctor's search for a murderer who is
a carrier of a highly contagious disease.

The Sniper (1952). Co-writers: Edward Anhalt, Harry Brown
87 min, b/w, r: BUD, KPF.
Adolphe Menjou, Arthur Franz
d: Edward Dmytryk
Franz stars as a mentally disturbed man who kills women.

The Member Of The Wedding (1953). Co-writer: Edward Anhalt
91 min, b/w, r: FNC.
Julie Harris, Ethel Waters
d: Fred Zinnemann
Excellent motion picture set in the South based on Carson McCullers'
story of a young girl facing the pain of growing up.

Not As A Stranger (1955). Co-writer: Edward Anhalt
135 min, b/w, r: MGM.
Olivia de Havilland, Robert Mitchum
d: Stanley Kramer
Drama starring Mitchum as a medical student being supported by
a nurse.

The Pride And The Passion (1957). Co-writer: Edward Anhalt
132 min, c, r: MGM.
Sophia Loren, Cary Grant, Frank Sinatra
d: Stanley Kramer
Historical drama set during the Spanish revoution.

BRACKETT, LEIGH

The Vampire's Ghost (1945)
54 min, b/w, r: IVY.
Charles Gordon, Adele Mara
d: Lesley Selander
Unusual film with vampire as a soft-spoken owner of an African
bar and gambling house.

The Big Sleep (1946). Co-writers: William Faulkner, Jules Furthman
114 min, b/w, r: MGM.
Humphrey Bogart, Lauren Bacall
d: Howard Hawks
Excellent mystery which stars Bogart as private detective
Philip Marlowe.

Rio Bravo (1959). Co-writer: Jules Furthman
141 min, c, r: FNC.
John Wayne, Dean Martin, Angie Dickinson, Ricky Nelson
d: Howard Hawks
Superb western featuring Wayne as a sheriff who must protect
his town against a group of hoods with only a gunslinger
(Nelson), a drunk (Martin), and an old man (Walter Brennan)
to help him.

Hatari! (1962)
158 min, c, r: FNC.
John Wayne, Red Buttons
d: Howard Hawks
Adventure film set in Africa with Wayne as a hunter of wild
animals for preservation.

El Dorado (1967)
126 min, c, r: FNC.
John Wayne, Robert Mitchum
d: Howard Hawks
Mitchum is an alcoholic sheriff who is helped by Wayne when
villains threaten to take over the town.

Rio Lobo (1970). Co-writer: Burton Wohl
114 min, c, r: SWA.
d: Howard Hawks
Retelling of Rio Bravo with Wayne as a soldier seeking revenge
for the death of a friend with the help of a farmer, three
women, and two Confederate soldiers.

The Long Goodbye (1973)
112 min, c, cinemascope only, r: MGM.
Elliott Gould, Sterling Hayden
d: Robert Altman
Interesting remake of The Big Sleep with Gould as detective
Marlowe in a contemporary setting.

COMDEN, BETTY
    NOTE: All scripts and songs were co-written with Adolph Green.
    Good News (1947)
    92 min, c, r: MGM.
    June Allyson, Peter Lawford
    d: Charles Walters
    Great musical containing several hit songs which stars Allyson
    and Lawford as college students.

    Take Me Out To The Ball Game (1949)
    (Songs co-written with Roger Edens).
    See SEWELL, BLANCHE (Editors).

The Barkleys Of Broadway (1949)
110 min, c, r: MGM.
Fred Astaire, Ginger Rogers, Oscar Levant
d: Charles Walters
Fred and Ginger are a married couple in show business who
separate because one wants to stay in musicals, while the
other wants to perform in dramas.

On The Town (1949)
98 min, c, r: MGM.
Gene Kelly, Frank Sinatra, Vera-Ellen
d: Gene Kelly/Stanley Donen
(Songs co-written with Roger Edens).
Exeptional musical involving three sailors on leave in New
York City.

Singin' In The Rain (1952)
(Songs co-written with Roger Edens).
See FAZAN, ADRIENNE (Editors).

The Band Wagon (1953)
111 min, c, r: MGM.
Fred Astaire, Nanette Fabray, Jack Buchanan
d: Vincente Minnelli
Excellent musical about an aging star's comeback with the
help of his friends.

It's Always Fair Weather (1955)
See FAZAN, ADRIENNE (Editors).

Bells Are Ringing (1960)
(Songs co-written with Jule Styne).
See FAZAN, ADRIENNE (Editors).

What A Way To Go! (1964)
See FOWLER, MARJORIE (Editors).

FRANK, JR., HARRIET
Silver River (1948). Co-writer: Stephen Longstreet
110 min, b/w, r: MGM.
Errol Flynn, Ann Sheridan
d: Raoul Walsh
Western which takes place during the 1860's and features
Flynn as a gambler who becomes power crazy.

Whiplash (1949). Co-writer: Maurice Geraghty
91 min, b/w, r: MGM.
Dane Clark, Alexis Smith, Eve Arden
d: Lewis Seiler
Drama concerning an artist who becomes involved with a woman
who is married to a boxer.

The Long, Hot Summer (1958). Co-writer: Irving Ravetch
115 min, c, available in cinemascope, r: FNC.
Orson Welles, Paul Newman, Joanne Woodward
d: Martin Ritt
Newman is an attractive stranger who disrupts a Southern
and its most powerful family.

The Sound And The Fury (1959). Co-writer: Irving Ravetch
115 min, c, available in cinemascope, r: FNC.
Joanne Woodward, Yul Brynner
d: Martin Ritt
Drama based on William Faulkner's novel concerning the members
of a decaying Southern family.

Home From The Hill (1960). Co-writer: Irving Ravetch
150 min, c, available in cinemascope, r: FNC.
Robert Mitchum, George Peppard, Eleanor Parker, George Hamilton
d: Vincente Minnelli
Intense drama set in the South with a fine cast concerning a
man and his two sons - one of whom is illegitimate.

The Dark At The Top Of The Stairs (1960). Co-writer: Irving Ravetch
124 min, c, r: SWA.
Robert Preston, Dorothy McGuire, Eve Arden
d: Delbert Mann
Drama based on William Inge's play about a family living in
Oklahoma during the 1920's.

Hud (1963). Co-writer: Irving Ravetch
112 min, b/w, available in cinemascope, r: FNC.
Paul Newman, Patricia Neal, Melvyn Douglas
d: Martin Ritt
Superb film involving a young man who has no regard for anything
or anyone but himself, despite the problems of his aging
father, and the family ranch.

Hombre (1967). Co-writer: Irving Ravetch
111 min, c, available in cinemascope, r: FNC.
Paul Newman, Fredric March
d: Martin Ritt
Western concerning a white man, raised since youth by Indians,
who returns to cililization when he inherits a boarding house.

The Reivers (1969). Co-writer: Irving Ravetch
107 min, c, available in cinemascope, r: SWA.
Steve McQueen, Sharon Farrell, Mitch Vogel
d: Mark Rydell
Film Based on Faulkner's novel about a young teenager who
learns his first lessons about growing up from his older
friend as they drive through the South around the turn of
the century.

The Cowboys (1972). Co-writers: William Dale Jennings, Irving
Ravetch
128 min, c, r: BUD, FNC.
John Wayne, Bruce Dern
d: Mark Rydell
Violent western concerning a group of young boys who must
take over a cattle drive when their boss is fatally shot.

Conrack (1974). Co-writer: Irving Ravetch
106 min, c, available in cinemascope, r: FNC.
Jon Voight, Hume Cronyn

d: Martin Ritt
Fine motion picture about a young teacher and the frustrations
he encounters as he tries to educate a group of illiterate
children in the Deep South.

Norma Rae (1979). Co-writer: Irving Ravetch
115 min, c, available in cinemascope, r: FNC.
Sally Field, Ron Liebman, Beau Bridges
d: Martin Ritt
Drama based on a true story about a young woman who risks
everything in order to organize the mill where she works
into a union.

GOODRICH, FRANCES
NOTE: All scripts were co-written with Albert Hackett.
The Secret Of Madame Blanche (1933)
78 min, b/w, r: MGM.
Irene Dunne, Douglas Walton
d: Charles Brabin
Drama concerning woman who hides her identity from her son.

Penthouse (1933)
90 min, b/w, r: MGM.
Myrna Loy, Warner Baxter
d: W. S. Van Dyke
Witty mystery film concerning the murder of a young woman
and the search for her killer.

Fugitive Lovers (1934). Co-writer: George B. Seitz
90 min, b/w, r: MGM.
Robert Montgomery, Madge Evans, Three Stooges
d: Richard Boleslawski
Montgomery is a escaped convict traveling from New York to
Los Angeles on a bus in this film.

The Thin Man (1934)
100 min, b/w, r: MGM.
William Powell, Myrna Loy
d: W. S. Van Dyke
Outstanding mixture of mystery and wit involving Powell and
Loy as crime-solving detectives Nick and Nora Charles.

Hideout (1934)
92 min, b/w, r: MGM.
Robert Montgomery, Maureen O'Sullivan, Edward Arnold
d: W. S. Van Dyke
City hood falls in love with a farmer's daughter while hiding
out in the countryside.

Naughty Marietta (1935). Co-writer: John Lee Mahin
See SEWELL, BLANCHE (Editors).

Ah, Wilderness! (1935)
101 min, b/w, r: MGM.
Wallace Beery, Lionel Barrymore, Mickey Rooney
d: Clarence Brown
Good study of a young boy going through the pain of growing
up, based on Eugene O'Neill's play.

<u>Rose Marie</u> (1936). Co-writer: Alice Duer Miller
See SEWELL, BLANCHE (Editors).

<u>After The Thin Man</u> (1939)
110 min, b/w, r: MGM.
William Powell, Myrna Loy, James Stewart
d: W. S. Van Dyke
Good sequel to <u>The Thin Man</u>.

<u>The Firefly</u> (1937). Co-writer: Ogdan Nash
131 min, b/w, r: MGM.
Jeanette MacDonald, Allan Jones
d: Robert Z. Leonard
Operetta set in Spain concerning a young woman who falls in
love with a soldier.

<u>Society Lawyer</u> (1939). Co-writers: Hugo Butler, Leon Gordon
77 min, b/w, r: MGM.
Virginia Bruce, Walter Pidgeon
d: Edward L. Marin
Remake of <u>Penthouse</u>.

<u>Another Thin Man</u> (1939)
102 min, b/w, r: MGM.
William Powell, Myrna Loy
d: W. S. Van Dyke
Third film in the <u>Thin Man</u> series.

<u>Lady In The Dark</u> (1944)
See MACRORIE, ALMA RUTH (Editors).

<u>The Virginian</u> (1946)
87 min, c, r: SWA.
Joel McCrea, Brian Donlevy
d: Stuart Gilmore
Western featuring McCrea in the title role as a quiet but
determined cowboy.

<u>It's A Wonderful Life</u> (1946). Co-writer: Frank Capra
130 min, b/w, r: FNC.
James Stewart, Donna Reed, Thomas Mitchell
d; Frank Capra
A suicidal man is shown how his life has affected different
people by his guardian angel in this outstanding film.

<u>The Pirate</u> (1945)
See SEWELL, BLANCHE (Editors).

<u>Summer Holiday</u> (1948)
92 min, b/w, r: MGM.
Mickey Rooney, Gloria De Haven, Agnes Moorehead
d: Rouben Mamoulian
Musical remake of <u>Ah Wilderness!</u>

<u>Easter Parade</u> (1948). Co-writer: Sidney Sheldon
103 min, c, r: MGM.
Fred Astaire, Judy Garland, Peter Lawford

d: Charles Walters
Delightful musical containing several songs by Irving Berlin concerning a dance team.

In The Good Old Summertime (1949). Co-writer: Ivan Tors
See FAZAN, ADRIENNE (Editors).

Father Of The Bride (1950)
92 min, b/w, r: MGM.
Spencer Tracy, Elizabeth Taylor, Joan Bennett
d: Vincente Minnelli
Excellent comedy about a husband and wife's struggle to survive their daughter's wedding.

Father's Little Dividend (1951)
82 min, b/w, r: MGM.
Spencer Tracy, Elizabeth Taylor
d: Vincente Minnelli
Sequel to Father Of The Bride.

Too Young To Kiss (1951)
89 min, b/w, r: MGM.
June Allyson, Van Johnson, Gig Young
d: Robert Z. Leonard
A frustrated pianist disguises herself as a little girl in order that she will appear to be a child prodigy in this romantic comedy.

Give A Girl A Break (1953)
See FAZAN, ADRIENNE (Editors).

The Long, Long Trailer (1954)
95 min, c, r: MGM.
Lucille Ball, Desi Arnaz
d: Vincente Minnelli
Everything that could possibly go wrong, does, in this comedy about a newly married couple who go on their honeymoon in a mobile home.

Seven Brides For Seven Brothers (1954). Co-writer: Dorothy Kingsley
102 min, c, available in cinemascope, r: MGM.
Jane Powell, Howard Keel
d: Stanley Donen
Energetic musical about six brothers who decide to get married after their eldest brother marries.

Gaby (1956). Co-writer: Charles Lederer
97 min, c, r: MGM.
Leslie Caron, John Kerr
d: Curtis Bernhardt
A young soldier falls in love with a ballerina during World War II.

A Certain Smile (1958)
106 min, c, cinemascope only, r: FNC.
Rossano Brazzi, Joan Fontaine, Bradford Dillman
d: Jean Negulesco
Film concerning a young woman's romances with a student and an older man.

The Diary Of Anne Frank   (1959)
170 min, b/w, available in cinemascope, r: FNC.
Millie Perkins, Shelley Winters, Ed Wynn
d: George Stevens
Strong drama taken from a young Jewish girl's diary
written in hiding from the Nazis during World War II.

Five Finger Exercise   (1962)
109 min, b/w, r: FNC.
Rosalind Russell, Jack Hawkins, Maximilian Schell
d: Daniel Mann
Drama based on Peter Shaffer's play concerning a
dominant mother who causes her family great unhappiness.

GORDON, RUTH
A Double Life   (1947). Co-writer: Garson Kanin
103 min, b/w, r: BUD.
Ronald Colman, Signe Hasso, Shelley Winters
d: George Cukor
Excellent drama about an actor who begins to take on
the character of Othello off-stage in his daily life
as well as on-stage.

Adam's Rib   (1949). Co-writer: Garson Kanin
101 min, b/w, r: MGM.
Spencer Tracy, Katharine Hepburn
d: George Cukor
A married couple are opposing lawyers in a court case
in this superb comedy.

The Marrying Kind   (1951)
93 min, b/w, r: FNC.
Judy Holliday, Aldo Ray
d: George Cukor
Beautifully directed comedy drama told mostly in flashbacks about a couple's marital problems.

Pat And Mike   (1952). Co-writer: Garson Kanin
95 min, b/w, r: MGM.
Spencer Tracy, Katharine Hepburn, Aldo Ray
d: George Cukor
Hepburn is an all-round athlete and Tracy is her wily
manager in this comedy.

The Actress   (1953)
90 min, b/w, r: MGM.
Spencer Tracy, Jean Simmons, Teresa Wright
d: George Cukor
Unconventional film based on Gordon's early life about a
young woman and her decision to go into acting despite
the opinions of her boyfriend and family.

HARRISON, JOAN
Jamaica Inn (1939). Co-writer: Sidney Gilliat
98 min, b/w, r: FNC.
Charles Laughton, Maureen O'Hara
d: Alfred Hitchcock
Film based on Daphne du Maurier's novel about a young
woman who becomes involved with a pirate after moving
to the coast of England.

Rebecca (1940). Co-writer: Robert E. Sherwood
115 min, b/w, r: FNC.
Laurence Olivier, Joan Fontaine
d: Alfred Hitchcock
Joan Fontaine is excellent as a young bride who is
constantly reminded by objects and events of her husband's first wife who died mysteriously.

Foreign Correspondent (1940). Co-writer: Charles Bennet
See SPENCER, DOROTHY (Editors).

Suspicion (1941). Co-writers: Samson Raphaelson, Alma
Reville
99 min, b/w, r: FNC.
Cary Grant, Joan Fontaine
d: Alfred Hitchcock
Tense mystery involving a woman who slowly begins to
believe that her husband is trying to murder her.
See REVILLE, ALMA (Screenwriters).

Saboteur (1942). Co-writers: Dorothy Parker, Peter
Viertel
98 min, b/w, r: CLE.
Robert Cummings, Priscilla Lane
d: Alfred Hitchcock
Cummings stars as a young man wrongly accused of sabo-
taging a World War II munitions plant who must prove
his innocence.

Dark Waters (1944). Co-writer: Marian Cockrell
90 min, b/w, r: IVY.
Merle Oberon, Franchot Tone, Thomas Mitchell
d: Andre de Toth
Oberon is a young woman who, because of certain odd
happenings, begins to suspect someone wants to drive
her crazy.

JHABVALA, RUTH PRAWER (British)
  Gharbar (The Householder) (1963)
  101 min, b/w, r: COR.
  d: James Ivory
  Film about a young couple's marital problems.

  Shakespeare-Wallah (1965)
  110 min, b/w, r: COR.
  d: James Ivory
  The story of an English theatre troupe and their adventures while touring through India.

  The Guru (1969)
  112 min, c, r: FNC.
  Michael York
  d: James Ivory
  York is a singer who journeys through India to learn
  the art of the sitar from a guru.

  Bombay Talkie (1970)
  110 min, c, r: FNC.
  d: James Ivory
  Wonderful spoof of the film industry in India.

  Roseland (1977)
  103 min, c, r: FNC.
  Teresa Wright, Lou Jacobi, Geraldine Chaplin
  d: James Ivory
  Three vignettes concerning lonely people who go to
  Roseland, a ballroom in New York City, to find romance.

  The Europeans (1979)
  90 min, c, r: FNC.
  Lee Remick, Lisa Eichhorn
  d: James Ivory
  Drama based on Henry James' novel about a family who is
  surprised when their cousins arrive from Europe to
  visit them.

  Hullabaloo Over Georgie And Bonnie's Pictures (1979)
  85 min, c, r: COR.
  Dame Peggy Ashcroft, Victor Banerjee
  d: James Ivory
  Everybody is after Georgie's priceless miniature paintings, including his sister Bonnie, in this funny film.

KANIN, FAY
    NOTE: All scripts were co-written with Michael Kanin.
    Sunday Punch (1942)
    77 min, b/w, r: MGM.
    William Lundigan, Guy Kibbee, Dan Dailey
    d: David Miller
    This comedy concerns a young woman boarding with a
    group of prizefighters.

    My Pal Gus (1952)
    83 min, b/w, r: FNC.
    Richard Widmark, Joanne Dru
    d: Robert Parrish
    Drama about a little boy from a broken home who is
    sent away to school.

    Rhapsody (1954)
    116 min, b/w, r: MGM.
    Elizabeth Taylor, Vittorio Gassman
    d: Charles Vidor
    Drama concerning a young woman's romantic affairs with
    a pianist and a violinist.

    The Opposite Sex (1956)
    116 min, c, r: MGM.
    June Allyson, Ann Sheridan, Joan Blondell
    d: David Miller
    Musical remake of The Women concerns a woman who hears
    through gossip that her husband is having an affair.

    Teacher's Pet (1958)
    See MACRORIE, ALMA RUTH (Editors).

    Swordsman Of Siena (1962). Co-writers: Alec Coppel,
    Anthony Marshall
    96 min, c, r: MGM.
    Stewart Granger, Sylva Koscina
    d: Etienne Perier
    Adventure film set in Italy during the 1500's concerning
    a mercenary who helps to overthrow the dishonest governor
    by working for the underground.

LENNART, ISOBEL
    A Stranger In Town (1943). Co-writer: William Kozlenko
    68 min, b/w, r: MGM.
    Richard Carlson, Jean Rogers, Frank Morgan
    d: Roy Rowland
    Morgan is the stranger in town in this film.

The Affairs Of Martha (1943). Co-writer: Lee Gold
67 min, b/w, r: MGM.
Marsha Hunt, Richard Carlson, Virginia Weidler
d: Jules Dassin
Servant writes a provocative book based on happenings
at the home where she works and starts a scandal.

Lost Angel (1943)
90 min, b/w, r: MGM.
Margaret O'Brien, James Craig
d: Roy Rowland
Drama featuring O'Brien as an orphan who is being used
for a scientific experiment, and a reporter who wants
her to be given the chance to grow up like a normal
little girl.

Anchors Aweigh (1945)
See FAZAN, ADRIENNE (Editors).

Holiday In Mexico (1946)
See FAZAN, ADRIENNE (Editors).

It Happened In Brooklyn (1947)
See SEWELL, BLANCHE (Editors).

The Kissing Bandit (1948). Co-writer: John Briard Harding
See FAZAN, ADRIENNE (Editors).

Holiday Affair (1949)
87 min, b/w, r: FNC.
Robert Mitchum, Janet Leigh
d: Don Hartman
Gentle film concerning a widow with a young son who
finds herself involved with two men.

East Side, West Side (1950)
106 min, b/w, r: MGM.
Barbara Stanwyck, James Mason, Ava Gardner
d: Mervyn LeRoy
Drama involving the marital problems of a New York
society couple.

A Life Of Her Own (1950)
108 min, b/w, r: MGM.
Lana Turner, Ray Milland, Ann Dvorak
d: George Cukor
Drama about a model who must decide whether she wants
a career or marriage.

It's A Big Country (1951)
89 min, b/w, r: MGM.
Film consisting of eight episodes by various directors and
screenwriters which tell stories about Americans in different
parts of the United States. Lennart wrote the "Rosika, the
Rose" sequence, which was directed by Charles Vidor and
starred Gene Kelly and Janet Leigh.

Skirts Ahoy (1952)
109 min, c, r: MGM.
Esther Williams, Vivian Blaine
d: Sidney Lanfield
Funny film about three female sailors on leave and their romances.

My Wife's Best Friend (1952)
87 min, b/w, r: FNC.
Anne Baxter, MacDonald Carey
d: Richard Sale
When a couple thinks that the plane they are on is going to
crash, they both reveal secrets about themselves.

The Girl Next Door (1953)
92 min, b/w, r: FNC.
Dan Dailey, June Haver
d: Richard Sale
Musical about the romance between a cartoonist and a singer.

Latin Lovers (1953)
104 min, c, r: MGM.
Lana Turner, Ricardo Montalban
d: Mervyn LeRoy
A young woman on vacation in South America becomes involved
with a Latin lover.

Love Me Or Leave Me (1955). Co-writer: Daniel Fuchs
112 min, c, r: MGM.
Doris Day, James Cagney
d: Charles Vidor
Well-cast film with good music based on the life of singer
Ruth Etting.

Meet Me In Las Vegas (1956)
112 min, c, r: MGM.
Dan Dailey, Cyd Charisse
d: Roy Rowland
Musical set in Las Vegas about a romance between a rancher
and a ballet dancer who brings him good luck with his gambling.

This Could Be The Night (1957)
104 min, b/w, available in cinemascope, r: MGM.
Jean Simmons, Paul Douglas
d: Robert Wise
Comedy concerning a secretary who is unaware that she is
working for a group of hoods.

Merry Andrew (1958). Co-writer: I.A.L. Diamond
103 min, c, available in cinemascope, r: MGM.
Danny Kaye, Pier Angeli
d: Michael Kidd
Kaye joins a circus in this musical comedy.

The Inn Of The Sixth Happiness (1958)
158 min, c, available in cinemascope, r: FNC.
Ingrid Bergman, Robert Donat
d: Mark Robson
Drama which features Bergman as a missionary in China who
struggles to get a group of children to shelter.

The Sundowners (1960)
133 min, c, r: FNC.
Deborah Kerr, Robert Mitchum
d: Fred Zinnemann
Excellent film set in Australia concerning a sheepherding
family.

Please Don't Eat The Daisies (1960)
111 min, c, available in cinemascope, r: MGM.
Doris Day, David Niven
d: Charles Walters
Hilarious motion picture about what happens when a drama
critic moves his family from the city to a big house in the
country.

Two For The Seesaw (1962)
120 min, b/w, r: MGM.
Robert Mitchum, Shirley MacLaine
d: Robert Wise
Film based on William Gibson's play involving the romance
between a lawyer and a young woman in New York City.

Period Of Adjustment (1962)
112 min, b/w, r: MGM.
Jane Fonda, Tony Franciosa
d: George Roy Hill
Fine film version of Tennessee Williams' comedy/drama concerning two couple's marital problems.

Fitzwilly (1967)
102 min, c, r: MGM.
Dick Van Dyke, Barbara Feldon
d: Delbert Mann
Comedy about a butler who robs to support his employer who is
writing a dictionary.

Funny Girl (1968)
151 min, c, available in cinemascope, r: FNC, SWA.
Barbra Streisand, Omar Sharif
d: William Wyler
Excellent musical based on Ziegfeld comedienne Fanny Brice's
life.

LEVIEN, SONYA
  The Power Of The Press (1928). Co-writer: Frederick
  A. Thompson
  70 min, b/w, silent, r: KPF.
  Douglas Fairbanks, Jobyna Ralston
  d: Frank Capra
  A reporter works with a young woman in order to clear
  her name of scandal.

  The Younger Generation (1929)
  80 min, b/w, sound sequences, r: KPF.
  Jean Hersholt, Ricardo Cortez
  d: Frank Capra
  A young emigrant becomes wealthy, moves out of his old
  neighborhood, but finds that he still has problems.

  Delicious (1931)
  106 min, b/w, r: FNC.
  Janet Gaynor, Charles Farrell, El Brendel
  d: David Butler
  Delightful musical about a young Scottish woman who
  escapes immigration officials on a ship by hiding in
  a wealthy man's horse stall.

  Daddy Long Legs (1931)
  73 min, b/w, r: FNC.
  Janet Gaynor, Warner Baxter
  d: Alfred Santell
  A benefactor falls in love with the orphan that he
  has helped.

  State Fair (1933). Co-writer: Paul Green
  60 min, b/w, r: FNC.
  Will Rogers, Janet Gaynor
  d: Henry King
  Gentle film which is centered around some small town
  residents who have entered their products and animals
  in a state fair.

  Cavalcade (1933)
  115 min, b/w, r: FNC.
  Clive Brook, Diana Wynyard
  d: Frank Lloyd
  Drama concerning British family during wartime.

  The Country Doctor (1936)
  See MCLEAN, BARBARA (Editors).

  In Old Chicago (1938). Co-writer: Lamar Trotti
  See MCLEAN, BARBARA (Editors).

The Cowboy And The Lady   (1938)
91 min, b/w, r: FNC.
Gary Cooper, Merle Oberon
d: H.C. Potter
Oberon is a senator's daughter who falls in love with
a cowboy.

Kidnapped   (1938). Co-writers: Edwin Blum, Eleanor
Harris, Ernest Pascal
90 min, b/w, r: FNC.
Warner Baxter, Freddie Bartholomew
d: Alfred Werker
Film based on Robert Louis Stevenson's novel, concerning
a young boy who is kidnapped while on a trip to claim
his inheritance.

The Hunchback Of Notre Dame   (1939)
114 min, b/w, r: FNC.
Charles Laughton, Maureen O'Hara
d: William Dieterle
Laughton gives a wonderful performance as the hunchback in this drama based on Victor Hugo's classic
novel.

Drums Along The Mohawk   (1939)
103 min, c, r: FNC.
Henry Fonda, Claudette Colbert
d: John Ford
Drama set during the Revolutionary War featuring Fonda
and Colbert as husband and wife.

Ziegfeld Girl   (1941). Co-writer: Marguerite Roberts
See SEWELL, BLANCHE   (Editors).

The Valley Of Decision (1945). Co-writer: John Meehan
120 min, b/w, r: MGM.
Greer Garson, Gregory Peck, Lionel Barrymore
d: Tay Garnett
Drama about the relationship between a maid and her
employer's son.

Rhapsody In Blue   (1945). Co-writers: Howard Koch,
Elliot Paul
93 min, b/w, r: MGM.
Joan Leslie, Robert Alda, Oscar Levant
d: Irving Rapper
Film based on the life of composer George Gershwin.

State Fair (1945). Co-writers: Paul Green, Oscar
Hammerstein II
100 min, c, r: FNC.
Dana Andrews, Vivian Blain, Jeanne Crain
d: Walter Lang
Remake of the 1933 hit movie.

The Green Years (1946). Co-writer: Robert Ardrey
128 min, b/w, r: MGM.
Dean Stockwell, Tom Drake, Charles Coburn
d: Victor Saville
Film set in Scotland concerning a young Irish boy's
growth into manhood.

Cass Timberlane (1947)
120 min, b/w, r: MGM.
Spencer Tracy, Lana Turner, Mary Astor
d: George Sidney
Romantic drama about a girl from the wrong side of
the tracks.

Three Daring Daughters (1947). Co-writers: Frederick
Kohner, Albert Mannheimer, John Meehan
See FAZAN, ADRIENNE (Editors).

The Great Caruso (1951). Co-writer: William Ludwig
109 min, c, r: MGM.
Mario Lanza, Ann Blyth
d: Richard Thorpe
Good drama based on tenor Caruso's life and career.

Quo Vadis (1951). Co-writers: S.N. Behrman, John Lee Mahin
168 min, c, r: MGM.
Robert Taylor, Deborah Kerr
d: Mervyn LeRoy
Spectacular film set in Rome during Nero's reign featuring Taylor and Kerr as lovers.

The Merry Widow (1952). Co-writer: William Ludwig
105 min, c, r: MGM.
Fernando Lamas, Lana Turner
d: Curtis Bernhardt
Musical based on Franz Lehar's operetta.

The Student Prince (1954). Co-writer: William Ludwig
107 min, c, available in cinemascope, r: MGM.
Ann Blyth, Edmund Purdom
d: Richard Thorpe
A prince, who is sent away to school, falls in love
with a waitress.

Hit The Deck   (1955). Co-writer: William Ludwig
112 min, c, available in cinemascope, r: MGM.
Walter Pidgeon, Debbie Reynolds
d: Roy Rowland
All-star musical involving sailors on leave in San
Francisco.

Interrupted Melody   (1955). Co-writer: William Ludwig
106 min, c, available in cinemascope, r: MGM.
Eleanor Parker, Glenn Ford
d: Curtis Bernhardt
Drama based on the life of soprano Marjorie Lawrence, who contracted polio in the prime of her
career.

Oklahoma! (1955). Co-writer: William Ludwig
148 min, c, available in cinemascope, r: TWY.
Gordon Macrae, Shirley Jones
d: Fred Zinnemann
Fine film based on the Broadway musical by Rodgers
and Hammerstein concerning the people in a small town
around the time that Oklahoma gained statehood.

Bhowani Junction   (1956). Co-writer: Ivan Moffatt
110 min, c, available in cinemascope, r: MGM.
d: George Cukor
Film set in India about a woman and her relationships with three different men.

Pepe   (1960). Co-writer: Leonard Spigelgass
See LAWRENCE, VIOLA (Editors).

LOOS, ANITA
The New York Hat   (1912)
77 min, b/w, silent, r: MMA.
Mary Pickford, Lionel Barrymore
d: D.W. Griffith
Pickford plays a young girl who dreams of having
the New York hat in a shop window.

The Social Secretary   (1916)
50 min, b/w, silent, r: EMG.
Norma Talmadge, Erich von Stroheim
d: John Emerson
Talmadge is a young woman, who, in order to get a
job as a secretary, must make herself appear ugly
so that she will not attract the attention of the
employer's son.

His Picture In The Papers (1916). Co-writer: John
Emerson
60 min, b/w, silent, r: EMG. s: BLA.
Douglas Fairbanks
d: John Emerson
To impress a woman he likes, a young man engages
in dangerous stunts in order to get his picture in
the newspaper.

The Matrimaniac (1916). Co-writer: John Emerson
45 min, b/w, silent, r: EMG. s: BLA.
Douglas Fairbanks, Constance Talmadge
d: John Emerson
Energetic film in which a man is determined to elope
with his girlfriend though the elopement is delayed
by several bizarre events.

Intolerance (1916). Co-writer: D.W. Griffith
154 min, b/w, silent, r: BUD. s: BLA. 120 min, tinted,
r: FNC.
Lillian Gish, Robert Harron, Mae Marsh
d: D.W. Griffith
Early epic which shows the intolerance of mankind
throughout history to the present.

The Americano (1917)
50 min, b/w, silent, r: IVY. s: BLA.
Douglas Fairbanks, Spottiswoode Aitken
d: John Emerson
Adventure film about a man who helps to stop a
South American uprising.

Wild And Woolly (1917)
70 min, b/w, silent, r: FNC.
Douglas Fairbanks, Eileen Percy
d: John Emerson
Funny western set in 1917 involving a young man
who goes West expecting to see gunfights, cowboys,
and Indians.

Reaching For The Moon (1917)
78 min, b/w, silent, r: MMA.
Douglas Fairbanks, Eileen Percy
d: John Emerson
Fantasy involving a man trying to become king of
a mythical kingdom.

The Struggle (1931). Co-writer: John Emerson
90 min, b/w, r: TWY.
Hal Skelly, Zita Johann
d: D.W. Griffith
Drama concerning a man's struggle against alcoholism.

Blondie Of The Follies (1932). Co-writer: Frances
Marion
90 min, b/w, r: MGM.
Marion Davies, Robert Montgomery
d: Edmund Goulding
Romantic comedy about a showgirl and her best friend
who are both in love with the same playboy.
See MARION, FRANCES (Screenwriters).

Red-Headed Woman (1932)
See SEWELL, BLANCHE (Editors).

Midnight Mary (1933). Co-writers: Gene Markey, Kathryn
Scola
71 min, b/w, r: MGM.
Loretta Young, Ricardo Cortez, Una Merkel
d: William Wellman
Young is a woman on trial for murder whose story is
told in flashbacks in this drama.

Hold Your Man (1933). Co-writer: Howard Emmett
Rogers
89 min, b/w, r: MGM.
Jean Harlow, Clark Gable
d: Sam Wood
A young woman becomes romantically involved with a
gangster when he hides from the police in her apartment.

The Girl From Missouri (1934)
75 min, b/w, r: MGM.
Jean Harlow, Franchot Tone, Lewis Stone
d: Jack Conway
Comedy about a young woman from Missouri who is
trying to catch a millionaire in the big city.

San Francisco (1936)
115 min, b/w, r: MGM.
Clark Gable, Jeanette MacDonald, Spencer Tracy
d: W.S. Van Dyke
Entertaining film with both romance and music which
is centered around the tragic San Francisco earthquake.

Riffraff (1936). Co-writers: Frances Marion,
H.W. Haneman
93 min, b/w, r: MGM.
Jean Harlow, Spencer Tracy, Una Merkel
d: J. Walter Ruben
Harlow and Tracy are a young couple who struggle
to make a life for themselves on the waterfront.
See MARION, FRANCES (Screenwriters).

Saratoga (1937). Co-writer: Robert Hopkins
94 min, b/w, r: MGM.
Jean Harlow, Clark Gable
d: Jack Conway
Harlow's last film is a comedy concerning horseracing.

Mama Steps Out (1937)
66 min, b/w, r: MGM.
Alice Brady, Guy Kibbee, Betty Furness
d: George B. Seitz
Comedy with Brady as Mama which takes place on the
French Riviera.

The Women (1939). Co-writer: June Murfin
134 min, b/w with color sequence, r: MGM.
Norma Shearer, Rosalind Russell, Joan Crawford
d: George Cukor
A married woman learns through gossip that her husband is having an affair with a perfume saleswoman
in this extraordinary comedy with an all-woman cast.

Susan And God   (1940)
117 min, b/w, r: MGM.
Joan Crawford, Fredric March, Rita Hayworth
d: George Cukor
Crawford stars in this drama about a woman who is so
devoted to her religious beliefs that it endangers
her relationship with her family.

They Met In Bombay (1941). Co-writers: Edwin Mayer,
Leon Gordon
86 min, b/w, r: MGM.
Clark Gable, Rosalind Russell, Peter Lorre
d: Clarence Brown
Gable and Russell are jewel thieves in this comedy.

When Ladies Meet   (1941). Co-writer: S.K. Lauren
108 min, b/w, r: MGM.
Joan Crawford, Robert Taylor, Greer Garson
d: Robert Z. Leonard
Crawford falls in love with Garson's husband in this
drama.

Blossoms In The Dust   (1941)
99 min, c, r: MGM.
Greer Garson, Walter Pidgeon
d: Mervyn LeRoy
Drama set in Texas and based on fact about a woman
who starts an orphanage.

I Married An Angel (1942)
84 min, b/w, r: MGM.
Jeanette MacDonald, Nelson Eddy
d: W.S. Van Dyke
Fantasy film with music involving a romance between
a playboy and an angel.

MACPHERSON, JEANIE
The Squaw Man   (1918).
See BAUCHENS, ANNE (Editors).

Male And Female   (1919)
See BAUCHENS, ANNE (Editors).

Manslaughter   (1922)
See BAUCHENS, ANNE (Editors).

The Ten Commandments   (1923)
See BAUCHENS, ANNE   (Editors).

The Road To Yesterday (1925). Co-writer: Beulah
Marie Dix
See BAUCHENS, ANNE (Editors).

The King Of Kings   (1927)
See BAUCHENS, ANNE (Editors).

Dynamite (1929). Co-writers: John Howard Lawson,
Gladys Unger
See BAUCHENS, ANNE (Editors).

Madame Satan (1930). Co-writers: Elsie Janis,
Gladys Unger
See BAUCHENS, ANNE (Editors).

The Devil's Brother (Fra Diavolo) (1933)
90 min, b/w, r: MGM.
Stan Laurel, Oliver Hardy
d: Hal Roach
Laurel and Hardy star as Stanlio and Ollio in this
film based on the comic opera Fra Diavolo.

MARION, FRANCES
  Tillie Wakes Up (1917)
  44 min, b/w, music and sound effects only, r: FCE.
  Marie Dressler
  d: Harry Davenport
  One of the comedy films in the Tillie series
  which stars Dressler as the innocent Tillie Blobbs.

  A Girl's Folly (1917). Co-writer: Maurice Tourneur
  60 min, b/w, silent, r: EMG.
  Doris Kenyon, Robert Warwick
  d: Maurice Tourneur
  Drama concerning the problems that a young woman
  encounters when she becomes a movie actress.

  Lazybones (1925)
  79 min, b/w, silent, r: KIL.
  Buck Jones, ZaSu Pitts
  d: Frank Borzage
  Drama concerning a young man who adopts an illegitimate
  child to save its mother from scandal.

  The Son Of The Sheik (1926). Co-writer: Fred De Gresac
  68 min, b/w, silent, r: CLE, IVY.
  Rudolph Valentino, Vilma Banky
  d: George Fitzmaurice
  Valentino plays both father and son in this romantic
  adventure story set in the desert.

  The Scarlet Letter (1926)
  86 min, b/w, silent, r: MGM.
  Lillian Gish, Lars Hanson
  d: Victor Seastrom
  Silent film based on Nathaniel Hawthorne's novel
  about a woman accused of committing adultery.

  Love (1927). Co-writer: Lorna Moon
  80 min, b/w, silent, r: MGM.
  John Gilbert, Greta Garbo
  d: Edmund Goulding
  Garbo stars as Anna Karenina, a married woman who
  leaves her husband and son for a lover.

  The Wind (1928)
  73 min, b/w, silent, r: MGM.
  Lillian Gish, Lars Hanson
  d: Victor Seastrom
  Dramatic film about the trials and tribulations of
  a young woman who moves to the West.

Anna Christie (1929)
102 min, b/w, r: MGM.
Greta Garbo, Marie Dressler
d: Clarence Brown
Based on Eugene O'Neill's drama, Anna Christie was
Garbo's first talking picture.

The Big House (1930)
See SEWELL, BLANCHE (Editors).

Min And Bill (1930)
66 min, b/w, r: MGM.
Wallace Beery, Marie Dressler
d: George Hill
Great comedy featuring Dressler and Beery in the
title roles.

The Secret Six (1931)
See SEWELL, BLANCHE (Editors).

The Champ (1931)
86 min, b/w, r: MGM.
Wallace Beery, Jackie Cooper
d: King Vidor
Moving story of a "has been" prizefighter who decides
to go back into the ring for the sake of his young
son.

Emma (1932)
72 min, b/w, r: MGM.
Marie Dressler, Richard Cromwell, Myrna Loy
d: Clarence Brown
Dressler was nominated for an Academy Award for her
portrayal of Emma, the family maid who sees attitudes
change when she marries her employer.

Blondie Of The Follies (1932)
See LOOS, ANITA (Screenwriters).

Cynara (1932). Co-writer: Lynn Starling
78 min, b/w, r: FNC.
Ronald Colman, Kay Francis
d: King Vidor
Tragic drama concerning a happily married man who
becomes romantically involved with a single woman.

Peg O' My Heart (1933)
See BOOTH, MARGARET (Editors).

Dinner At Eight (1933). Co-writers: Herman Mankiewicz, Donald Ogden Stewart
113 min, b/w, r: MGM.
Wallace Beery, Jean Harlow, John Barrymore
d: George Cukor
Extraordinary dialogue and a fine cast make this comedy/drama one of the best films made in the early 1930's.

The Prizefighter And The Lady (1933). Co-writers: John Lee Mahin, John Meehan
110 min, b/w, r: MGM.
Myrna Loy, Max Baer, Jack Dempsey
d: W.S. Van Dyke
Classic boxing drama with main bout between Primo Carnera and Baer with Dempsey as referee.

Going Hollywood (1933). Co-writer: Donald Ogden Stewart
77 min, b/w, r: MGM.
Bing Crosby, Marion Davies, Fifi D'Orsay
d: Raoul Walsh
Musical with Davies as a devoted fan of a young singer.

Riffraff (1936)
See LOOS, ANITA (Screenwriters).

Camille (1936). Co-writers: Zoe Akins, James Hilton
See BOOTH, MARGARET (Editors).

Love From A Stranger (1937)
82 min, b/w, r: KPF.
Basil Rathbone, Ann Harding
d: Rowland V. Lee
A murderer pursues a young woman in this suspenseful drama.

Knight Without Armor (1937)
105 min, b/w, r: FNC.
Robert Donat, Marlene Dietrich
d: Jacques Feyder
Romantic film set in Russia during 1918 about a commissar who falls in love with his prisoner.

PERRY, ELEANOR
David And Lisa (1962)
94 min, b/w, r: BUD, FNC.
Keir Dullea, Janet Margolin
d: Frank Perry
Sensitive drama about two young inmates in an asylum who help each other to overcome problems.

Ladybug, Ladybug (1963). Co-writer: Richard Harris
81 min, b/w, r: MGM.
Estelle Parsons, Jane Connell
d: Frank Perry
Timely drama involving the actions of a group of
school children who are sent home following an
alarm that a nuclear attack is imminent.

The Swimmer (1968)
94 min, c, r: BUD, FNC.
Burt Lancaster, Janice Rule
d: Frank Perry
An advertising man finds out a great deal about
himself and his relationships with others by stopping
and swimming in his friends' pools on his way home.

Last Summer (1969)
97 min, c, r: HCW.
Barbara Hershey, Richard Thomas
d: Frank Perry
Tense drama involving four teenagers who are spending
a summer vacation at the beach.

Trilogy (Truman Capote's Trilogy) (1969). Co-writer:
Truman Capote
99 min, c, r: HCW.
Maureen Stapleton, Mildred Natwick
d: Frank Perry
Film consisting of three of Capote's short stories:
"Miriam," "Among The Paths To Eden," and "A Christmas
Memory."

Diary Of A Mad Housewife (1970). Co-writer: Richard
Harris
100 min, c, r: CLE.
Carrie Snodgress, Richard Benjamin
d: Frank Perry
Excellent drama about a young woman who finds that
she can no longer cope with her nagging husband or
her life as a housewife.

The Man Who Loved Cat Dancing (1973)
114 min, c, available in cinemascope, r: MGM.
Burt Reynolds, Sarah Miles, George Hamilton
d: Richard Sarafin
Miles stars as a woman who runs away from her husband, only to be caught in the middle of a train
robbery and taken hostage in this western set in
the late 1800's.

REVILLE, ALMA   (MRS. ALFRED HITCHCOCK)   (British)
Juno And The Paycock   (1930)
85 min, b/w, r: CFM.
Sara Allgood, Edward Chapman
d: Alfred Hitchcock
Drama based on Sean O'Casey's play about a lawyer
who attempts to swindle a family's money that he
believes they will be inheriting.

Murder! (1930)
102 min, b/w, r: FNC, KPF.
Herbert Marshall, Norah Baring
D: Alfred Hitchcock
Interesting film about a juror who decides that he
must find the real killer when he is unconvinced of the
guilt of the woman on trial.

The Skin Game (1931). Co-writer: Alfred Hitchcock
88 min, b/w, r: FNC.
Edmund Gwenn, Jill Esmond
d: Alfred Hitchcock
Taken from Galsworthy's play, this film involves
the actions of two families against each other in
order to attain social prominence.

Rich And Strange (1932). Co-writer: Val Valentine
92 min, b/w, r: FNC.
Henry Kendall, Joan Barry
d: Alfred Hitchcock
A quiet man gets more adventure than he thought
possible when he inherits some money and takes a
trip with his wife around the world.

Waltzes From Vienna (1933). Co-writer: Guy Bolton
80 min, b/w, r: CFM.
Jessie Matthews, Esmond Knight
d: Alfred Hitchcock
A real oddity among Hitchcock's films, this motion
picture is an operetta based loosely on Johann
Strauss and his son.

The Thirty-Nine Steps (1935). Co-writer: Charles Bennett
80 min, b/w, r: FNC, KPF.
Robert Donat, Madeleine Carroll
d: Alfred Hitchcock
Donat stars as a young Canadian who must prove his
innocence when a woman spy is murdered in his apartment.

Young And Innocent (1937). Co-writer: Charles Bennett
80 min, b/w, r: BUD, FNC.
Derrick de Marney, Nova Pilbeam
d: Alfred Hitchcock
With the help of a young woman, a writer must clear
his name after circumstances cause him to be suspected of
murder.

Suspicion (1941)
See HARRISON, JOAN (Screenwriters).

Shadow Of A Doubt (1943). Co-writers: Sally Benson,
Thornton Wilder
108 min, b/w, r: CLE.
Joseph Cotten, Teresa Wright
d: Alfred Hitchcock
Fine suspense film concerning a young woman who
begins to believe that her uncle is trying to
murder her.

Stage Fright (1950). Co-writer: Whitfield Cook
110 min, b/w, r: FNC.
Marlene Dietrich, Michael Wilding, Jane Wyman,
Richard Todd
d: Alfred Hitchcock
Todd is a young man suspected of killing an actress's
husband in this thriller.

SILVER, JOAN MICKLIN
Hester Street
See SILVER, JOAN MICKLIN (Directors, Chapter I).

Limbo (1972). Co-writer: James Bridges
See SPENCER, DOROTHY (Editors).

Head Over Heels
See SILVER, JOAN MICKLIN (Directors, Chapter I).

See SILVER, JOAN MICKLIN (Directors, Chapter I).

TEWKESBURY, JOAN
Thieves Like Us (1974). Co-writers: Robert Altman,
Calder Willingham
123 min, c, r: MGM.
Keith Carradine, Shelley Duvall
d: Robert Altman
Carradine and Duvall are doomed lovers in this tragic
drama set during the Depression in rural Mississippi
about three bank robbers.

Nashville (1975)
159 min, c, cinemascope only, r: FNC.
Barbara Harris, Geraldine Chaplin, Keith Carradine
d: Robert Altman
Crazy film with an all-star cast about the lives and
careers of several people and how they interact.

See TEWKESBURY, JOAN (Directors, Chapter 2).

WEST, MAE

She Done Him Wrong
68 min, b/w, r: CLE
Mae West, Cary Grant
d: Lowell Sherman
West stars as Lady Lou, a woman who runs a bar, and
Grant is featured as a missionary who attempts to
save her soul.

Belle Of The Nineties   (1934)
76 min, b/w, r: SWA.
Mae West, Roger Pryor
d: Leo McCarey
Comedy with music by Duke Ellington concerning the
problems of a woman working in the Sensation House
in New Orleans during the 1890's.

Goin' To Town   (1935)
74 min, b/w, r: SWA.
Mae West, Paul Cavanagh
d: Alexander Hall
Mae inherits some oil fields and becomes part of
high society in this comedy.

Klondike Annie   (1936)
83 min, b/w, r: CLE.
Mae West, Voctor McLaglen
d: Raoul Walsh
West disguises herself as a missionary who is going
to the Klondike in order to escape the police in this
comedy.

Go West Young Man   (1936)
80 min, b/w, r: SWA.
Mae West, Randolph Scott
d: Henry Hathaway
Comedy in which West is a motion picture actress on a
personal tour around the United States.

Every Day's A Holiday   (1937)
79 min, b/w, r: SWA.
Mae West, Edmund Lowe
d: Edward Sutherland
West stars as Peaches O'Day, a woman who changes
her identity to Mlle. Fifi of Paris in order to
elude the police.

My Little Chickadee (1940). Co-writer: W.C. Fields
92 min, b/w, r: SWA.
W.C. Fields, Mae West
d: Edward Cline
Fields and West star as a couple who decide to get
married for reasons of convenience.

SELECTED FILMOGRAPHIES

DIRECTORS

DOROTHY ARZNER

FASHIONS FOR WOMEN   (1927)
TEN MODERN COMMANDMENTS   (1927)
GET YOUR MAN (1927)
MANHATTAN COCKTAIL   (1928)
THE WILD PARTY (1929)*
SARAH AND SON   (1930)
ANYBODY'S WOMAN   (1930)
WORKING GIRLS   (1930)
PARAMOUNT ON PARADE   (1930)*
HONOR AMONG LOVERS   (1931)
MERRILY WE GO TO HELL   (1932)
CHRISTOPHER STRONG   (1933)*
NANA   (1934)*
CRAIG'S WIFE   (1936)*
THE BRIDE WORE RED   (1937)*
DANCE, GIRL, DANCE   (1940)*
FIRST COMES COURAGE   (1943)*

IDA LUPINO

NOT WANTED   (1949)*
NEVER FEAR   (1950)*
OUTRAGE   (1950)*
HARD, FAST, AND BEAUTIFUL   (1951)*
THE HITCHHIKER   (1953)
THE BIGAMIST   (1953)*
THE TROUBLE WITH ANGELS   (1966)*

LENI RIEFENSTAHL

THE BLUE LIGHT (DAS BLAUE LICHT)   (1932)*
TRIUMPH OF THE WILL (TRIUMPH DES WILLENS)   (1935)*
DAY OF FREEDOM (TAG DER FREIGEIT)   (1935)*
OLYMPIA: I AND II   (1938)*
BERCHTESGADEN UBER SALZBURG   (1938)
TIEFLAND   (1954)*
SCHWARZE FRACHT   (1956)

STEPHANIE ROTHMAN

BLOOD BATH   (1966)
IT'S A BIKINI WORLD   (1966)
THE STUDENT NURSES   (1970)*
THE VELVET VAMPIRE   (1971)
GROUP MARRIAGE   (1972)
TERMINAL ISLAND   (1973)
THE WORKING GIRLS   (1974)*

LOIS WEBER

THE EYES OF GOD (1913)
THE JEW'S CHRISTMAS (1913)
THE MERCHANT OF VENICE (1914)
TRAITOR (1914)
LIKE MOST WIVES (1914)
THE HYPOCRITES (1914)
IT'S NO LAUGHING MATTER (1914)
SUNSHINE MOLLY (1915)
A CIGARETTE (1915)
THAT'S ALL (1915)
SCANDAL (1915)
DISCONTENT (1916)
HOP, THE DEVIL'S BREW (1916)
WHERE ARE MY CHILDREN? (1916)
THE FRENCH DOWNSTAIRS (1916)
ALONE IN THE WORLD (1916)
THE ROCK OF RICHES (1916)
JOHN NEEDHAM'S DOUBLE (1916)
SAVING THE FAMILY NAME (1916)
SHOES (1916)
THE DUMB GIRL OF PORTICI (1916)
THE HAND THAT ROCKS THE CRADLE (1917)
EVEN AS YOU AND I (1917)
THE MYSTERIOUS MRS. M. (1917)
THE PRICE OF A GOOD TIME (1917)
THE MAN WHO DARED GOD (1917)
THERE'S NO PLACE LIKE HOME (1917)
FOR HUSBANDS ONLY (1917)
THE DOCTOR AND THE WOMAN (1918)
BORROWED CLOTHES (1918)
WHEN A GIRL LOVES (1919)
MARY REGAN (1919)
MIDNIGHT ROMANCE (1919)
SCANDAL MANAGERS (1919)
HOME (1919)
FORBIDDEN (1919)
TOO WISE WIVES (1921)
WHAT'S WORTH WHILE? (1921)
TO PLEASE ONE WOMAN (1921)
THE BLOT (1921)*
WHAT DO MEN WANT? (1921)
A CHAPTER IN HER LIFE (1923)*
THE MARRIAGE CLAUSE (1926)
SENSATION SEEKERS (1927)
THE ANGEL OF BROADWAY (1927)
WHITE HEAT (1934)

CLAUDIA WEILL

METROPOLE (1968)
RADCLIFFE BLUES (1968)
PUTNEY SCHOOL (1969)

THIS IS THE HOME OF MRS. LEVANT GRAHAM (1970)*
IDCA-1970 (1971)
COMMUTERS (1972)*
YOGA (1972)*
MARRIAGE (1972)*
LOST AND FOUND (1972)*
ROACHES (1972)
BELLY DANCING CLASS (1972)
JOYCE AT 34 (1972)*
MATINE HORNER - PORTRAIT OF A PERSON (1974)*
THE OTHER HALF OF THE SKY: A CHINA MEMOIR (1974)*
GIRL FRIENDS (1977)*
IT'S MY TURN (1980)*

EDITORS

DEDE ALLEN

ENDOWING YOUR FUTURE (1957)
TERROR FROM THE YEAR 5000 (1958)*
ODDS AGAINST TOMORROW (1959)*
THE HUSTLER (1961)*
AMERICA, AMERICA (1963)
IT'S ALWAYS NOW (1965)
BONNIE AND CLYDE (1968)*
RACHEL, RACHEL (1968)*
LITTLE BIG MAN (1971)*
SLAUGHTERHOUSE FIVE (1972)*
VISIONS OF EIGHT (1973)*
SERPICO (1974)*
DOG DAY AFTERNOON (1975)*
NIGHT MOVES (1975)*
THE MISSOURI BREAKS (1976)*
SLAP SHOT (1977)*
THE WIZ (1978)*
REDS (1982)*

ANNE BAUCHENS

THE SQUAW MAN (1918)*
TILL I COME BACK TO YOU (1918)
WE CAN'T HAVE EVERYTHING (1918)
DON'T CHANGE YOUR HUSBAND (1919)
FOR BETTER, OR WORSE (1919)
MALE AND FEMALE (1919)*
SOMETHING TO THINK ABOUT (1920)
WHY CHANGE YOUR WIFE (1920)
THE AFFAIRS OF ANATOL (1921)
FOOL'S PARADISE (1921)
FORBIDDEN FRUIT (1921)
MANSLAUGHTER (1922)*
SATURDAY NIGHT (1922)*

ADAM'S RIB   (1923)
THE TEN COMMANDMENTS   (1923)*
FEET OF CLAY   (1924)
TRIUMPH   (1924)
THE GOLDEN BED   (1925)
THE ROAD TO YESTERDAY   (1925)*
THE KING OF KINGS   (1927)*
CHICAGO   (1928)
CRAIG'S WIFE   (1928)*
DYNAMITE   (1929)*
THE GODLESS GIRL   (1929)
NED McCOBB'S DAUGHTER   (1929)
NOISY NEIGHBORS   (1929)
LORD BYRON OF BROADWAY   (1930)
MADAM SATAN   (1930)*
THIS MAD WORLD   (1930)
THE GREAT MEADOW   (1931)
GUILTY HANDS   (1931)
THE SQUAW MAN   (1931)
BEAST OF THE CITY   (1932)
THE SIGN OF THE CROSS   (1932)*
THE WET PARADE   (1932)
CRADLE SONG   (1933)
THIS DAY AND AGE   (1933)*
CLEOPATRA   (1934)*
FOUR FRIGHTENED PEOPLE   (1934)*
MENACE   (1934)
ONE LATE HOUR   (1934)
THE CRUSADES   (1935)*
THE PLAINSMAN   (1937)*
THIS WAY PLEASE   (1937)
THE BUCCANEER   (1938)
BULLDOG DRUMMOND IN AFRICA   (1938)
HUNTED MEN   (1938)
SONS OF THE LEGION   (1938)
TELEVISION SPY   (1939)
UNION PACIFIC   (1939)*
NORTHWEST MOUNTED POLICE   (1940)*
WOMEN WITHOUT NAMES   (1940)
COMMANDOS STRIKE AT DAWN   (1942)
MRS. WIGGS OF THE CABBAGE PATCH   (1942)
REAP THE WILD WIND   (1942)*
THE STORY OF DR. WASSELL   (1944)*
TOMORROW, THE WORLD!   (1944)
LOVE LETTERS   (1945)
UNCONQUERED (1947)
SAMSON AND DELILAH   (1949)*
THE GREATEST SHOW ON EARTH   (1952)*
THE TEN COMMANDMENTS   (1956)*

MARGARET BOOTH

HUSBANDS AND LOVERS   (1924)
WHY MEN LEAVE HOME   (1924)
FINE CLOTHES   (1925)

MEMORY LANE (1926)
THE GAY DECEIVER (1926)
BRINGING UP FATHER (1927)
THE ENEMY (1927)
IN OLD KENTUCKY (1927)
LOVERS (1927)
A LADY OF CHANCE (1928)
THE MYSTERIOUS LADY (1928)*
TELLING THE WORLD (1928)
THE BRIDGE OF SAN LUIS REY (1929)
WISE GIRLS (1929)*
THE LADY OF SCANDAL (1930)*
A LADY'S MORALS (1930)*
REDEMPTION (1930)*
THE ROGUE SONG (1930)*
STRICTLY UNCONVENTIONAL (1930)*
THE CUBAN LOVE SONG (1931)*
FIVE AND TEN (1931)*
IT'S A WISE CHILD (1931)
NEW MOON (1931)*
THE SOUTHERNER (1931)
SUSAN LENOX, HER FALL AND RISE (1931)*
SMILIN' THROUGH (1932)*
THE SON-DAUGHTER (1932)*
STRANGE INTERLUDE (1932)*
BOMBSHELL (1933)*
DANCING LADY (1933)*
PEG O' MY HEART (1933)*
STORM AT DAYBREAK (1933)*
THE BARRETTS OF WIMPOLE STREET (1934)*
RIPTIDE (1934)
RECKLESS (1935)*
MUTINY ON THE BOUNTY (1935)*
CAMILLE (1936)*
ROMEO AND JULIET (1936)*
A YANK AT OXFORD (1937)*
THE OWL AND THE PUSSYCAT (1970)*
TO FIND A MAN (1972)*
FAT CITY (1972)*
THE WAY WE WERE (1973)*
FUNNY LADY (1975)*
SUNSHINE BOYS (1975)*
MURDER BY DEATH (1976)*
THE GOODBYE GIRL (1977)*
CALIFORNIA SUITE (1978)*
CHAPTER TWO (1979)*
ANNIE (1982)*

ADRIENNE FAZAN

DAY OF RECKONING (1933)*
THE BRIDE WORE RED (1937)*
YOU'RE ONLY YOUNG ONCE (1937)*

BARBARY COAST GENT   (1944)*
BETWEEN TWO WOMEN   (1944)*
ANCHORS AWEIGH   (1945)*
SHE WENT TO THE RACES   (1945)*
HOLIDAY IN MEXICO   (1946)*
THE SECRET HEART   (1946)*
THE KISSING BANDIT   (1948)*
THREE DARING DAUGHTERS   (1948)*
IN THE GOOD OLD SUMMERTIME   (1949)*
THE DUCHESS OF IDAHO   (1950)*
NANCY GOES TO RIO   (1950)*
THE PAGAN LOVE SONG   (1950)*
AN AMERICAN IN PARIS   (1951)*
TEXAS CARNIVAL   (1951)*
EVERYTHING I HAVE IS YOURS   (1952)*
SINGIN' IN THE RAIN   (1952)*
GIVE A GIRL A BREAK   (1953)*
I LOVE MELVIN   (1953)*
DEEP IN MY HEART   (1954)*
IT'S ALWAYS FAIR WEATHER   (1955)*
KISMET   (1955)*
INVITATION TO THE DANCE   (1956)*
LUST FOR LIFE   (1956)*
DESIGNING WOMAN   (1957)*
DON'T GO NEAR THE WATER   (1957)*
GIGI   (1958)*
THE RELUCTANT DEBUTANTE   (1958)*
SOME CAME RUNNING   (1958)*
THE BIG CIRCUS   (1959)*
THE GAZEBO   (1959)*
BELLS ARE RINGING   (1960)*
THE FOUR HORSEMEN OF THE APOCALYPSE   (1962)*
TWO WEEKS IN ANOTHER TOWN   (1962)*
THE COURTSHIP OF EDDIE'S FATHER   (1963)*
THE PRIZE   (1963)*
LOOKING FOR LOVE   (1964)*
BILLIE   (1965)*
THIS PROPERTY IS CONDEMNED   (1966)*
WHO'S MINDING THE MINT?   (1967)*
WHERE ANGELS GO.....TROUBLE FOLLOWS!   (1968)*
WITH SIX YOU GET EGGROLL   (1968)*
THE COMIC   (1969)*
THE CHEYENNE SOCIAL CLUB   (1970)*

VERNA FIELDS

STUDS LONIGAN   (1960)*
THE SAVAGE EYE   (1960)
AN AFFAIR OF THE SKIN   (1963)
CRY OF BATTLE   (1963)
NOTHING BUT A MAN   (1964)*
THE BUS   (1965)
COUNTRY BOY   (1966)
DEATHWATCH   (1966)

LEGEND OF THE BOY AND THE EAGLE   (1967)
TRACKS OF THUNDER   (1968)
THE WILD RACERS   (1968)
MEDIUM COOL   (1969)*
WHAT'S UP, DOC?   (1972)
AMERICAN GRAFFITI   (1973)*
PAPER MOON   (1973)*
DAISY MILLER   (1974)*
THE SUGARLAND EXPRESS   (1974)*
JAWS   (1975)*

AGNES GUILLEMOT

LA FAUTE DES AUTRES   (1953)
VOUS N'AVEZ RIEN CONTRE LA JEUNESSE   (1958)
VOYAGE EN BOSCAVIE   (1958)
VOILE A VAL   (1959)
LE GAZ DE LACQ   (1960)
THAUMETOPEA   (1960)
LE PETIT SOLDAT   (1960)
UN STEAK TROUP CUIT   (1960)
UNE FEMME EST UNE FEMME   (1961)
UNE GROSSE TETE   (1961)
VIVRE SA VIE   (1962)
LES HOMMES DE LA WAGHI   (1962)
ROGOPAG   (1952)*
LES CARABINIERS   (1963)*
UNE FILLE A LA DERIVE   (1963)
LES PLUS BELLES ESCROQUERIES DU MONDE   (1963)
LE MEPRIS   (1963)*
JEROME BOSCH   (1963)
BANDE A PART   (1964)*
UNE FEMME MARIEE   (1964)*
LA JONQUE   (1964)
RUES DE HONG KONG   (1964)
LES TOMBIERS   (1964)
DE L'AMOUR   (1964)
ALPHAVILLE   (1965)*
MASCULIN FEMININ   (1966)*
DIALECTIQUE   (1966)
LE CHIEN FOU   (1966)
LES PLUS VIEUX METIER DU MONDE   (1966)
MADE IN U.S.A.   (1966)
LA CHINOISE   (1967)*
VANGELO '70   (1967)
WEEKEND   (1967)*
LES GAULOISES BLEUES
BAISERS VOLES   (1968)
ONE PLUS ONE   (1968)
LA TREVE   (1968)
LA SIRENE DU MISSISSIPPI   (1969)*
L'ENFANT SAUVAGE   (1969)*
DOMICILE CONJUGAL   (1970)*

LE GRAND MAIN   (1972)
L'AGE TENDRE TV   (1974)
COUSIN COUSINE   (1975)

VIOLA LAWRENCE

O'HENRY   (1916)
AN ALABASTER BOX   (1917)
WITHIN THE LAW   (1917)
THE HEART OF HUMANITY   (1919)
HIS DIVORCED WIFE   (1919)
LOOT   (1919)
ONCE TO EVERY WOMAN   (1920)
THE VIRGIN OF STAMBOUL   (1920)
MAN-WOMAN-MARRIAGE   (1921)
FIGHTING THE FLAMES   (1925)
THE WINNING OF BARBARA WORTH   (1926)
THE NIGHT OF LOVE   (1927)
THE MAGIC FLAME   (1927)
THE DEVIL DANCER   (1927)
THE AWAKENING   (1928)
QUEEN KELLY   (1928)
TWO LOVERS   (1928)
BULLDOG DRUMMOND   (1929)
THIS IS HEAVEN   (1929)
THE GREAT PARADE   (1930)
WHAT A WIDOW!   (1930)
PAGAN'S LADY   (1931)
A MAN'S CASTLE   (1933)*
SAILOR BE GOOD   (1933)
LADY BY CHOICE   (1934)
NO GREATER GLORY   (1934)
THE PARTY'S OVER   (1934)
WHOM THE GODS DESTROY   (1934)
A FEATHER IN HER HAT   (1935)
LOVE ME FOREVER   (1935)
PARTY WIRE   (1935)
THE WHOLE TOWN'S TALKING   (1935)
CRAIG'S WIFE   (1936)*
THE KING STEPS OUT   (1936)*
LADY OF SECRETS   (1936)
THE LONE WOLF RETURNS   (1936)
DEVIL'S PLAYGROUND   (1937)
LIFE BEGINS WITH LOVE   (1937)
SHE MARRIED AN ARTIST   (1937)
SPEED TO SPARE   (1937)
CITY STREETS   (1938)
I AM THE LAW   (1938)
PENITENTIARY   (1938)
THERE'S ALWAYS A WOMAN   (1938)
THERE'S THAT WOMAN AGAIN   (1938)
THE AMAZING MR. WILLIAMS   (1939)

BLONDIE TAKES A VACATION (1939)
ONLY ANGELS HAVE WINGS (1939)*
THE DOCTOR TAKES A WIFE (1940)
FIVE LITTLE PEPPERS AT HOME (1940)
GLAMOUR FOR SALE (1940)
HE STAYED FOR BREAKFAST (1940)
BEDTIME STORY (1941)
THE BIG BOSS (1941)
HERE COMES MR. JORDAN (1941)*
THE LONE WOLF TAKES A CHANCE (1941)
THIS THING CALLED LOVE (1941)
TWO IN A TAXI (1941)
YOU BELONG TO ME (1941)
MY SISTER EILEEN (1942)*
THEY ALL KISSED THE BRIDE (1942)
TWO YANKS IN TRINIDAD (1942)
FIRST COMES COURAGE (1943)*
ONE DANGEROUS NIGHT (1943)
COVER GIRL (1944)*
SECRET COMMAND (1944)
THE FIGHTING GUARDSMAN (1945)
SHE WOULDN'T SAY YES (1945)
TONIGHT AND EVERY NIGHT (1945)*
HIT THE HAY (1946)
PERILOUS HOLIDAY (1946)
DOWN TO EARTH (1947)*
THE DARK PAST (1948)
THE GALLANT BLADE (1948)
THE LADY FROM SHANGHAI (1948)*
LEATHER GLOVES (1948)
MARY LOU (1948)
AND BABY MAKES THREE (1949)
KNOCK ON ANY DOOR (1949)*
TOKYO JOE (1949)
TRAVELLING SALESWOMAN (1949)
THE FLYING MISSILE (1950)
HARRIET CRAIG (1950)*
IN A LONELY PLACE (1950)*
SIROCCO (1951)
AFFAIR IN TRINIDAD (1952)*
THE FIRST TIME (1952)
PAULA (1952)
MAN IN THE DARK (1953)
MISS SADIE THOMPSON (1953)*
SALOME (1953)*
BATTLE OF ROGUE RIVER (1954)
JESSE JAMES VS. THE DALTONS (1954)
THE MIAMI STORY (1954)
CHICAGO SYNDICATE (1955)
QUEEN BEE (1955)

THREE FOR THE SHOW   (1955)*
TIGHT SPOT   (1955)*
THE EDDY DUCHIN STORY   (1956)*
JEANNE ENGELS   (1957)
PAL JOEY   (1957)*
PEPE   (1960)*
WHO WAS THAT LADY?   (1960

McLEAN, BARBARA

THE BOWERY   (1933)*
THE AFFAIRS OF CELLINI   (1934)
GALLANT LADY   (1934)
THE HOUSE OF ROTHSCHILD   (1934)*
THE MIGHTY BARNUM   (1934)
CLIVE OF INDIA   (1935)*
METROPOLITAN   (1935)
LES MISERABLES   (1935)*
THE COUNTRY DOCTOR   (1936)*
LLOYDS OF LONDON   (1936)*
PROFESSIONAL SOLDIER   (1936)
SING, BABY, SING   (1936)*
SINS OF MAN   (1936)
SEVENTH HEAVEN   (1937)*
ALEXANDER'S RAGTIME BAND   (1938)
THE BARONESS AND THE BUTLER   (1938)
IN OLD CHICAGO   (1938)*
SUEZ   (1938)*
JESSE JAMES   (1939)*
THE RAINS CAME   (1939)*
STANLEY AND LIVINGSTONE   (1939)*
DOWN ARGENTINE WAY   (1940)*
CHAD HANNA   (1940)
LITTLE OLD NEW YORK   (1940)*
MARYLAND   (1940)*
REMEMBER THE DAY   (1941)*
TOBACCO ROAD   (1941)*
A YANK IN THE R.A.F.   (1941)*
THE BLACK SWAN   (1942)*
THE MAGNIFICENT DOPE   (1942)*
RINGS ON HER FINGERS   (1942)*
HELLO, FRISCO, HELLO   (1943)*
THE SONG OF BERNADETTE   (1943)*
WILSON   (1944)*
WINGED VICTORY   (1944)
A BELL FOR ADANO   (1945)*
THE DOLLY SISTERS   (1945)*
MARGIE   (1946)*
THREE LITTLE GIRLS IN BLUE   (1946)*
CAPTAIN FROM CASTILE   (1947)*

NIGHTMARE ALLEY   (1947)*
DEEP WATERS   (1948)*
WHEN MY BABY SMILES AT ME   (1948)
PRINCE OF FOXES   (1949)*
ALL ABOUT EVE   (1950)*
THE GUNFIGHTER   (1950)*
NO WAY OUT   (1950)*
TWELVE O'CLOCK HIGH   (1950)*
DAVID AND BATHSHEBA   (1951)*
FOLLOW THE SUN   (1951)*
I'D CLIMB THE HIGHEST MOUNTAIN   (1951)*
PEOPLE WILL TALK   (1951)*
LURE OF THE WILDERNESS   (1952)*
O. HENRY'S FULL HOUSE   (1952)*
THE SNOWS OF KILIMANJARO   (1952)
VIVA ZAPATA   (1952)*
WAIT 'TIL THE SUN SHINES, NELLIE   (1952)*
THE DESERT RATS   (1953)*
KING OF THE KHYBER RIFLES   (1953)*
NIAGARA   (1953)*
THE ROBE   (1953)*
THE EGYPTIAN   (1954)*
UNTAMED   (1955)*

DOROTHY SPENCER

FOUR MARRIED MEN   (1929)
MARRIED IN HOLLYWOOD   (1929)
NIX ON DAMES   (1929)
AS HUSBANDS GO   (1934)
COMING OUT PARTY   (1934)
SHE WAS A LADY   (1934)
THE CASE AGAINST MRS. AMES   (1936)
THE LUCKIEST GIRL IN THE WORLD   (1936)
THE MOON'S OUR HOME   (1936)
STAND-IN   (1937)*
VOGUES OF 1938   (1937)
BLOCKADE   (1938)*
TRADE WINDS   (1938)*
ETERNALLY YOURS   (1939)*
STAGECOACH   (1939)*
WINTER CARNIVAL   (1939)*
FOREIGN CORRESPONDENT   (1940)*
THE HOUSE ACROSS THE BAY   (1940)*
SLIGHTLY HONORABLE   (1940)*
SUNDOWN   (1941)*
TO BE OR NOT TO BE   (1942)*
HAPPY LAND   (1943)*
HEAVEN CAN WAIT   (1943)*
LIFEBOAT   (1943)*

SWEET AND LOW-DOWN   (1944)
A ROYAL SCANDAL   (1945)*
A TREE GROWS IN BROOKLYN   (1945)
CLUNY BROWN   (1946)*
DRAGONWYCK   (1946)*
MY DARLING CLEMENTINE   (1946)*
THE GHOST AND MRS. MUIR   (1947)*
THE SNAKE PIT   (1948)*
THAT LADY IN ERMINE   (1948)
DOWN TO THE SEA IN SHIPS   (1949)*
IT HAPPENS EVERY SPRING   (1949)*
THREE CAME HOME   (1950)*
UNDER MY SKIN   (1950)*
DECISION BEFORE DAWN   (1951)*
14 HOURS   (1951)*
LYDIA BAILEY   (1952)
WHAT PRICE GLORY   (1952)
MAN ON A TIGHTROPE   (1953)*
TONIGHT WE SING   (1953)*
VICKI   (1953)*
BLACK WIDOW   (1954)*
BROKEN LANCE   (1954)*
DEMETRIUS AND THE GLADIATORS   (1954)*
NIGHT PEOPLE   (1954)*
THE LEFT HAND OF GOD   (1955)*
PRINCE OF PLAYERS   (1955)*
THE RAINS OF RANCHIPUR   (1955)*
SOLDIER OF FORTUNE   (1955)*
THE BEST THINGS IN LIFE ARE FREE   (1956)*
THE MAN IN THE GRAY FLANNEL SUIT   (1956)*
A HATFUL OF RAIN   (1957)*
THE YOUNG LIONS   (1958)*
THE JOURNEY   (1959)*
A PRIVATE AFFAIR   (1959)
FROM THE TERRACE   (1960)*
NORTH TO ALASKA   (1960)*
SEVEN THIEVES   (1960)*
WILD IN THE COUNTRY   (1961)
CLEOPATRA   (1963)*
CIRCUS WORLD   (1964)*
VON RYAN'S EXPRESS   (1965)*
LOST COMMAND   (1966)
A GUIDE FOR THE MARRIED MAN   (1967)*
VALLEY OF THE DOLLS   (1967)*
DADDY'S GONE A-HUNTING   (1969)*
HAPPY BIRTHDAY, WANDA JUNE   (1971)*
LIMBO   (1972)*
EARTHQUAKE   (1974)*
CHAINED TO YESTERDAY   (1974)
THE CONCORDE - AIRPORT '79   (1979)*

SCREENWRITERS

LEIGH BRACKETT

THE VAMPIRE'S GHOST   (1945)*
CRIME DOCTOR'S MAN-HUNT   (1945)
THE BIG SLEEP   (1946)*
RIO BRAVO   (1959)*
GOLD OF THE SEVEN SAINTS   (1961)
HATARI!   (1962)*
13 WEST STREET   (1962)*
EL DORADO   (1967)*
RIO LOBO   (1970)*
THE LONG GOODBYE   (1973)*
THE EMPIRE STRIKES BACK   (1980)

ANITA LOOS

THE POWER OF THE CAMERA   (1912)
THE ROAD TO PLAINDALE   (1912)
THE NEW YORK HAT   (1912)*
HE WAS A COLLEGE BOY   (1912)
THE EARL AND THE TOMBOY   (1912)
A HORSE ON BILL   (1913)
A HICKSVILLE EPICURE   (1913)
A FALLEN HERO   (1913)
A FIREMAN'S LOVE   (1913)
A CURE FOR SUFFRAGETTES   (1913)
THE SUICIDE PACT   (1913)
BINKS RUNS AWAY   (1913)
HOW THE DAY WAS SAVED   (1913)
WHEN A WOMAN GUIDES   (1913)
FALL OF HICKSVILLE'S FINEST   (1913)
THE WEDDING GOWN   (1913)
YIDDISH LOVE   (19193)
GENTLEMEN AND THIEVES   (1913)
A BUNCH OF FLOWERS (1913)
PA SAYS   (1913)
THE WIDOW'S KIDS   (1913)
THE LADY IN BLACK   (1913)
THE DEACON'S WHISKERS   (1913)
HIS AWFUL VENGEANCE   (1913)
ALL FOR MABEL   (1913)
THE FATAL DECEPTION   (1913)
FOR HER FATHER'S SINS   (1913)
UNLUCKY FIM   (1913)
ALL ON ACCOUNT OF A COLD   (1913)
THE SAVING GRACE   (1913)
A NARROW ESCAPE   (1913)
TWO WOMEN   (1913)
THE WALL FLOWER   (1913)
QUEEN OF THE CARNIVAL   (1913)

THE MAYOR ELECT (1913)
THE MAKING OF A MASHER (1913)
PATH OF TRUE LOVE (1913)
A GIRL LIKE MOTHER (1913)
THE MOTHER (1913)
THE GREAT MOTOR RACE (1913)
HIS HOODOO (1913)
THE MEAL TICKET (1914)
THE SAVING PRESENCE (1914)
THE SUFFERING OF SUSAN (1914)
THE CHIEFTAIN'S DAUGHTER (1914)
THE FATAL DRESS SUIT (1914)
THE GIRL IN THE SHACK (1914)
THE SAVING PRESENCE (1914)
HIS HATED RIVAL (1914)
A COMER IN HATS (1914)
NEARLY A BURGLAR'S BRIDE (1914)
THE FATAL CURVE (1914)
THE MILLION-DOLLAR BRIDE (1914)
A FLURRY IN ART (1914)
NELLIE, THE FEMALE VILLAIN (1914)
HIS RIVAL (1914)
WHERE THE ROADS PART (1914)
A NO BULL SPY (1914)
A BALKED HEREDITY (1914)
A BLASTED ROMANCE (1914)
MORTIMER'S MILLIONS (1914)
A LIFE AND DEATH AFFAIR (1914)
THE SENSIBLE GIRL (1914)
AT THE TUNNEL'S END (1914)
THE DEADLY GLASS OF BEER (1914)
THE STOLEN MASTERPIECE (1914)
THE LAST DRINK OF WHISKEY (1914)
NELL'S EUGENIC WEDDING (1914)
THE SCHOOL OF ACTING (1914)
A HICKSVILLE REFORMER (1914)
THE WHITE SLAVE CATCHERS (1914)
THE STYLE ACCUSTOMED (1914)
THE DECEIVER (1914)
HOW THEY MET (1914)
THE COST OF A BARGAIN (1915)
SYMPATHY SAL (1915)
NELLY, THE FEMALE VICTIM (1915)
MIXED VALUES (1915)
PENNINGTON'S CHOICE (1915)
THE TEAR ON THE PAGE (1915)
HOW TO KEEP A HUSBAND (1915)
THE BURLESQUERS (1915)
THE FATAL FOURTH (1915)
THE FATAL FINGERPRINTS (1915)
WARDS OF FATE (1915)
HEART THAT TRULY LOVED (1915)

THE LITTLE LIAR (1915)
MOUNTAIN BRED (1915)
MACBETH (1916)
A COMER IN COTTON (1916)
WILD GIRL OF THE SIERRAS (1916)
CALICO VAMPIRE (1916)
LAUNDRY LIZ (1916)
FRENCH MILLINER (1916)
THE WHARF RAT (1916)
STRANDED (1916)
THE SOCIAL SECRETARY (1916)*
HIS PICTURE IN THE PAPERS (1916)*
THE HALF-BREED (1916)
AMERICAN ARISTOCRACY (1916)
MANHATTAN MADNESS (1916)
THE MATRIMANIAC (1916)*
INTOLERANCE (1916)*
THE AMERICANO (1917)*
IN AGAIN, OUT AGAIN (1917)
WILD AND WOOLLY (1917)*
REACHING FOR THE MOON (1917)*
DOWN TO EARTH (1917)
LET'S GET A DIVORCE (1918)
COME ON IN (1918)
GOODBYE BILL (1918)
HIT-THE-TRAIL HOLIDAY (1918)
OH, YOU WOMEN! (1919)
GETTING MARY MARRIED (1919)
A TEMPERAMENTAL WIFE (1919)
A VIRTUOUS VAMP (1919)
THE ISLE OF CONQUEST (1919)
TWO WEEKS (1920)
IN SEARCH OF A SINNER (1920)
THE LOVE EXPERT (1920)
THE PERFECT WOMAN (1920)
THE BRANDED WOMAN (1920)
DANGEROUS BUSINESS (1921)

MAMA'S AFFAIR (1921)

A WOMAN'S PLACE (1921)

RED HOT ROMANCE (1922)

POLLY OF THE FOLLIES (1922)

DULCY (1923)
THREE MILES OUT (1924)
LEARNING TO LOVE (1925)
PUBLICITY MADNESS (1927)
GENTLEMENT PREFER BLONDES (1928)
THE STRUGGLE (1931)*
RED-HEADED WOMAN (1932)*
BLONDIE OF THE FOLLIES (1932)*
HOLD YOUR MAN (1933)*
MIDNIGHT MARY (1933)*
THE BARBARIAN (1933)
SOCIAL REGISTER (1934)

THE GIRL FROM MISSOURI (1934)*
BIOGRAPHY OF A BACHELOR GIRL (1934)
RIFFRAFF (1935)*
SAN FRANCISCO (1936)*
MAMA STEPS OUT (1937)*
SARATOGA (1937)*
THE GREAT CANADIAN (1938)
ALASKA (1938)
THE WOMEN (1939)*
SUSAN AND GOD (1940)*
THEY MET IN BOMBAY (1941)*
WHEN LADIES MEET (1941)*
BLOSSOMS IN THE DUST (1941)*
I MARRIED AN ANGEL (1942)*

ADDRESSES

AFA
The American Federation of Arts
41 East 65th Street
New York, NY
212-988-7700

ASF
Association Films
866 Third Avenue
New York, NY 10022
212-935-4210

BAC
Balkan Arts Center, Inc.
P.O. Box 315
Franklin Lakes, NF 07417
201-891-8240

BAU
Bauer International
695 West 7th Street
Plainfield, NJ 07060
201-757-6090

Constance Beeson
99 West Shore Road
Belvedere, CA 94920
415-435-3002

Cathey Billian
456 Broome Street
New York, NY 10013

BKW
Blackwood Productions, Inc.
251 West 57th Street
New York, NY 10019
212-247-4710

BLA
Blackhawk Films
Eastin-Phelan Corp.
Davenport, IA 52808
319-323-9736

BUD
Budget Films
4590 Santa Monica Boulevard
Los Angeles, CA 90020
213-660-0187
213-660-0800

CAL
California Newsreel
630 Natoma Street
San Francisco, CA 94103
415-621-6196

CAM
Cambridge Documentary Films
P.O. Box 385
Cambridge, MA 02139
617-354-3677

CAN
Canyon Cinema Cooperative
2325 Third Street
Suite 338
San Francisco, CA 94107
415-626-2255

Vince Cannon
365 Beloit Avenue
Los Angeles, CA 90049
213-472-0488

CAR
Carousel Films
241 East 34th Street
Room 304
New York, NY 10016
212-683-1660

CST
Castelli-Sonnabend Tapes & Films,
Inc.
142 Green Street
New York, NY 10012

CEN
Centre Productions
2006 Broadway
Boulder, Colo. 80302

Doris Chase
Chelsea Hotel
222 West 23rd Street
New York, NY 10011
212-929-7285

CHU
Churchill Films
662 North Robertson Boulevard
Los Angeles, CA 90069
213-657-5110

CCC
Cine-Craft Co.
1720 West Marshall
Portland, Oregon   97209
513-228-7484

CFM
Classic Film Museum
4 Union Square
Dover-Foxcroft, ME   04426
207-564-8371

CLE
Clem Williams
2240 Noblestown Road
Pittsburgh, PA   15205
412-921-5810

CFS
Creative Film Society
7237 Canby Avenue
Reseda, CA   91355
213-881-3887

CIN
Cine 16 Films
2233 - 40th Place, NW
Washington, DC   20007
202-333-3639

CIV
Cinema 5
595 Madison Avenue
New York, NY
212-421-5555

Jeanne Collachia
21205-4 Lassen Street
Chatsworth, CA   91311

COF
The Conservation Foundation
1717 Massachusetts Avenue, NW
Washington, DC   20036
202-797-4358

COR
Corinth Films
410 East 62nd Street
New York, NY   10021
212-421-4770

Sally Cruikshank
15143 Hartsook Street
Sherman Oaks, CA   91403

Davenport Films
Box 124
Delaplane, VA   22025
703-592-3701

Direct Cinema
Mitchell Block, President
Box 69589
Los Angeles, CA   90069
213-656-4700

EBE
Encyclopedia Britannica
Educational Corporation
426 North Michigan Avenue
Chicago, ILL   60611

EDC
Education Development Center
39 Chapel Street
Newton, MA   02160
617-969-7100

Martha Edelheit
1140 Fifth Avenue
New York, NY   10028

EXP
Expanded Cinema Group
204-1/2 West John Street
Champaign, ILL   61820
217-352-7353

FAC
FACSEA
972 Fifth Avenue
New York, NY   10021
212-570-4440

Farenthold
P.O. Box 315
Franklin Lakes, NJ   07417

FCE
Film Classic Exchange
1914 South Vermont Avenue
Los Angeles, CA   90007
213-877-3191

FFC
FILMFAIR Communications
10900 Ventura Boulevard
P.O. Box 1728
Studio City, CA 91604
213-877-3191

FIC
The Film Center
938 K Street
Washington, DC 20001
202-393-1205

FIM
Film Images
1034 Lake Street
Oak Park, IL 60301
312-386-4826

FMC
Filmmakers Cooperative
175 Lexington Avenue
New York, NY 10016
212-889-3820

FML
Filmmakers Library
133 East 58th Street
Suite 703A
New York, NY 10022
212-355-6545

FNC
Films Incorporated
733 Green Bay Road
Wilmette, Ill. 60091
312-256-3200

FOC
Focus International
1 East 53rd Street
New York, NY 10022
212-799-0491

FOR
Ford Foundation
320 East 43rd Street
New York, NY 10017
212-573-4825

Monica Freeman
62 Hamilton Terrace
New York, NY 10031

FRO
Frontline Management
9044 Melrose Avenue
Los Angeles, CA 90069

Amy Greenfield
135 St. Paul's Avenue
Staten Island, NY 10301

GRO
Grove Press, Inc.
196 West Houston Street
New York, NY 10014
212-242-4900

Barbara Hammer/Goddess Films
P.O. Box 2446
Berkeley, CA 94702
415-658-6959

HER
Herstory Films
137 East 13th Street
New York, NY 10003
212-260-0324

Victoria Hochberg
6825 Alta Loma Terrace
Los Angeles, CA 90068

Nancy Holt
799 Greenwich Street
New York, NY 10004

Faith Hubley
Hubley Studio
971 Madison Avenue
New York, NY 10021

HUR
Hurlock Cine-World
13 Arcadia Road
Old Greenwich, CT 06870
203-637-4319

ICA
Icarus Films Inc.
200 Park Avenue South
Suite 1319
New York, NY 10003
212-674-3375

IAI
Ideas and Images, Inc.
P.O. Box 5354
Atlanta, GA 30307
404-523-8023

ICS
Institutional Cinema Services
915 Broadway
New York, NY 10010
212-673-3990

IFC
Iris Feminist Collective, Inc.
Box 26463
Los Angeles, CA 90026
213-483-5793
film orders: Box 5353
Berkeley, CA
94705
415-835-9118

IMA
The Images Film Archive, Inc.
300 Phillips Park Road
Mamaroneck, NY 10543
914-381-2993

IMP
Impact Films
144 Bleeker Street
New York, NY 10012
212-674-3375

Louva Irvine
P.O. Box 189
Murray Hill, NY 10016

IVY
Ivy Films
165 West 46th Street
New York, NY 10036
212-765-3940

Kartemquin Films Ltd.
1901 West Wellington
Chicago, Ill. 60657
213-472-4366

KIL
Killiam Collection
Rental Division
6 East 39th Street
New York, NY 10016
212-684-3920

KPF
Kit Parker Films
Box 227
Carmel Valley, CA 93924
208-659-4131

LCA
Learning Corporation Of America
1350 Avenue of the Americas
New York, NY 10019
212-397-9353

LEA
Leacock-Pennebaker
56 West 45th Street
New York, NY 10036
212-986-7020

Janis Crystal Lipzin
633 San Bruno Avenue
San Francisco, CA 94107

Lucerne Films
37 Ground Pine Road
Morris Plains, NJ 07950
201-538-1401

Babette Mangolte
319 Greenwich Street
New York, NY 10013

Sue Marx
600 Woodbridge
Detroit, MI 48226
313-259-8505

MAY
Maysles Film
250 West 54th Street
New York, NY 10019
212-582-6050

MGM
MGM/United Artists
729 Seventh Avenue
New York, NY   10019

MIL
Milestone Movie Corporation
P.O. Box 75
Monroe, CT   06468

MMA
Museum of Modern Art
Circulating Film Program
11 West 53rd Street
New York, NY   10019
212-956-4204

MOD
Modern Sound Pictures
1402 Howard Street
Omaha, Nebraska   68102
402-341-8476

MOG
Mogull's
1280 North Avenue
Plainfield, NJ   07062
201-753-6004

Jane Morrison
218 Thompson Street
New York, NY   10012

Caroline and Frank Mouris
741 South Curson Avenue
Los Angeles, CA   90036

MTI
MTI Teleprograms
4825 North Scott Street
Schiller Park, ILL   60176
312-671-0141

MUL
Multi Media Resource Center
1525 Franklin Street
San Francisco, CA   94109
415-673-5100

National Film Board Of Canada
1251 Avenue of the Americas
New York, NY   10020
212-586-2400

NDF
New Day Films
P.O. Box 315
Franklin Lakes, NJ   07417
201-891-8240

NEF
National Film and Video Center
4321 Sykesville Road
Finksburg, MD   21048
301-795-3000

Gunvor Nelson
Box 263
Star Route, Muir Beach
Sausilito, CA   94965

Newsreel
See CAL, SFN, or TWN.

NLC
New Line Cinema
853 Broadway
New York, NY   10003
1-800-221-5150

NWU
Northwestern University
Film Division
Speech Annex
Evanston, ILL   60201
312-492-7317

NYF
New Yorker Films
16 West 61st Street
New York, NY   10023
212-247-6110

ODE
Odeon
P.O. Box 315
Franklin Lakes, NJ   07417

PEN
Pennsylvania State University
A.V. Services
Special Services Building
University Park, PA   16802
814-865-6316

PER
Perspective Films
369 West Erie Street
Chicago, ILL   60610
312-977-4100

Vicki Z. Peterson
500 East 63rd Street
New York, NY 10021

PIC
Pictura
111 Eighth Avenue
New York, NY 10011
212-691-1730

PNX
Phoenix Films
470 Park Avenue South
New York, NY 10016
212-684-5910

POY
Polymorph Films
331 Newbury Street
Boston, MA 02115
617-262-5960

PRE
Perennial Education, Inc.
477 Roger Williams
P.O. Box 855 Ravinia
Highland Park, ILL 60035
312-446-4153

PYR
Pyramid Films
P.O. Box 1048
Santa Monica, CA 90406
213-828-7577

QST
Quest Productions
630 Ninth Avenue
New York, NY 10036
212-247-0398

REE
Reel Images
495 Monroe Turnpike
Monroe, CT 06468

ROA
Roa Films
1696 North Astor Street
Milwaukee, WI 53202
414-271-0861

Joan Rosenfelt
204 West 10 Street
New York, NY 10014
212-929-0727

RFL
Runner Film Library
P.O. Box 315
Franklin Lakes, NJ 07417
201-891-8240

SBC
Serious Business Company
1145 Mandana Boulevard
Oakland, CA 94610
415-832-5600

Lillian Schwartz
Lilyan Productions
524 Ridge Road
Watchung, NJ 07060

SEL
Select Film Library
115 West 31st Street
New York, NY 10001
212-594-4500

SFM
Steigliz Film Market
Bay Ridge Station
P.O. Box 127
Brooklyn, NY 11220

SFN
San Francisco Newsreel
630 Natoma Street
San Francisco, CA 94103
415-621-6196

SPI
Spiral Productions
1301 North Harper Avenue
West Hollywood, CA 90046
213-654-9870

Cecile Starr
50 West 96th Street
New York, NY 10025

Joan Strommer
c/o Virginia Commonwealth Univ.
Photography Dept. Room 208
325 North Harrison Street
Richmond, VA 23284

SWA
Swank Motion Pictures
201 South Jefferson
St. Louis, MO 63166
314-534-6300

TEX
Texture Films
1600 Broadway
New York, NY 10019
212-586-6960

Anita Thacher Films
33 Second Avenue
New York, NY 10003

Dorothy Tod Films
P.O. Box 315
Franklin Lakes, NJ 07417

TOM
Tomato Productions Inc.
P.O. Box 1952
Evergreen, Colo. 80439
303-838-5359

TWN
Third World Newsreel
160 Fifth Avenue
Room 911
New York, NY 10010
212-243-2310

TWY
Twyman
329 Salem Avenue
P.O. Box 605
Dayton, Ohio 45401
1-800-543-9594

University of California
Extension Media Center
2223 Fulton Street
Berkeley, CA 94720
415-642-6000

Gail Vachon
8 Spring Street
New York, NY 10012

VCI
6555 East Skelly Drive
Tulsa, Okla. 74145
918-583-2681

VIE
Viewfinders
P.O. Box 1665
Evanston, ILL 60204
312-869-0600

W/A/F
Women/Artists/Filmmakers
79 Mercer Street
New York, NY 10012

Jane Warrenbrand
52 West 27th Street
New York, NY 10011
212-684-1290

WCF
Westcoast Films
25 Lusk Street
San Francisco, CA 94107
415-362-4700

WEL
Welling Motion Picture
454 Meacham Avenue
Elmont, NY 11003
516-354-1066

WES
Weston Woods
Weston, CT 06880
203-226-3355

WMM
Women Make Movies
257 West 19th Street
New York, NY 10011
212-929-6477

WOM
Wombat Productions
Little Lake
Glendale Road
P.O. Box 70
Ossining, NY 10562
914-762-0011

Women's Labor History
Film Project
1735 New Hampshire Avenue, NW
Washington, D.C. 20009
202-387-2213   ·

WRS
Walter Reade 16
241 East 34th Street
New York, NY 10016
212-683-6300

XEX
Xerox Films
245 Long Hill Road
Middletown, CT 06457
203-347-7251

YBW
Yellow Ball Workshop
62 Tarbell Avenue
Lexington, MA 02173
617-862-4283

ZPH
Zipporah
54 Lewis Wharf
Boston, MA 02210
617-742-6680

CATALOGS

Almi Libra Cinema V
Budget Films
Canyon
Clem Williams Films
Corinth
Filmmaker's Cooperative
Films Incorporated
Grove Press
Hurlock Cine-World
Images Film Archive
Ivy Films
Janus Classic Collection
Kit Parker Films
MGM/United Artists
Macmillan
New Line Cinema
New Yorker Films
Perspective Films
Phoenix
Pyramid
Serious Business Company
Swank
Twyman
Women Make Movies

BIBLIOGRAPHY

The American Film Institute Catalog of Motion Pictures:
   Feature Films, 1921-1930. New York: R.R. Bowker:
   1971.

The American Film Institute Catalog of Motion Pictures:
   Feature Films, 1961-1970. New York: R.R. Bowker,
   1976.

Ash, Rene L. The Motion Picture Film Editor. Metuchen,
   N.J.: Scarecrow Press, 1974.

Bauden, Liz-Anne. The Oxford Companion To Film. London:
   Oxford University Press, 1976.

Belafonte, Dennis with Alvin H. Marill. The Films of
   Tyrone Power. Secaucus, N.J.: The Citadel Press, 1979.

Betancourt, Jeanne. Women In Focus. Dayton, OH: Pflaum-
   Standard, 1974.

Carey, Gary. Doug & Mary: A Biography of Douglas Fairbanks
   & Mary Pickford. New York: E.P. Dutton, 1977.

Conway, Michael and Mark Ricci. The Films of Jean Harlow.
   New York: Bonanza, 1965.

Corliss, Richard. The Hollywood Screenwriters. New York:
   Avon, 1972.

Dawson, Bonnie, ed. Women's Films In Print. San Francisco:
   Booklegger Press, 1975.

Deschner, Donald. The Films of Cary Grant. Secaucus, N.J.:
   The Citadel Press, 1973.

Dickens, Homer. The Films of Katharine Hepburn. New York:
   The Citadel Press, 1971.

Eames, John Douglas. The MGM Story. New York: Crown, 1976.

Essoe, Gabe. The Films of Clark Gable. Secaucus, N.J.:
   The Citadel Press, 1970.

Higham, Charles. Cecil B. DeMille. New York: Scribner's
   Sons, 1973.

Hirschorn, Clive. The Warner Bros. Story. New York:
   Corwn, 1979.

Jackson, Arthur and John Russell Taylor. The Hollywood
   Musical. New York: McGraw-Hill, 1971.

Katz, Ephraim. The Film Encyclopedia. New York: G.P.
Putnam's Sons, 1979.

Kay, Karyn and Geral Peary, eds. Women And The Cinema:
A Critical Anthology. New York: E.P. Dutton, 1977.

Limbacher, James L., ed. Feature Films On 8mm, 16mm and
Videotape. New York: R.R. Bowker, 1979.

Loos, Anita. Cast Of Thousands. New York: Grosset and
Dunlap, 1977.

Maltin, Leonard, ed. TV Movies. New York: Signet (New
American Library), 1978.

Marion, Frances. Off With Their Heads: A Serio-Comic Tale
Of Hollywood. New York: Macmillan, 1972.

Slide, Anthony. Early Women Directors. New York: A.S.
Barnes, 1977.

Smith, Sharon. Women Who Make Movies. New York: Hopkinson
and Blake, 1975.

Thomas, Tony and Aubrey Solomon. The Films Of 20th Century
Fox. Secaucus, N.J.: Citadel Press, 1979.

Thomson, David. A Biographical Dictionary Of Film. New
York: William Morrow and Company, 1975.

Weaver, Kathleen, ed. Film Programmer's Guide to 16mm
Rentals. Reel Research, 1980.

Who Wrote The Movie And What Else Did He Write? An Index
Of Screen Writers and Film Works, 1936-1969. Los
Angeles: Academy of Motion Picture Arts and Sciences,
Writers Guild of America, West, 1970.

Women's Cinema. London: British Film Institute, April-May
1973.
This is a National Film Theatre Programme Booklet.

Women's Films - A Critical Guide. Bloomington, IN: Indiana
University Audio-Visual Center, 1975.

248

ARTICLES

Bodeen, De Witt. "Frances Marion." Films In Review,
Vol. 20, No. 2 (February 1969), p. 71-91.

Bodeen, De Witt. "Frances Marion: Part II." Films In
Review, Vol. 20, No. 3 (March 1969), p. 129-152.

De Lauretis, Teresa. "Cavani's Night Porter: A Woman's
Film?" Film Quarterly, Vol. 30, No. 2 (Winter 1976-
1977), p. 35-38.

"Fifty Filmographies." Film Comment, Vol. 6, No. 4
(Winter 1970-1971), p. 101-114.
Entire issue is devoted to Hollywood screenwriters.

Henshaw, Richard. "Women Directors." Film Comment,
Vol. 8, No. 4 (November - December 1972), p. 33-45.

Rich, B. Ruby. "The Crisis Of Naming In Feminist Film
Criticism." Jump Cut, No. 19 (December 1978), p. 9-12.

Sharples, Win, Fr. with Elias Savada. "75 Editors'
Filmographies." Film Comment, Vol. 13, No. 2 (March-
April 1977), p. 8-29.

Singer, Marilyn. "The Originals: Women In Art." Film
Library Quarterly, Vol 11, No. 3 (1978), p. 17-26.